# 13

## CLAMP

TRANSLATED AND ADAPTED BY
William Flanagan

LETTERED BY
Dana Hayward

DEL
REY

BOOKS • NEW YORK

COUNTY PUBLIC LIBRARY
hestnut Street
ton NC 28401

A Del Rey Manga/Kodansha Trade Paperback Original



Published in the United States by Del Rey Books, an imprint of The Random House Publishing Group, a division of Random House, Inc., New York.



Publication rights arranged through Kodansha Ltd.

First published in Japan in 2008 by Kodansha Ltd., Tokyo

ISBN 978-0-345-50566-8

Printed in the United States of America

www.delreymanga.com

9 8 7 6 5 4 3

Translator and Adapter—William Flanagan
Lettering—Dana Hayward
Cover Design—David Stevenson

*xxxHOLiC* crosses over with *Tsubasa*. Although it isn't necessary to read *Tsubasa* to understand the events in *xxxHOLiC*, you'll get to see the same events from different perspectives if you read both series!

# Contents

# Honorifics Explained

Throughout the Del Rey Manga books, you will find Japanese honorifics left intact in the translations. For those not familiar with how the Japanese use honorifics and, more important, how they differ from American honorifics, we present this brief overview.

Politeness has always been a critical facet of Japanese culture. Ever since the feudal era, when Japan was a highly stratified society, use of honorifics—which can be defined as polite speech that indicates relationship or status—has played an essential role in the Japanese language. When you address someone in Japanese, an honorific usually takes the form of a suffix attached to one's name (example: "Asuna-san"), is used as a title at the end of one's name, or appears in place of the name itself (example: "Negi-sensei," or simply "Sensei!").

Honorifics can be expressions of respect or endearment. In the context of manga and anime, honorifics give insight into the nature of the relationship between characters. Many English translations leave out these important honorifics and therefore distort the feel of the original Japanese. Because Japanese honorifics contain nuances that English honorifics lack, it is our policy at Del Rey not to translate them. Here, instead, is a guide to some of the honorifics you may encounter in Del Rey Manga.

**-san:** This is the most common honorific and is equivalent to Mr., Miss, Ms., or Mrs. It is the all-purpose honorific and can be used in any situation where politeness is required.

**-sama:** This is one level higher than "-san" and is used to confer great respect.

**-dono:** This comes from the word "tono," which means "lord." It is an even higher level than "-sama" and confers utmost respect.

**-kun:** This suffix is used at the end of boys' names to express familiarity or endearment. It is also sometimes used by men among friends, or when addressing someone younger or of a lower station.

**-chan:** This is used to express endearment, mostly toward girls. It is also used for little boys, pets, and even among lovers. It gives a sense of childish cuteness.

**Bozu:** This is an informal way to refer to a boy, similar to the English terms "kid" and "squirt."

**Sempai/Senpai:** This title suggests that the addressee is one's senior in a group or organization. It is most often used in a school setting, where underclassmen refer to their upperclassmen as "sempai." It can also be used in the workplace, such as when a newer employee addresses an employee who has seniority in the company.

**Kohai:** This is the opposite of "sempai" and is used toward underclassmen in school or newcomers in the workplace. It connotes that the addressee is of a lower station.

**Sensei:** Literally meaning "one who has come before," this title is used for teachers, doctors, or masters of any profession or art.

**-[blank]:** This is usually forgotten in these lists, but it is perhaps the most significant difference between Japanese and English. The lack of honorific means that the speaker has permission to address the person in a very intimate way. Usually, only family, spouses, or very close friends have this kind of permission. Known as *yobisute*, it can be gratifying when someone who has earned the intimacy starts to call one by one's name without an honorific. But when that intimacy hasn't been earned, it can be very insulting.

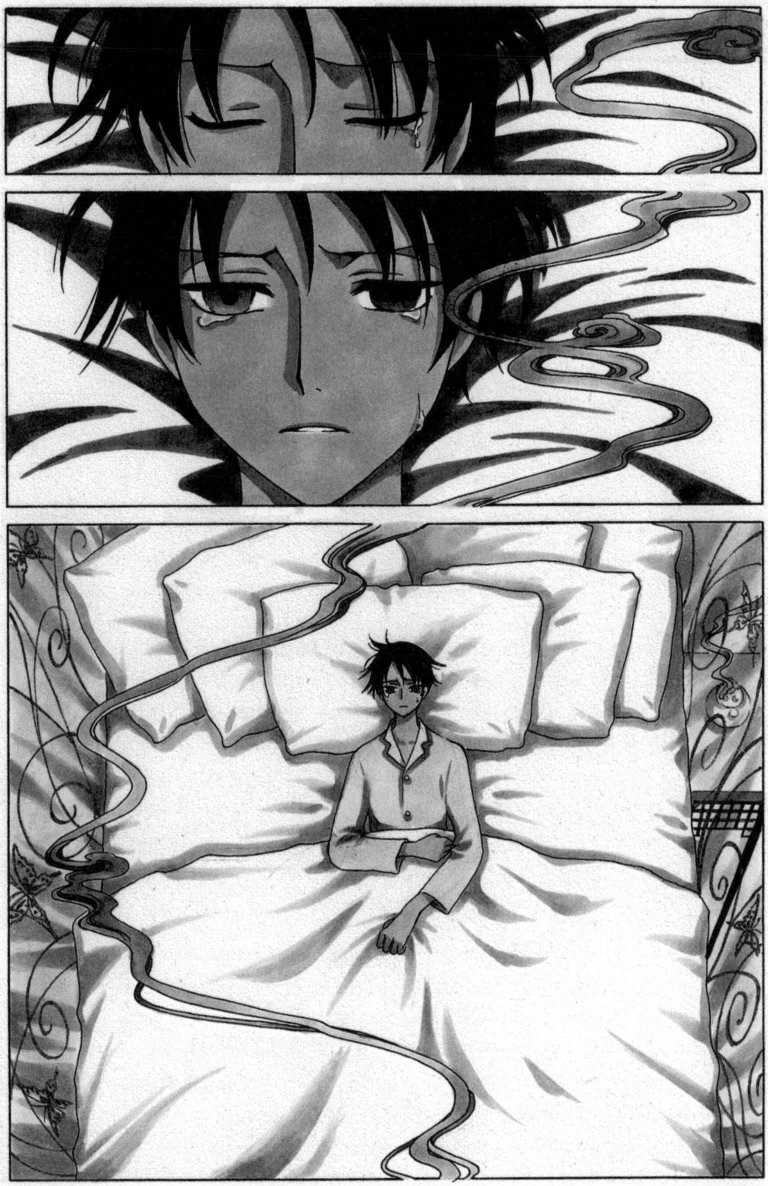

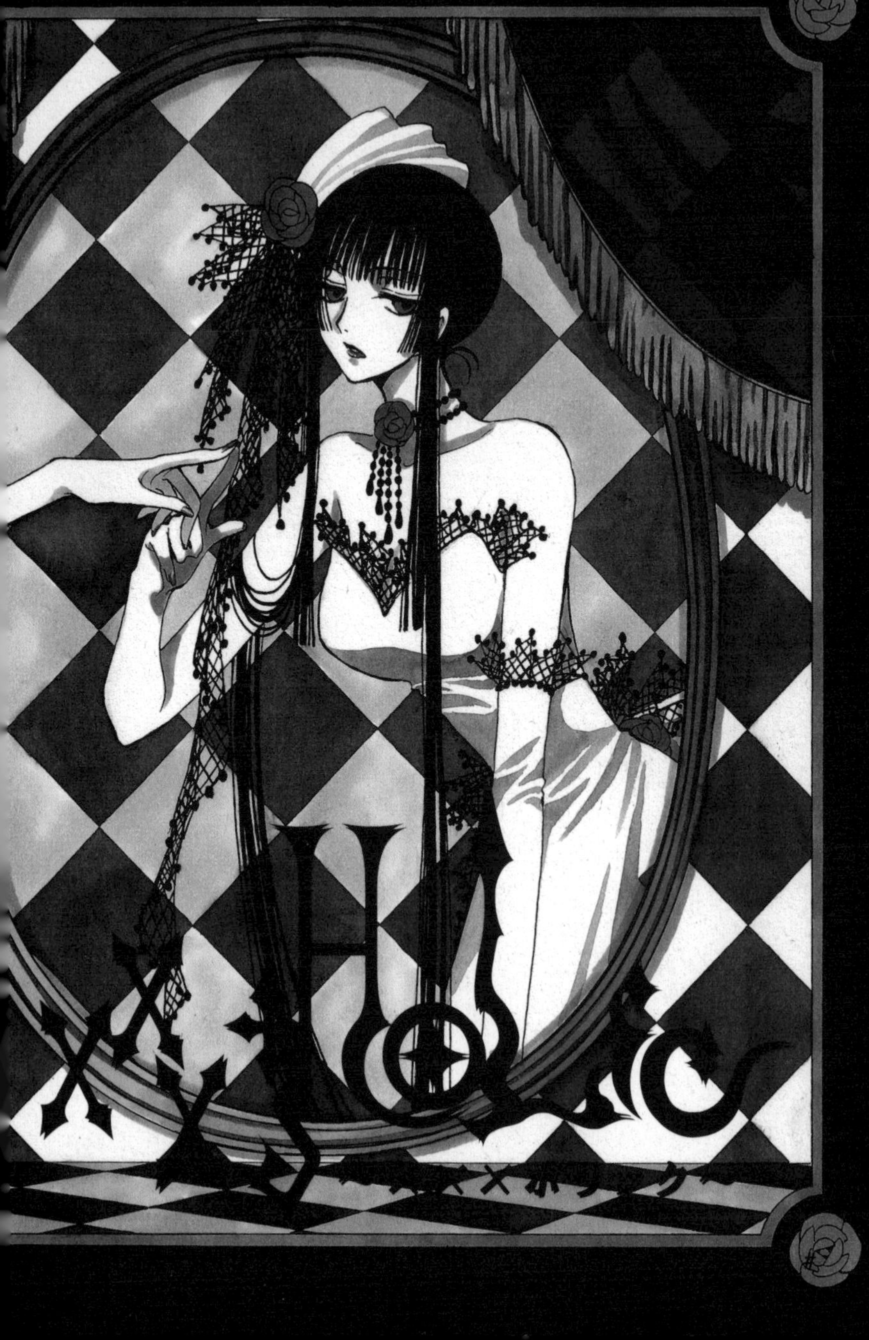

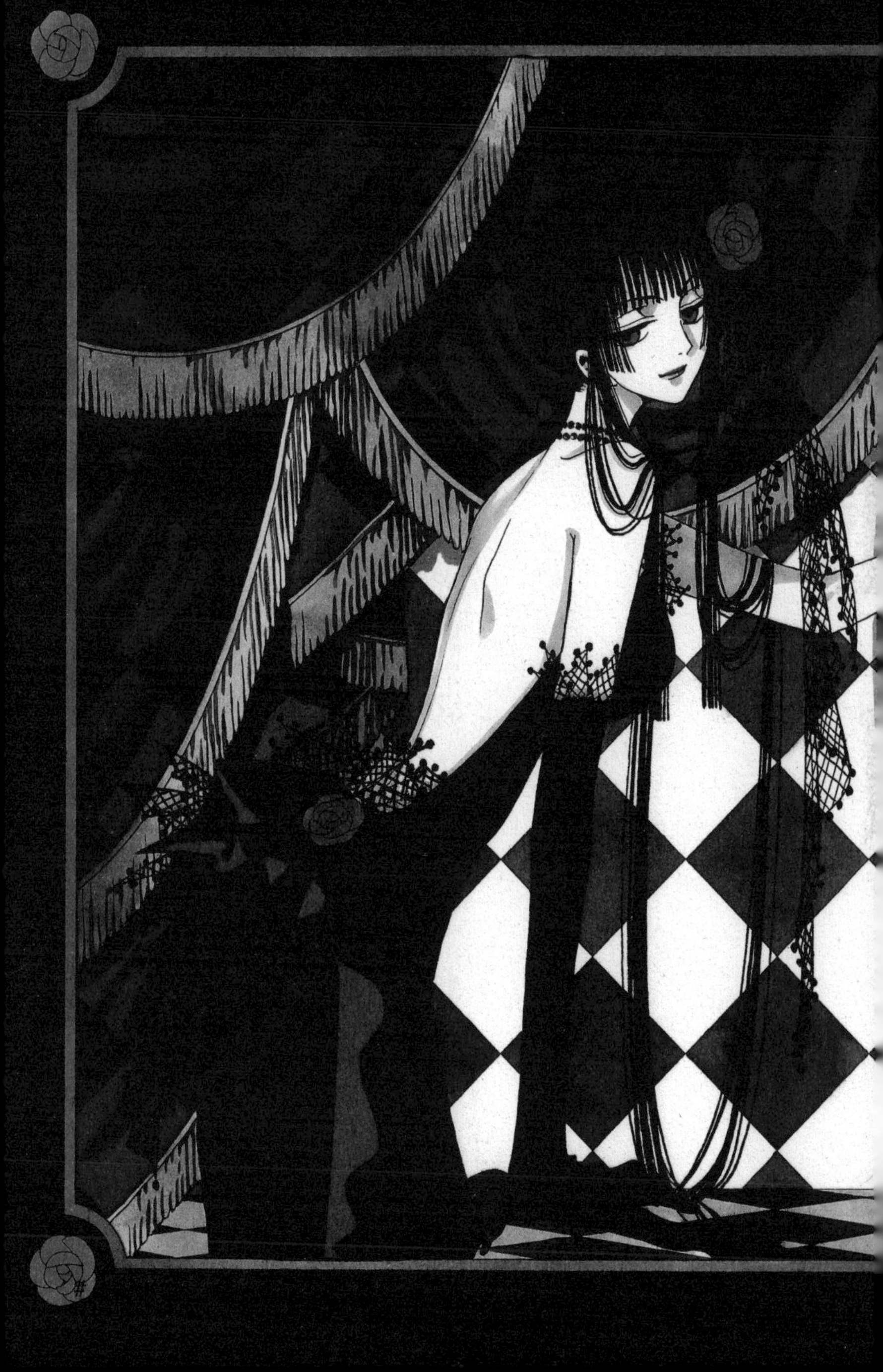

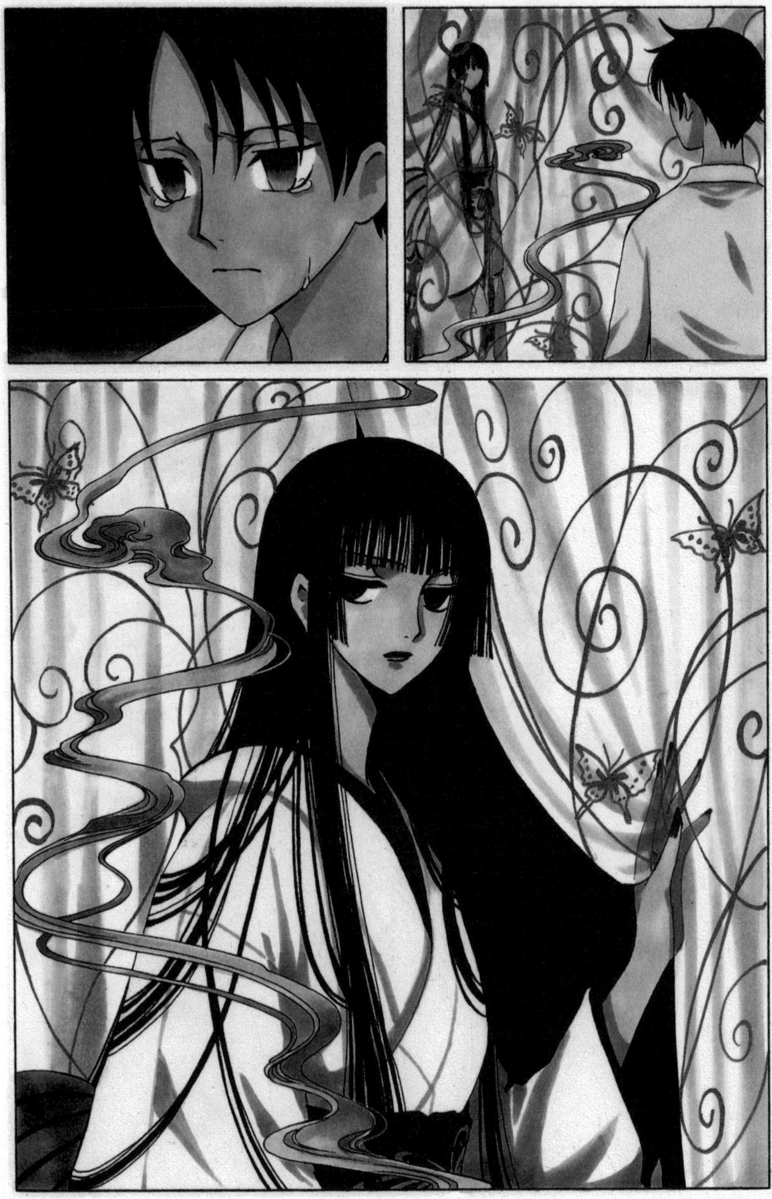

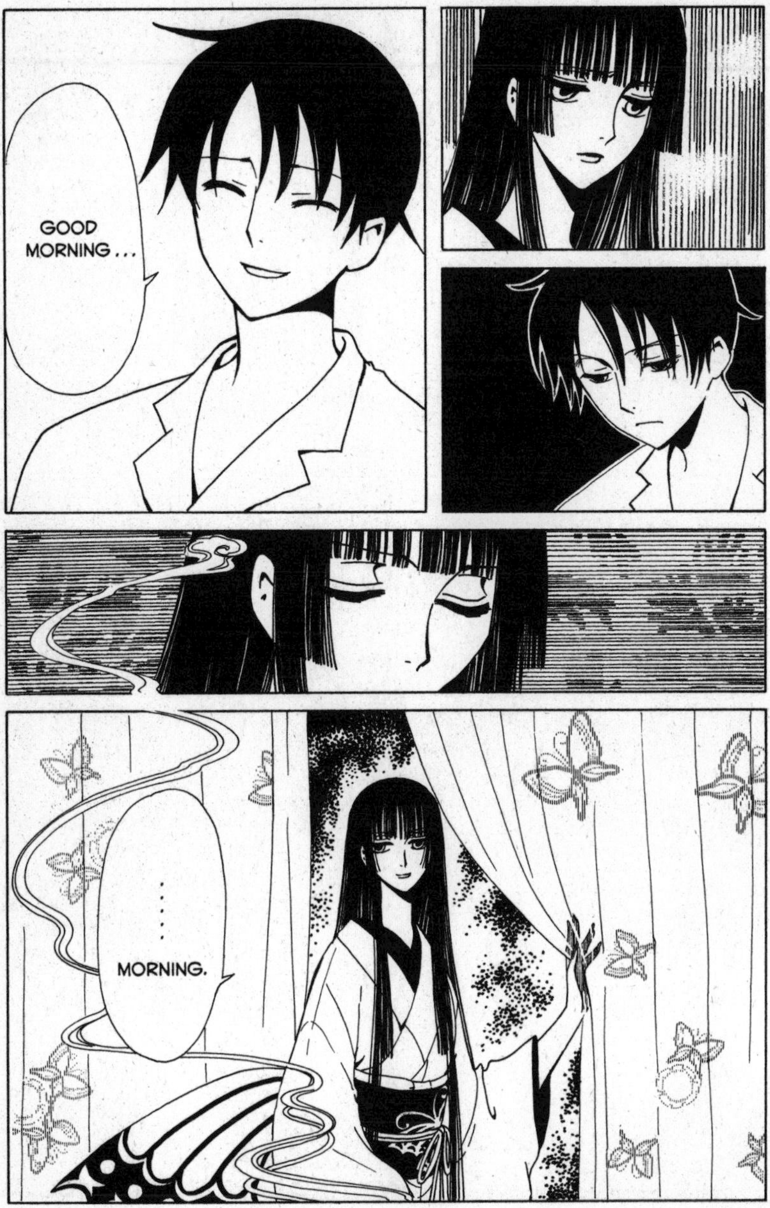
GOOD MORNING...
.....
MORNING.

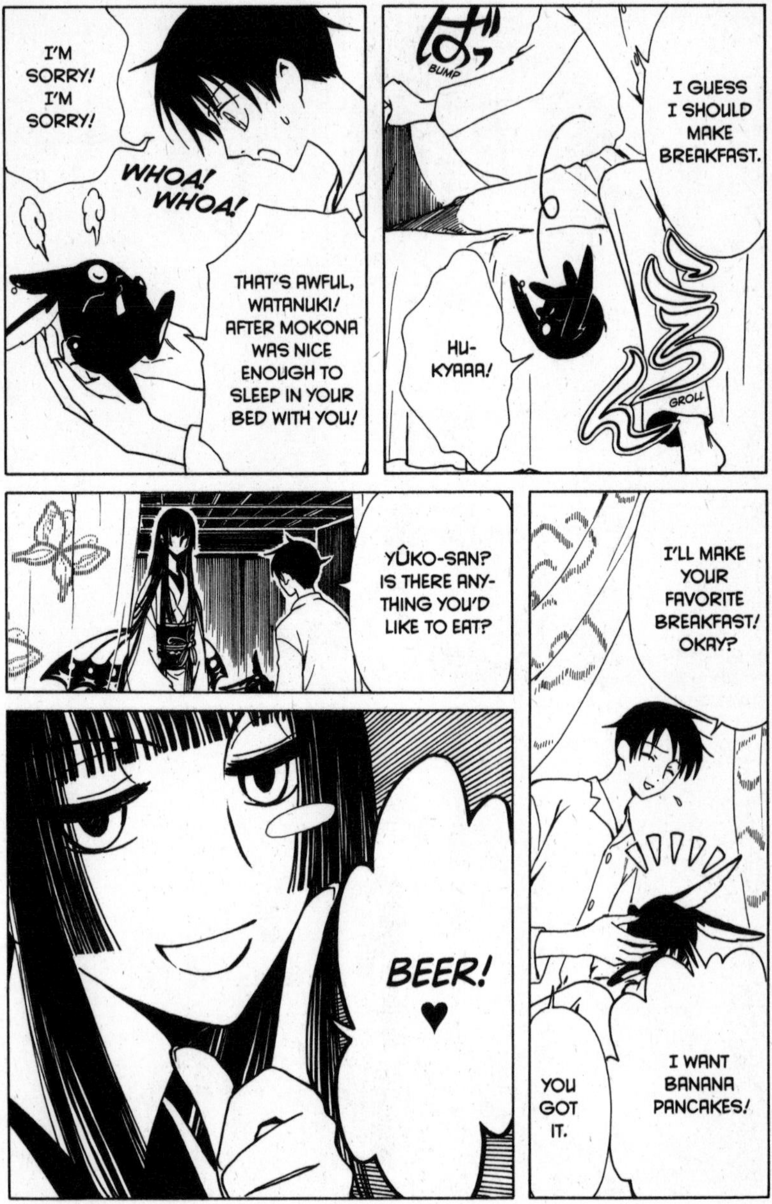

I GUESS I SHOULD MAKE BREAKFAST.
ばっ
BUMP
HU-KYAAA!
GROLL
THAT'S AWFUL, WATANUKI! AFTER MOKONA WAS NICE ENOUGH TO SLEEP IN YOUR BED WITH YOU!
WHOA! WHOA!
I'M SORRY! I'M SORRY!
I'LL MAKE YOUR FAVORITE BREAKFAST! OKAY?
I WANT BANANA PANCAKES!
YOU GOT IT.
YÛKO-SAN? IS THERE ANY-THING YOU'D LIKE TO EAT?
BEER! ♥

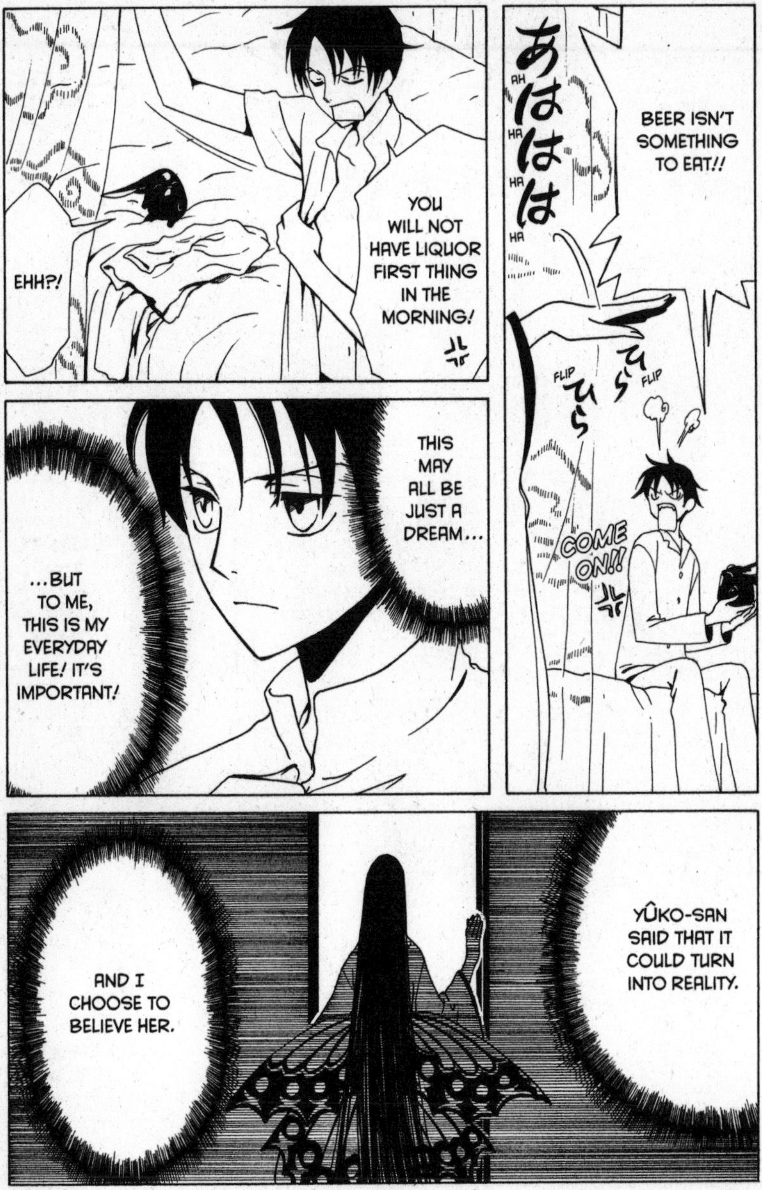
あはは は
AH HA HA HA
BEER ISN'T SOMETHING TO EAT!!
ひら ひら
FLIP FLIP
COME ON!!
YOU WILL NOT HAVE LIQUOR FIRST THING IN THE MORNING!
EHH?!
THIS MAY ALL BE JUST A DREAM...
...BUT TO ME, THIS IS MY EVERYDAY LIFE! IT'S IMPORTANT!
YÛKO-SAN SAID THAT IT COULD TURN INTO REALITY.
AND I CHOOSE TO BELIEVE HER.

SHU-
KUNK

はたん

じっ...

STAARE

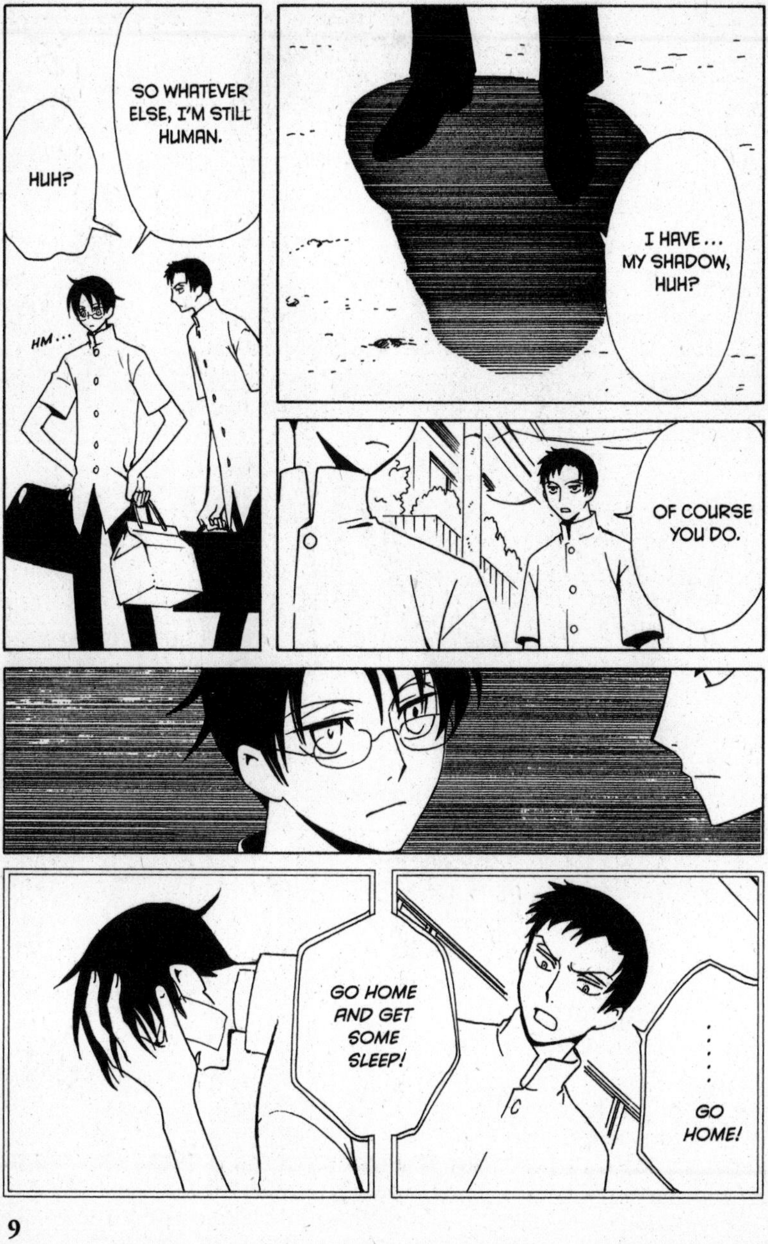
I HAVE... MY SHADOW, HUH?
OF COURSE YOU DO.
SO WHATEVER ELSE, I'M STILL HUMAN.
HUH?
HM...
....
GO HOME!
GO HOME AND GET SOME SLEEP!

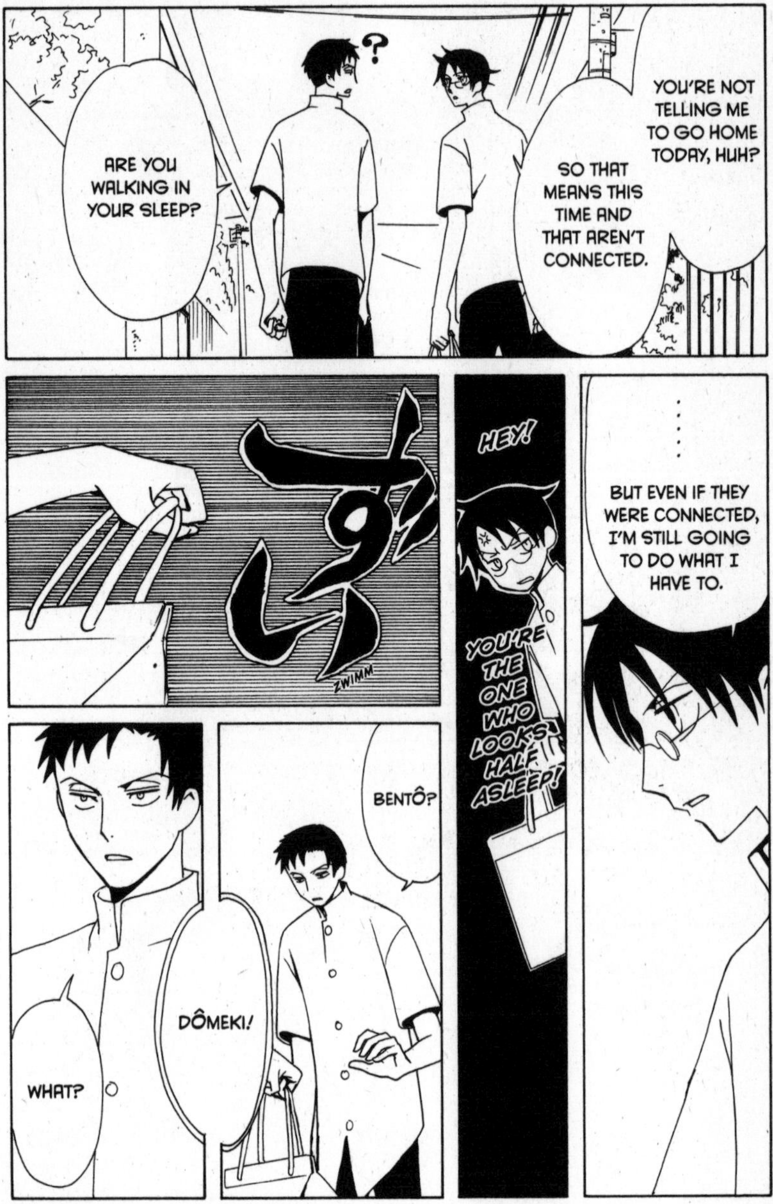
YOU'RE NOT TELLING ME TO GO HOME TODAY, HUH?
SO THAT MEANS THIS TIME AND THAT AREN'T CONNECTED.
ARE YOU WALKING IN YOUR SLEEP?
......
BUT EVEN IF THEY WERE CONNECTED, I'M STILL GOING TO DO WHAT I HAVE TO.
HEY!
YOU'RE THE ONE WHO LOOKS HALF ASLEEP!
ZWIMM
BENTÔ?
DÔMEKI!
WHAT?

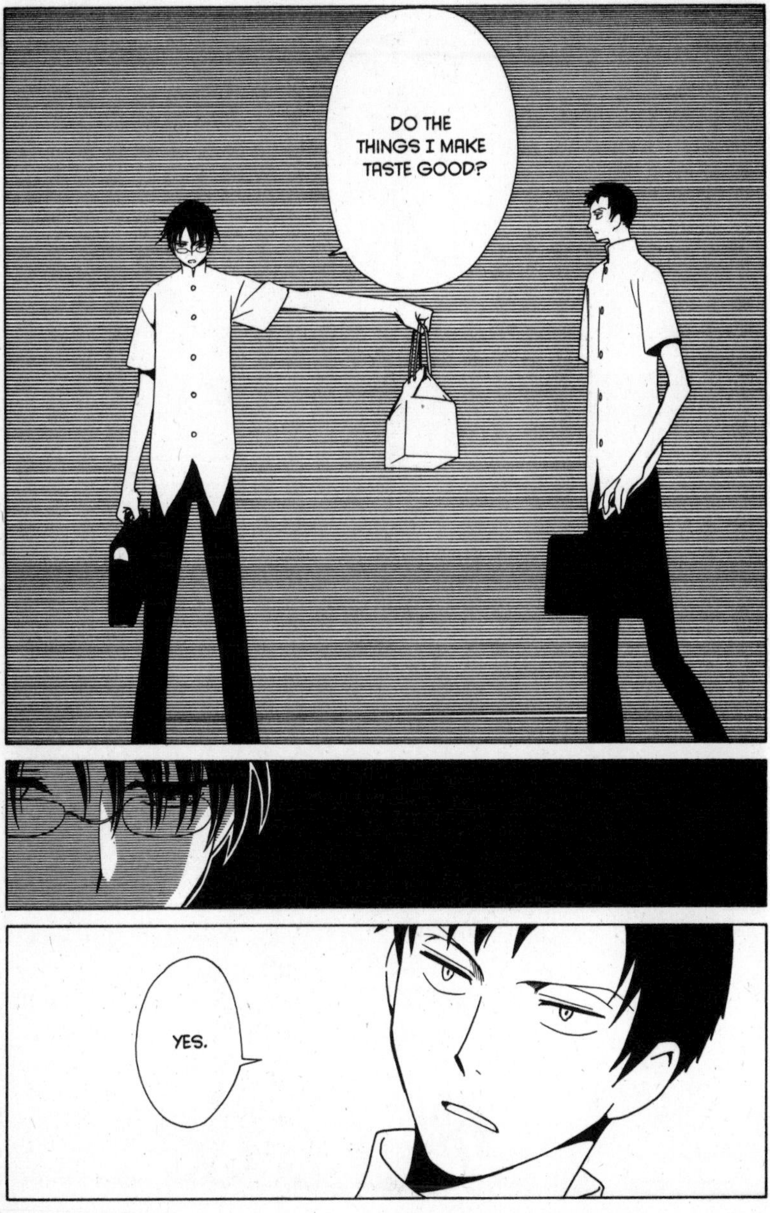
DO THE THINGS I MAKE TASTE GOOD?
YES.

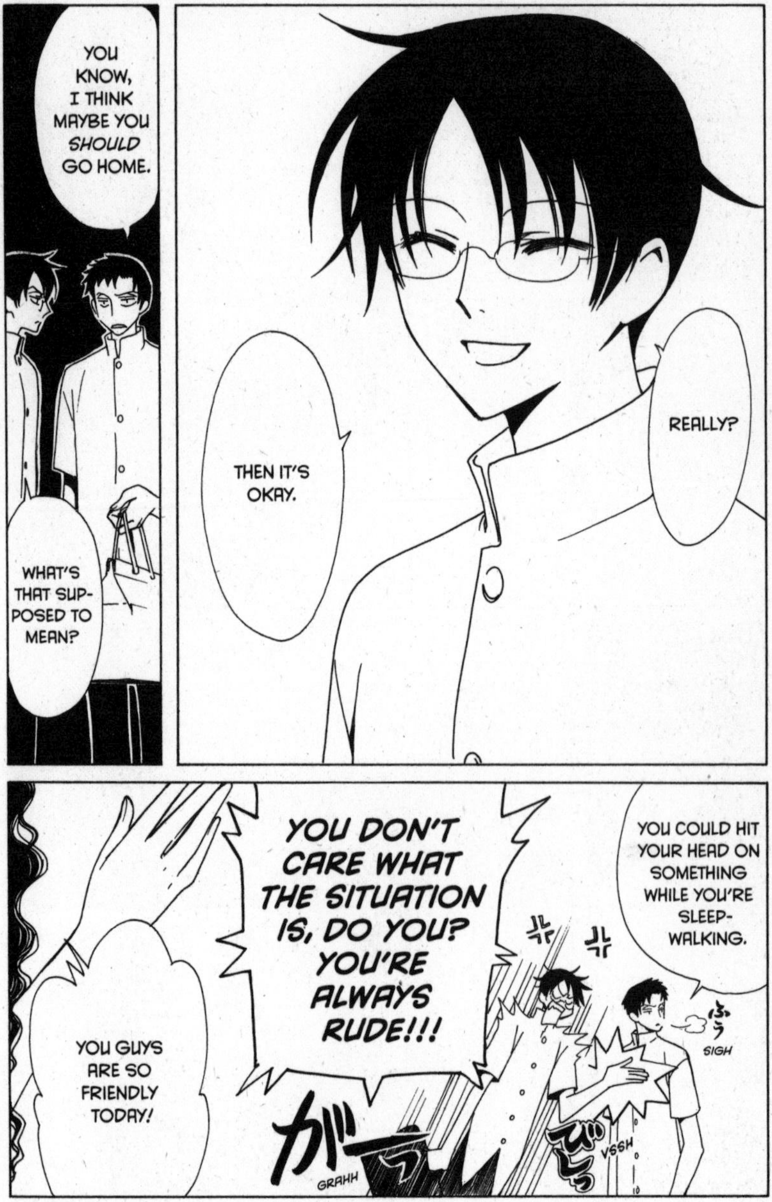
REALLY?
THEN IT'S OKAY.
YOU KNOW, I THINK MAYBE YOU *SHOULD* GO HOME.
WHAT'S THAT SUP-POSED TO MEAN?
YOU COULD HIT YOUR HEAD ON SOMETHING WHILE YOU'RE SLEEP-WALKING.
ふぅ SIGH
YOU DON'T CARE WHAT THE SITUATION IS, DO YOU? YOU'RE ALWAYS RUDE!!!
びくっ VSSH
がーっ GRAHH
YOU GUYS ARE SO FRIENDLY TODAY!

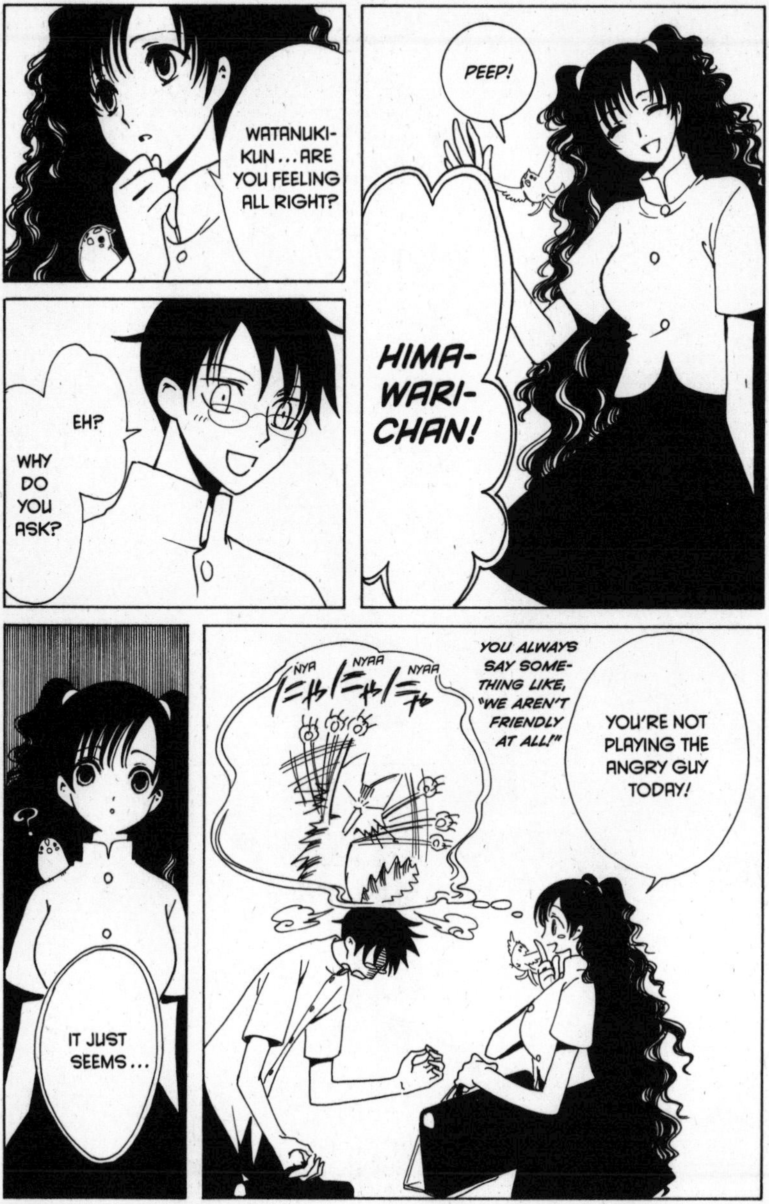
PEEP!
HIMA-WARI-CHAN!
WATANUKI-KUN ... ARE YOU FEELING ALL RIGHT?
EH?
WHY DO YOU ASK?
YOU'RE NOT PLAYING THE ANGRY GUY TODAY!
YOU ALWAYS SAY SOME-THING LIKE, "WE AREN'T FRIENDLY AT ALL!"
NYAA
NYAA
NYA
IT JUST SEEMS ...

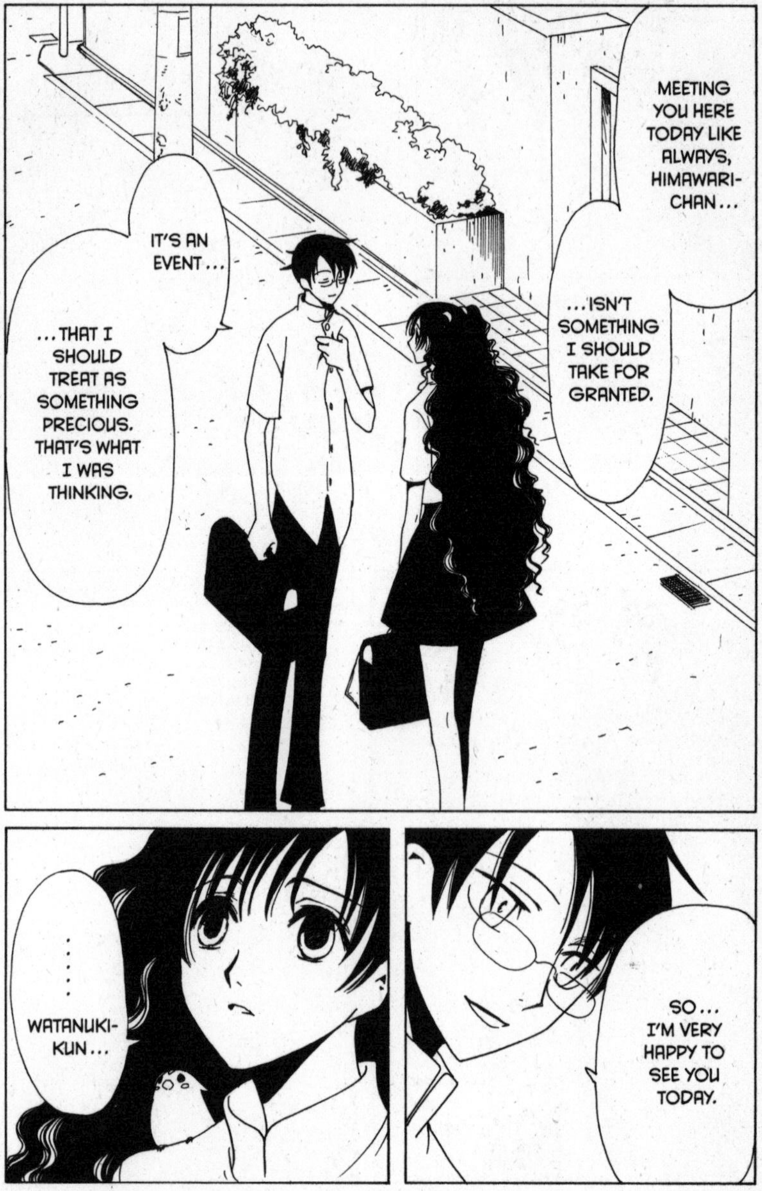
MEETING YOU HERE TODAY LIKE ALWAYS, HIMAWARI-CHAN...
...ISN'T SOMETHING I SHOULD TAKE FOR GRANTED.
IT'S AN EVENT...
...THAT I SHOULD TREAT AS SOMETHING PRECIOUS. THAT'S WHAT I WAS THINKING.
SO... I'M VERY HAPPY TO SEE YOU TODAY.
..... WATANUKI-KUN...

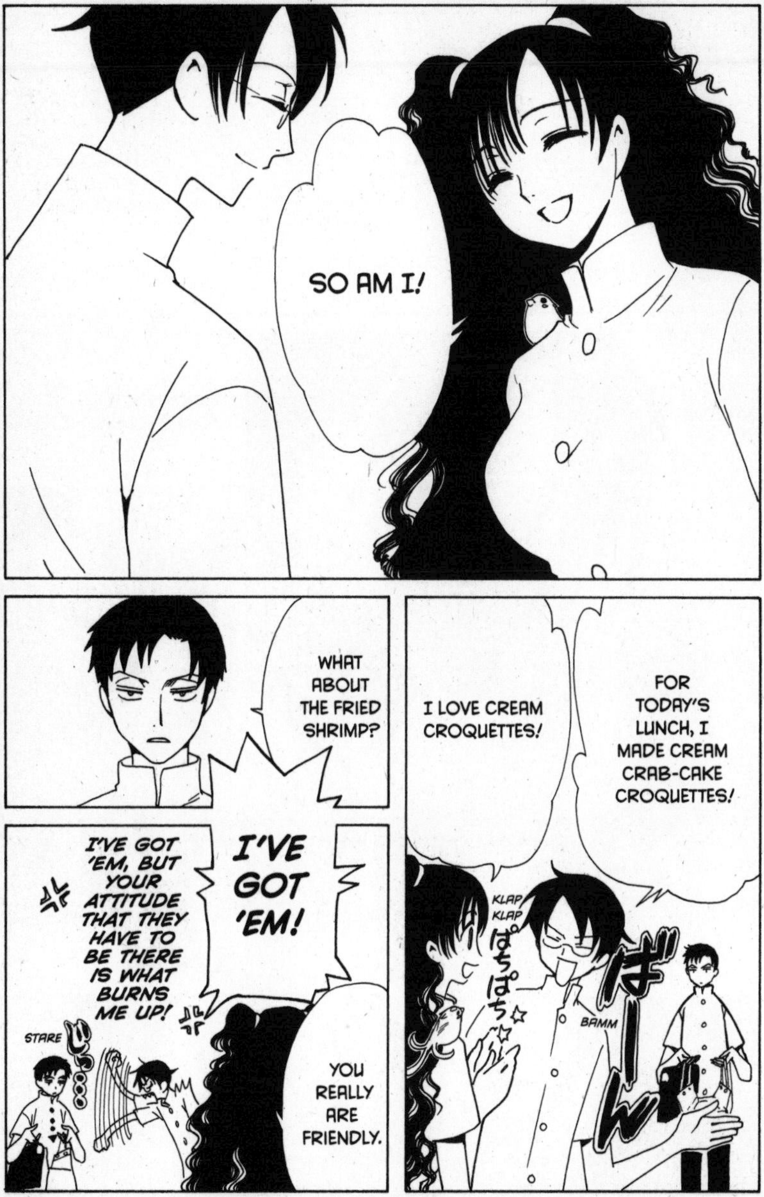
SO AM I!
FOR TODAY'S LUNCH, I MADE CREAM CRAB-CAKE CROQUETTES!
I LOVE CREAM CROQUETTES!
KLAP KLAP
ぱちぱち
ばーん
BAMM
WHAT ABOUT THE FRIED SHRIMP?
I'VE GOT 'EM!
I'VE GOT 'EM, BUT YOUR ATTITUDE THAT THEY HAVE TO BE THERE IS WHAT BURNS ME UP!
YOU REALLY ARE FRIENDLY.
STARE

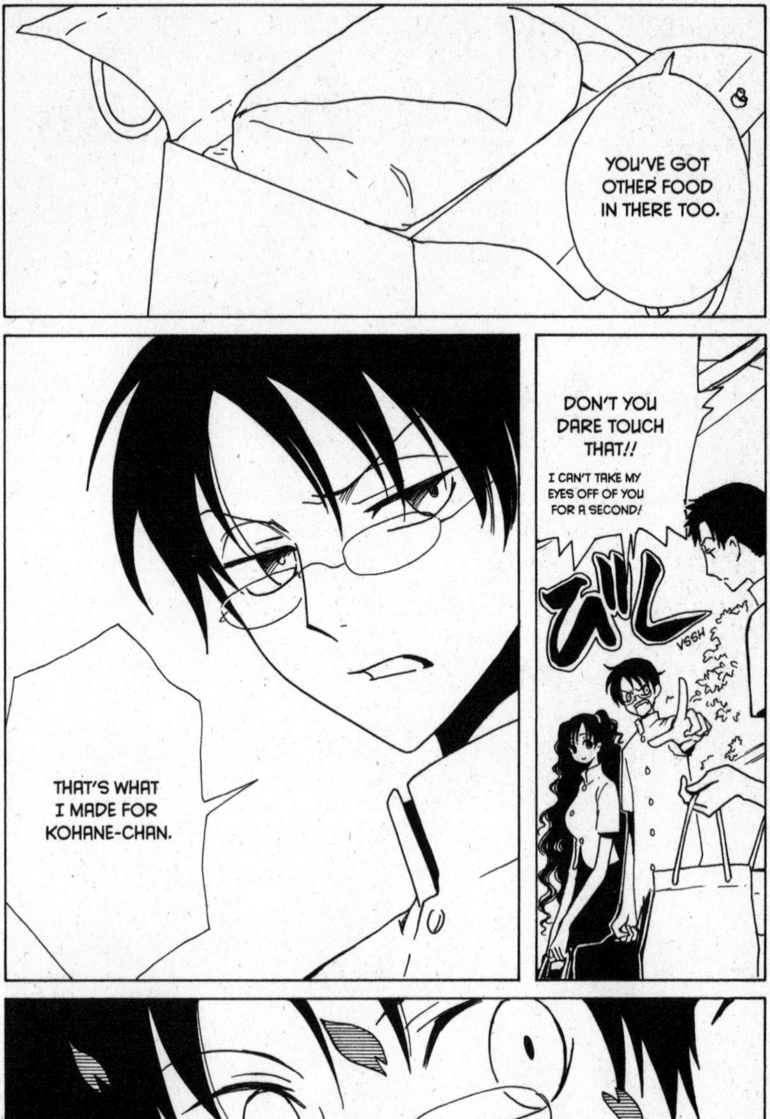
YOU'VE GOT OTHER FOOD IN THERE TOO.
DON'T YOU DARE TOUCH THAT!!
I CAN'T TAKE MY EYES OFF OF YOU FOR A SECOND!
VSSH
THAT'S WHAT I MADE FOR KOHANE-CHAN.

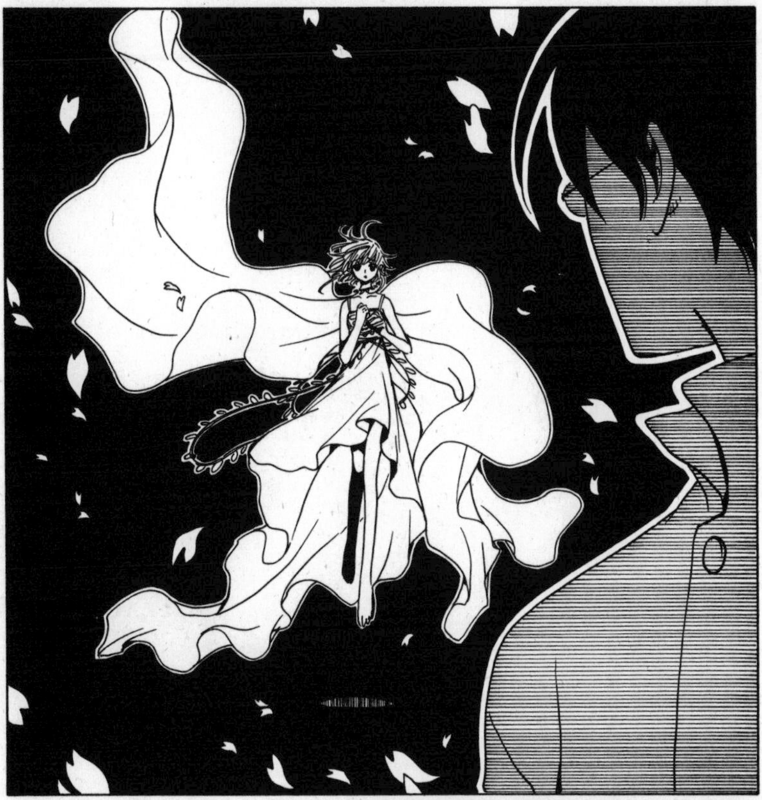

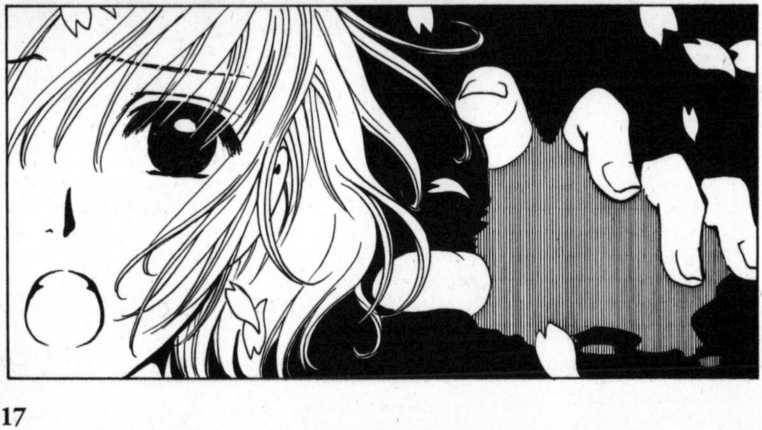

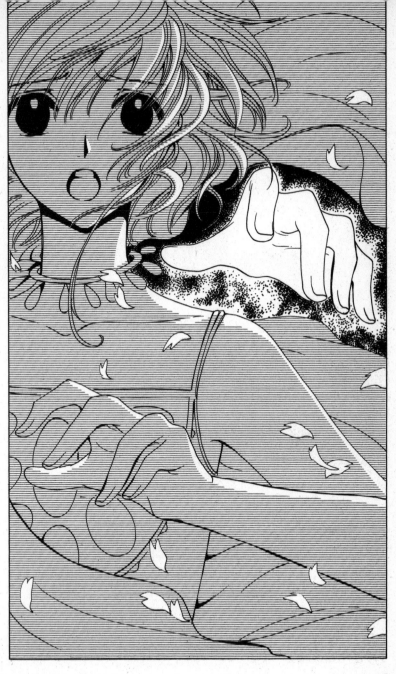

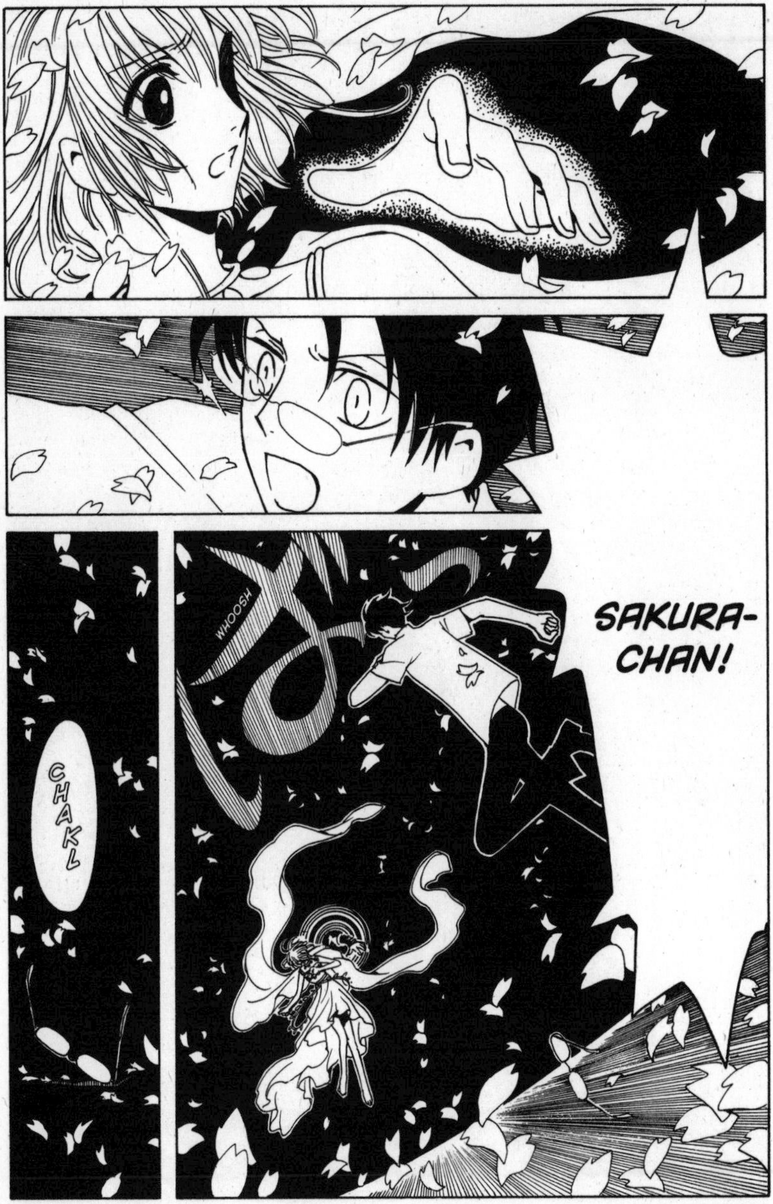
SAKURA-CHAN!
WHOOSH
CHAK!

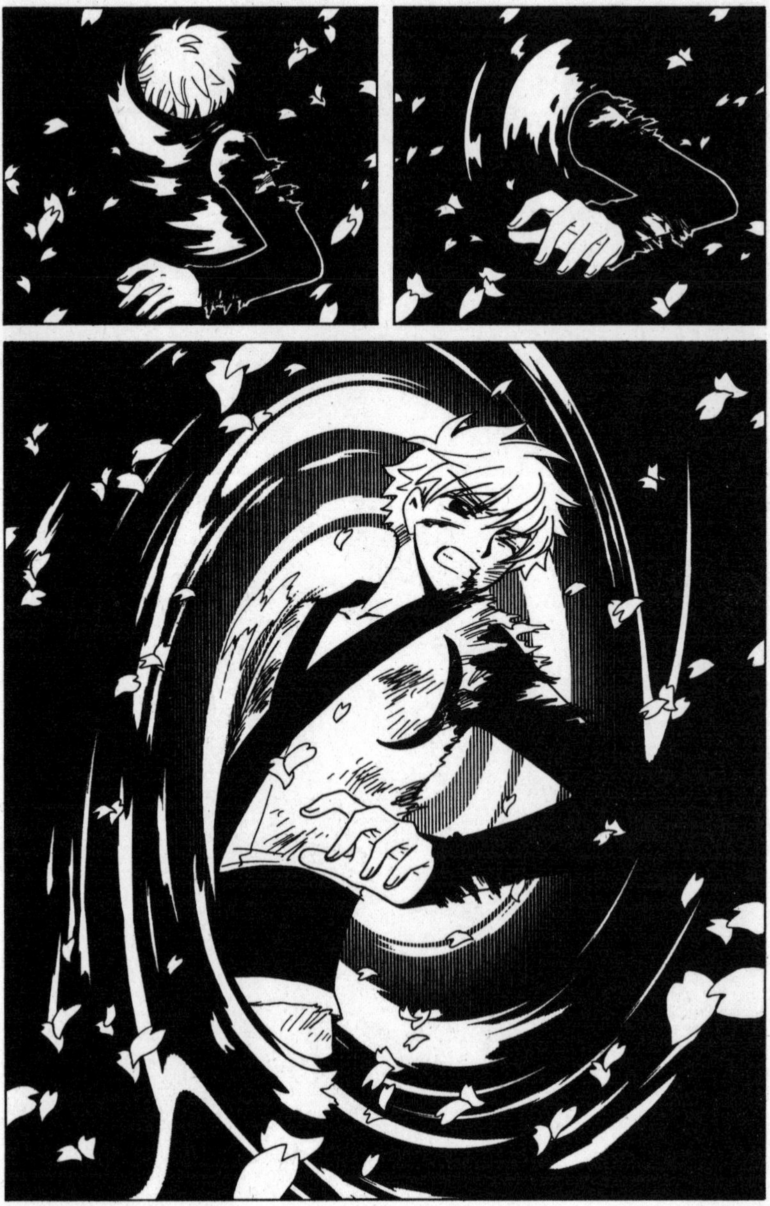

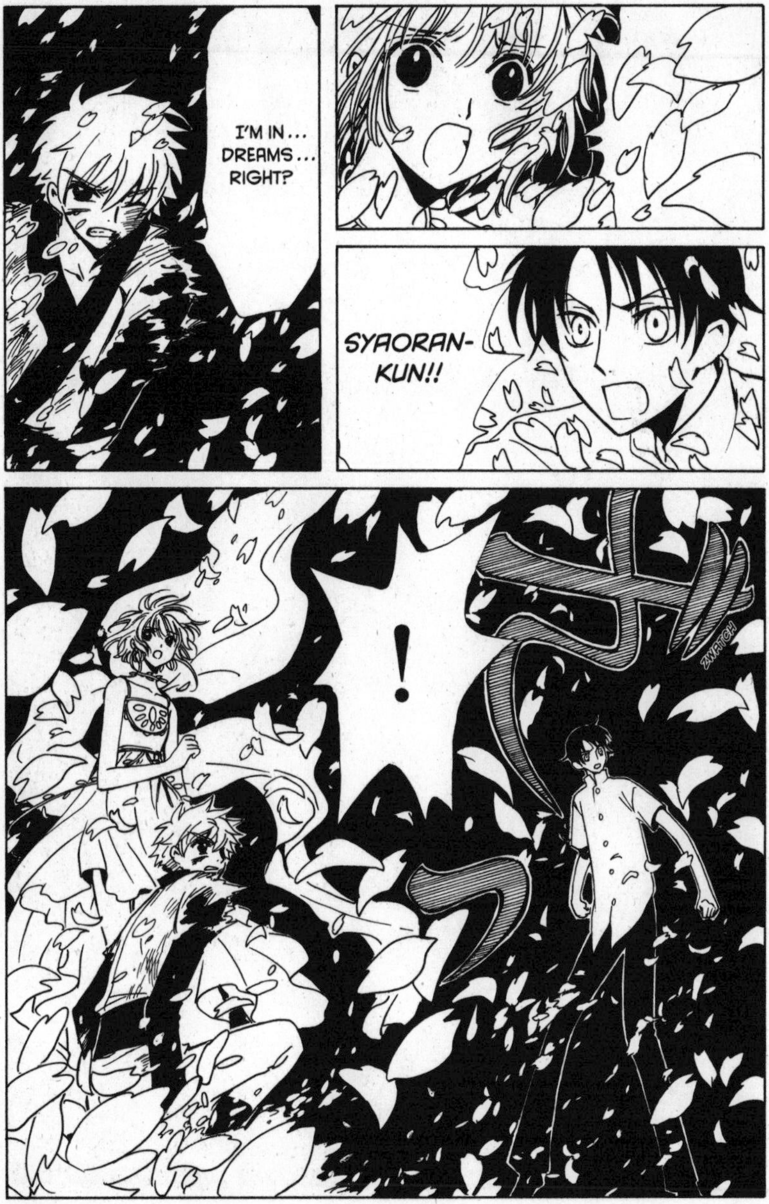
SYAORAN-KUN!!
I'M IN... DREAMS... RIGHT?
ZWATCH
!

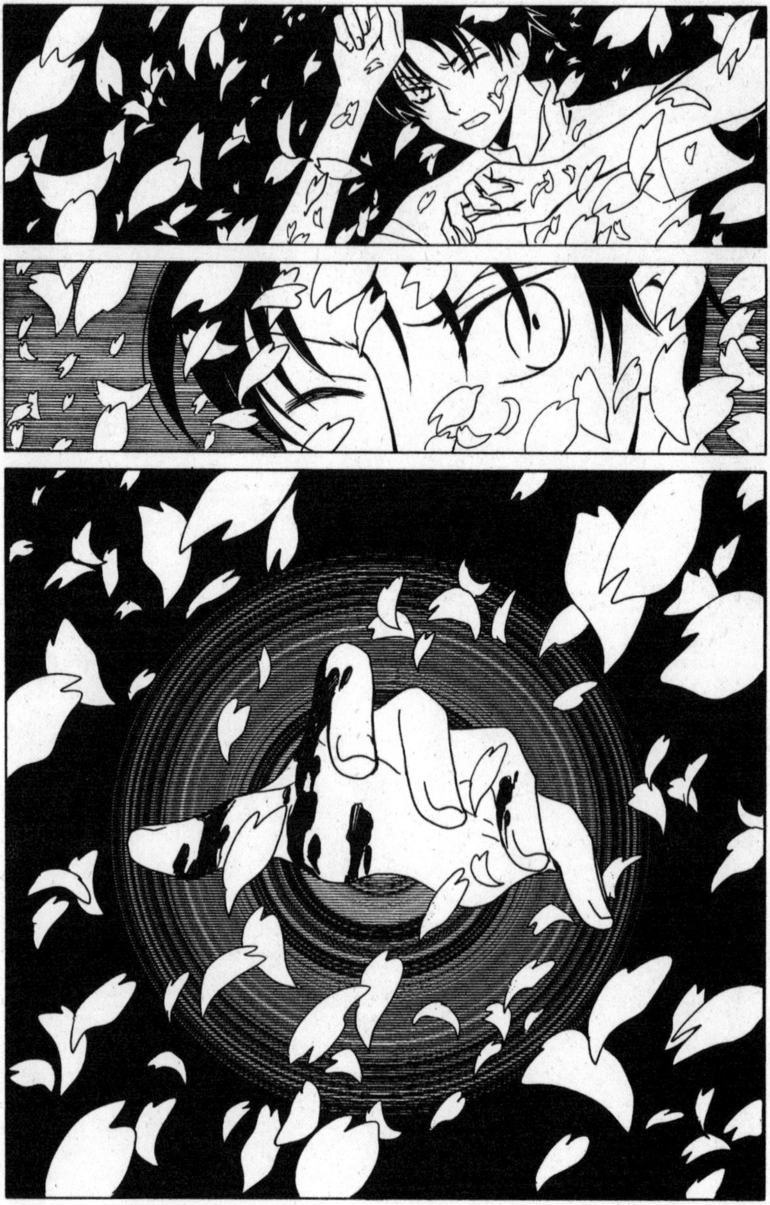

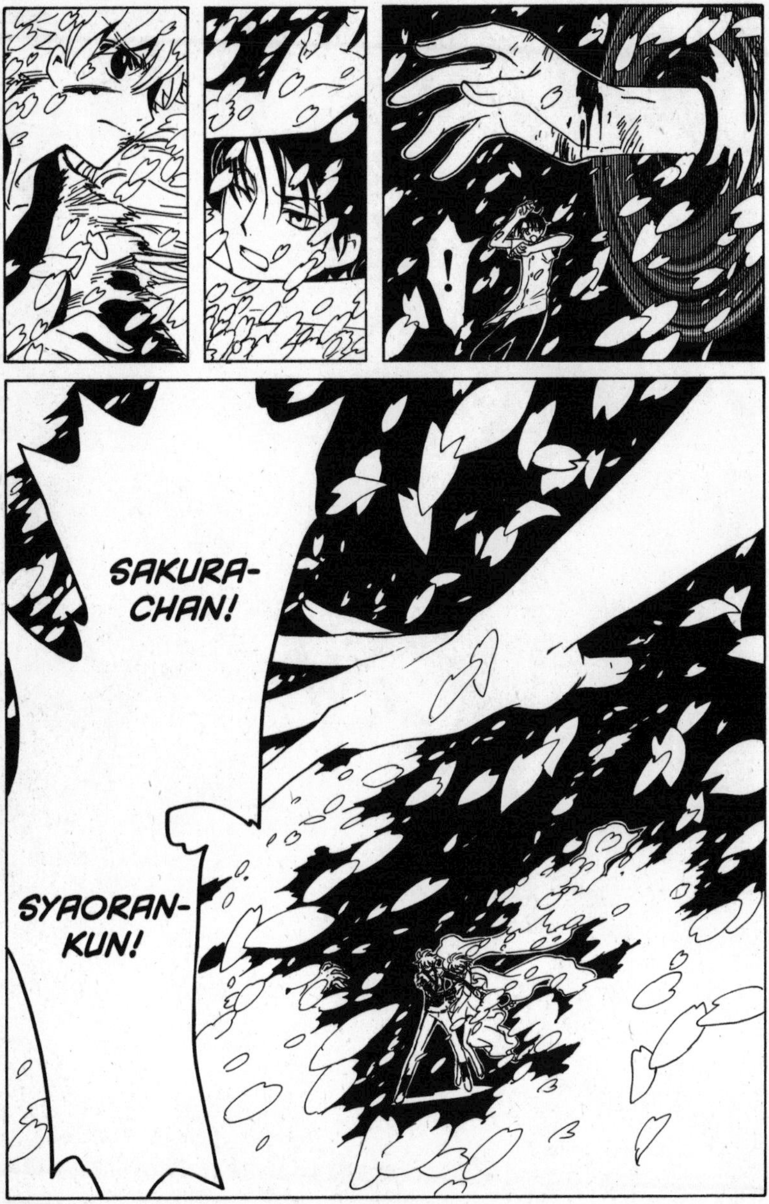
!
SAKURA-CHAN!
SYAORAN-KUN!

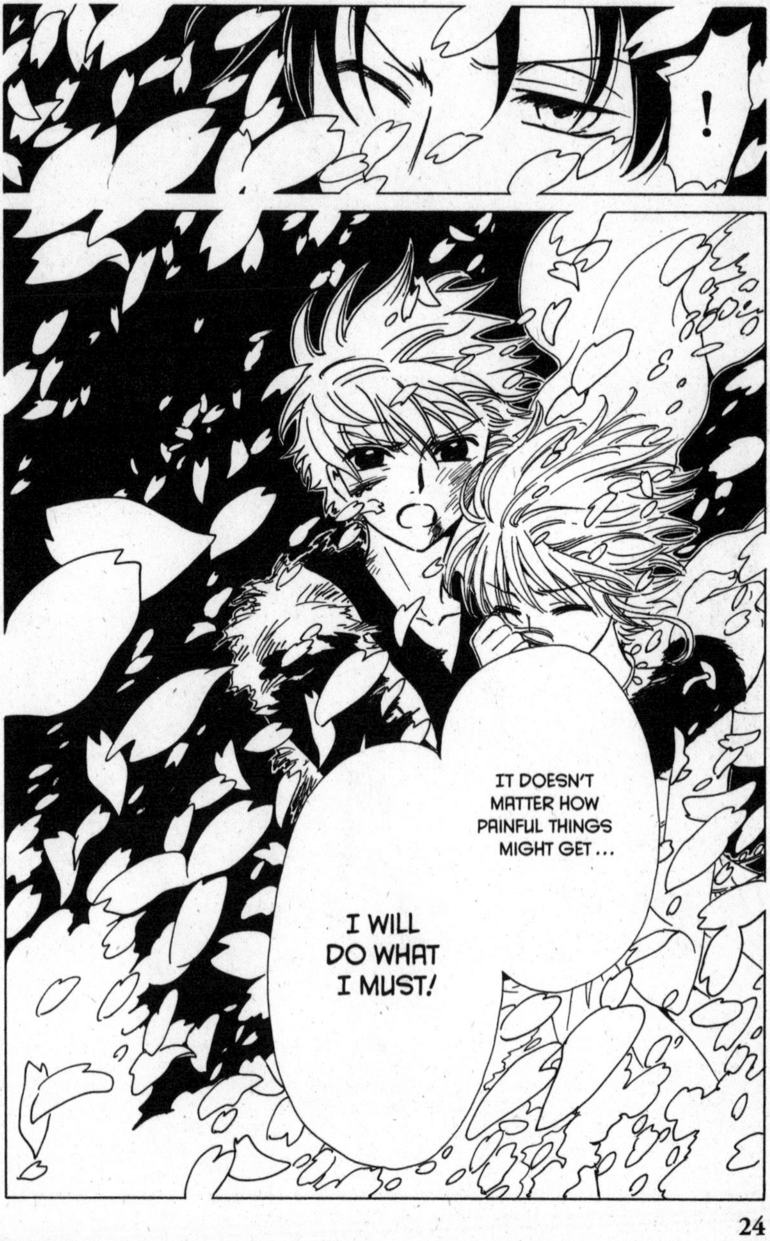
!
IT DOESN'T MATTER HOW PAINFUL THINGS MIGHT GET...
I WILL DO WHAT I MUST!

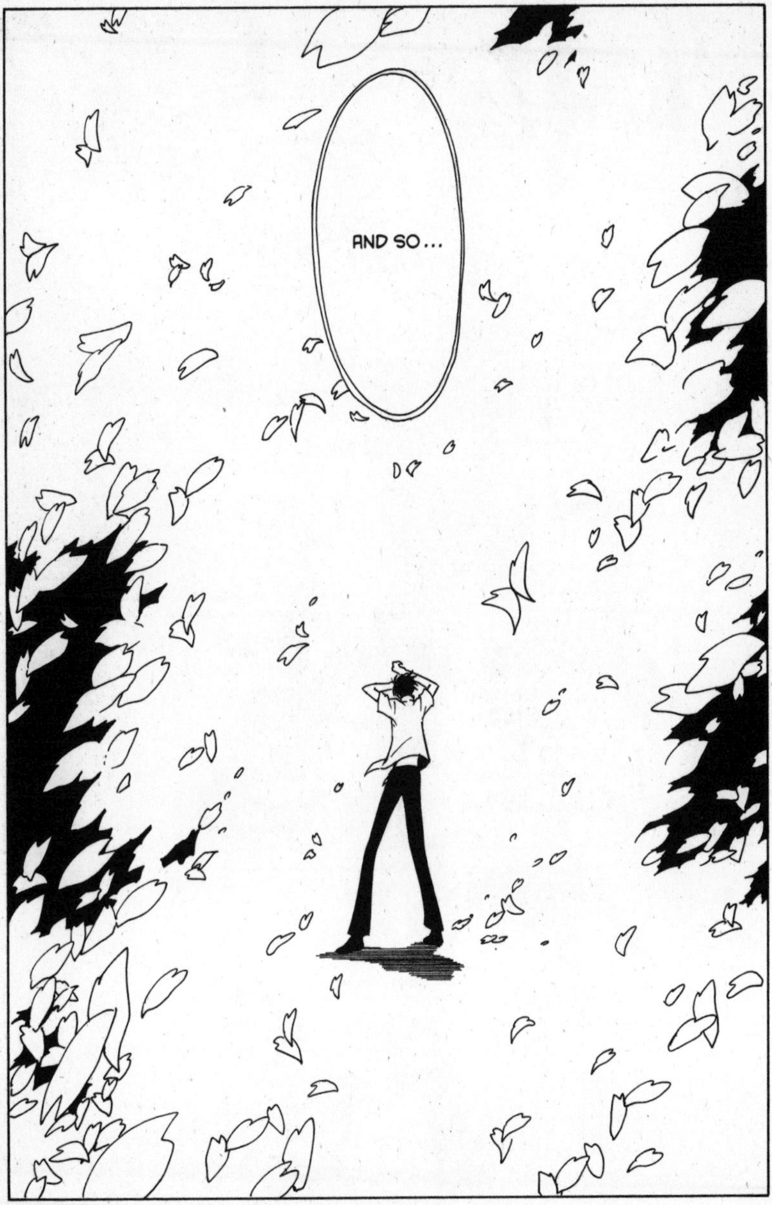
AND SO...

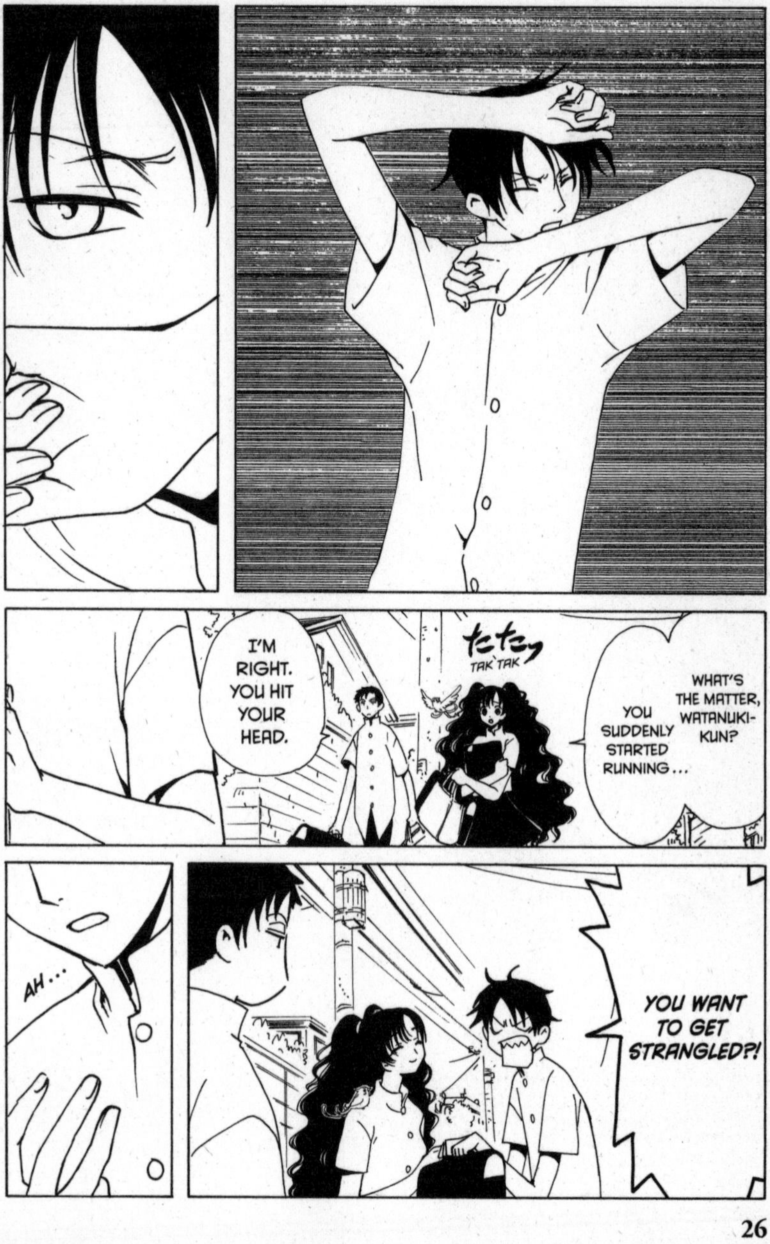
WHAT'S THE MATTER, WATANUKI-KUN?
YOU SUDDENLY STARTED RUNNING...
たたっ
TAK TAK
I'M RIGHT. YOU HIT YOUR HEAD.
YOU WANT TO GET STRANGLED?!
AH...

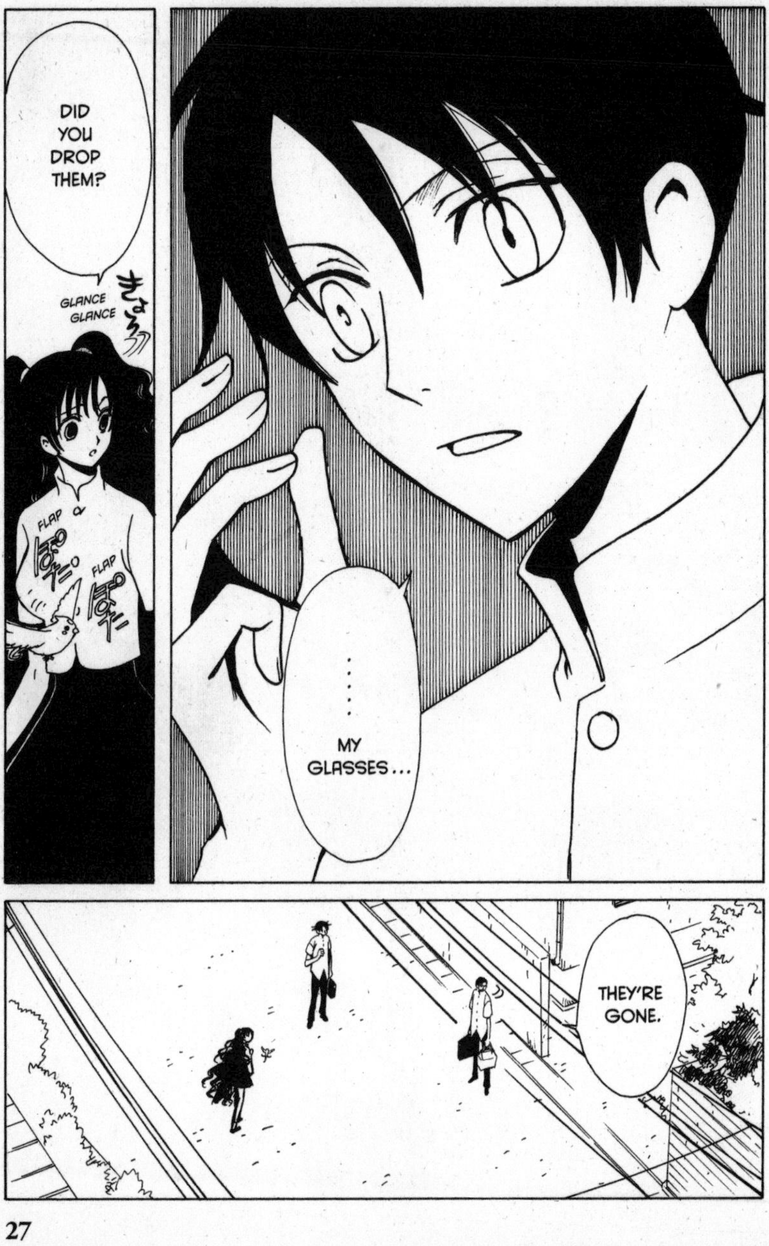

.....
MY GLASSES...
DID YOU DROP THEM?
GLANCE GLANCE
FLAP
FLAP
THEY'RE GONE.

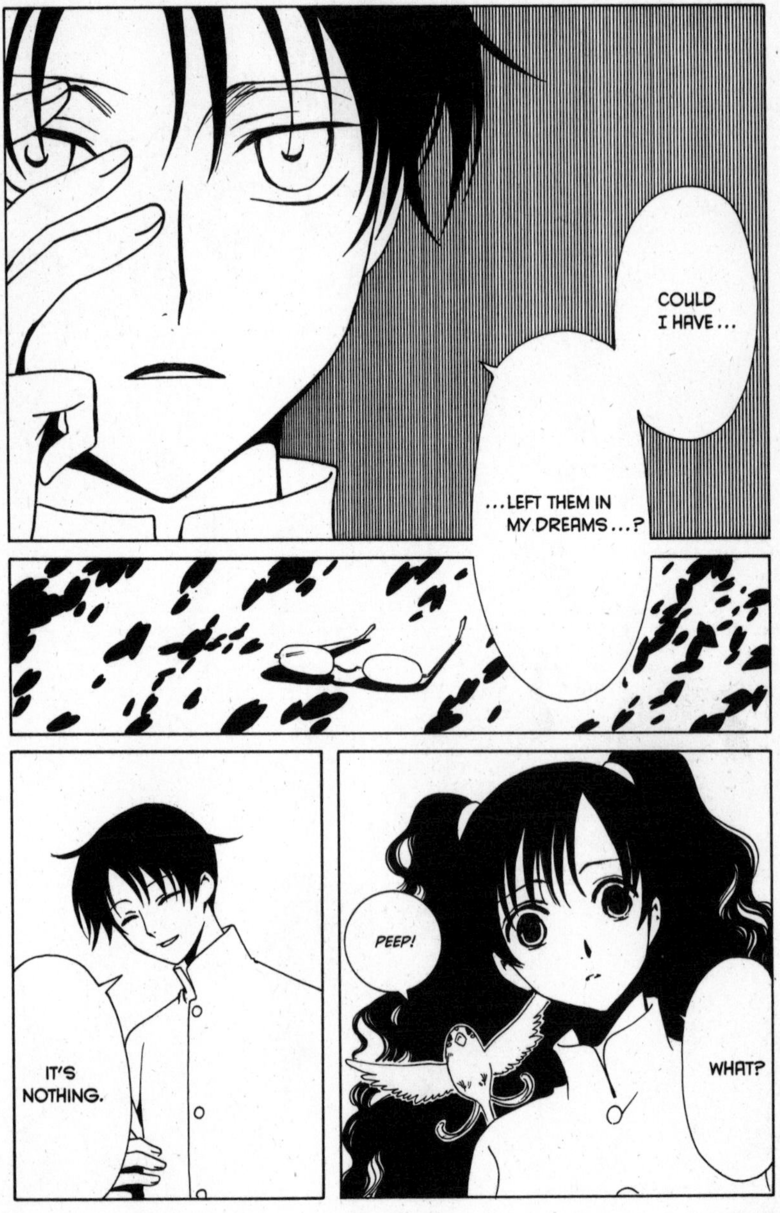
COULD I HAVE...
...LEFT THEM IN MY DREAMS...?
PEEP!
WHAT?
IT'S NOTHING.

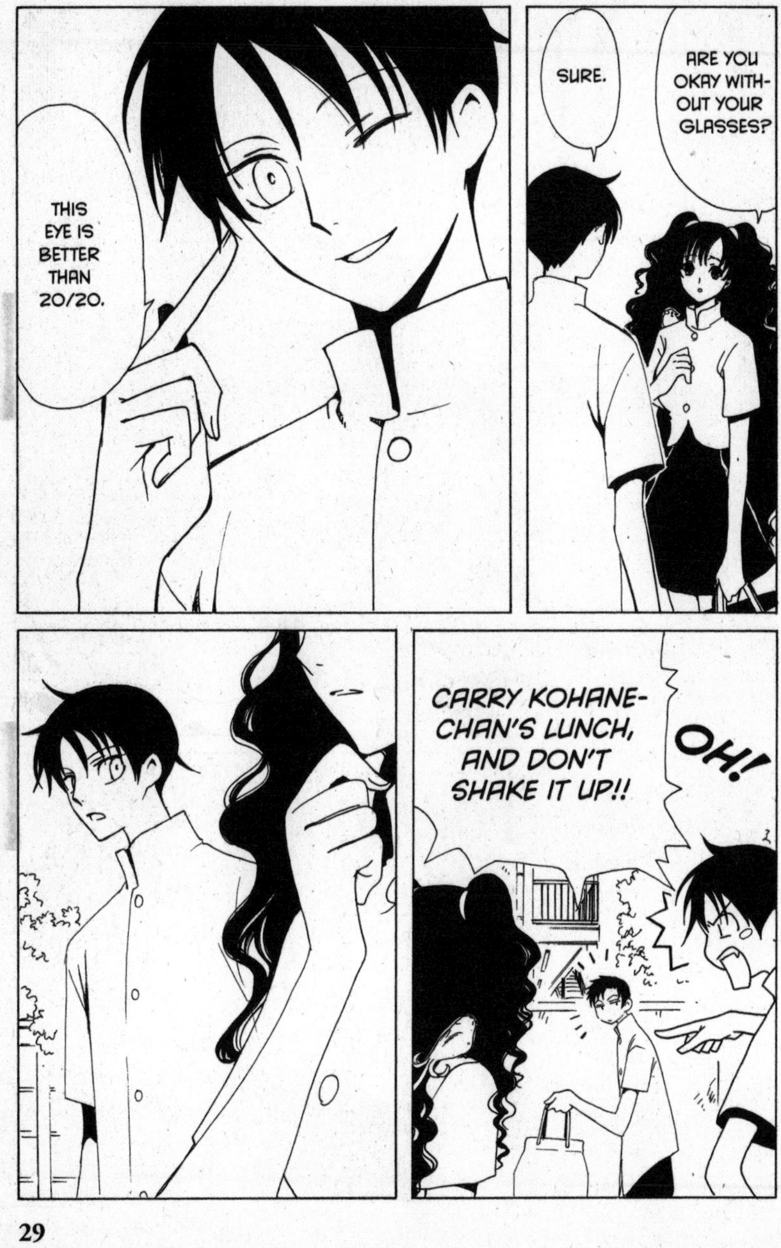
ARE YOU OKAY WITH-OUT YOUR GLASSES?
SURE.
THIS EYE IS BETTER THAN 20/20.
OH!
CARRY KOHANE-CHAN'S LUNCH, AND DON'T SHAKE IT UP!!

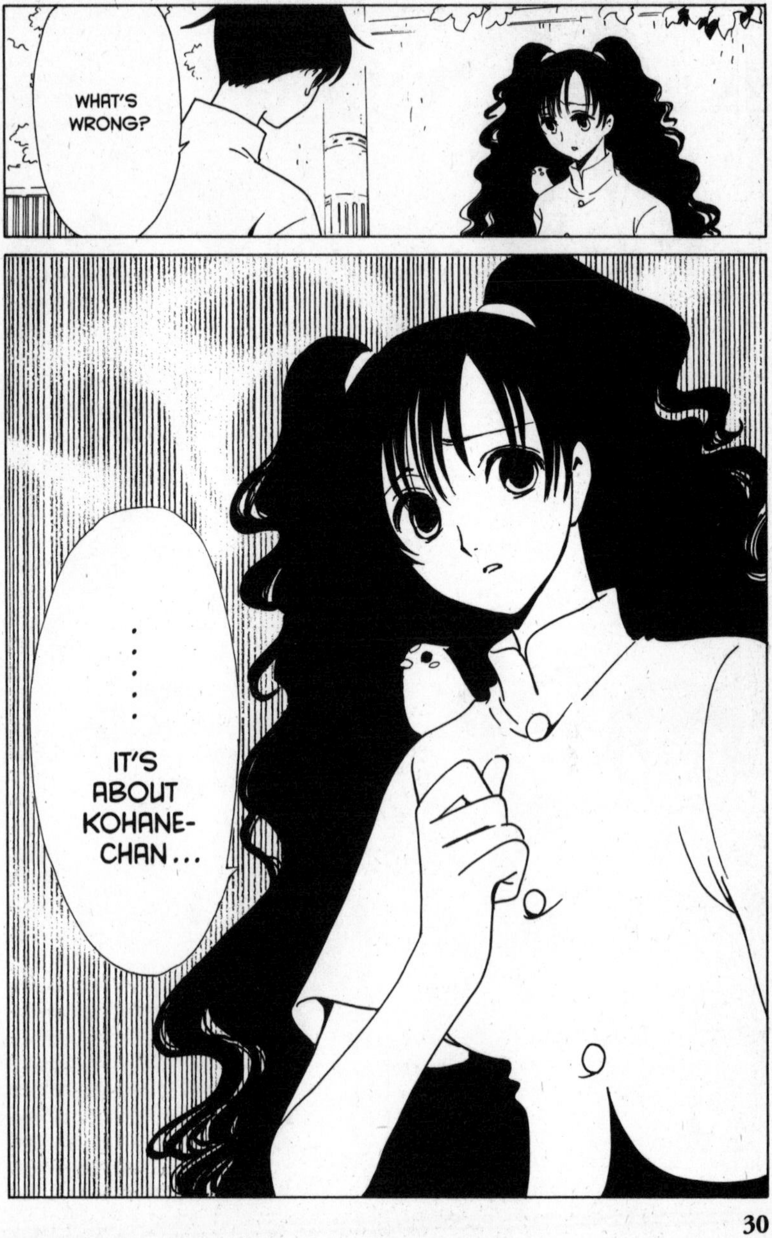
WHAT'S WRONG?
.....
IT'S ABOUT KOHANE-CHAN...

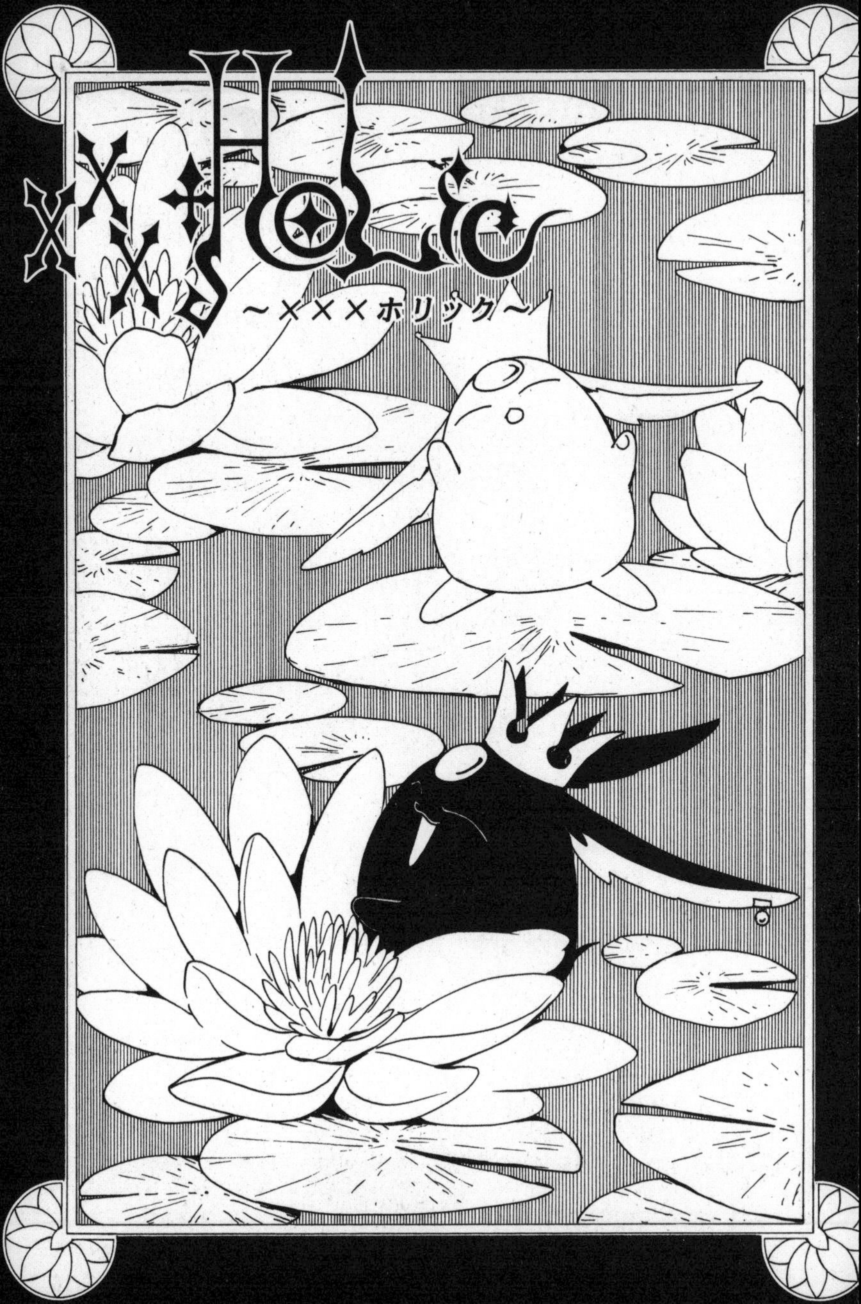
xxxHOLiC
~×××ホリック~

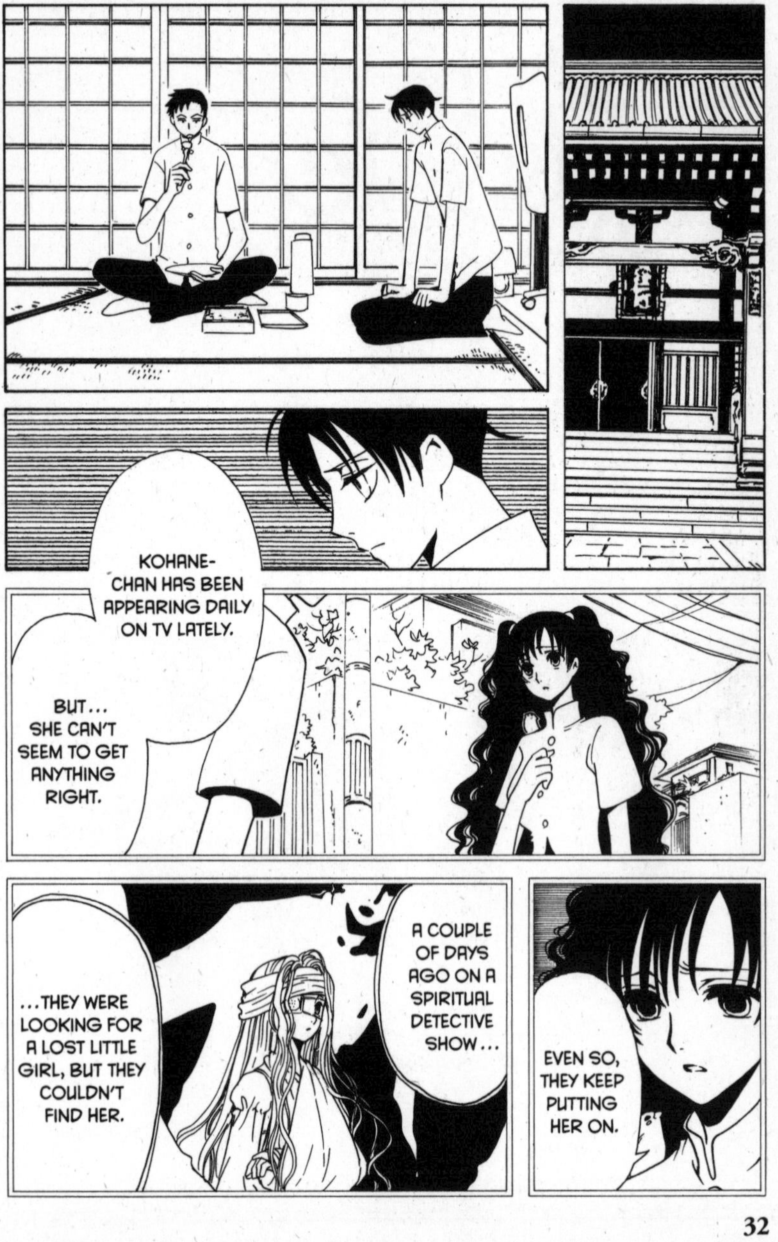
KOHANE-CHAN HAS BEEN APPEARING DAILY ON TV LATELY.
BUT… SHE CAN'T SEEM TO GET ANYTHING RIGHT.
EVEN SO, THEY KEEP PUTTING HER ON.
A COUPLE OF DAYS AGO ON A SPIRITUAL DETECTIVE SHOW…
…THEY WERE LOOKING FOR A LOST LITTLE GIRL, BUT THEY COULDN'T FIND HER.

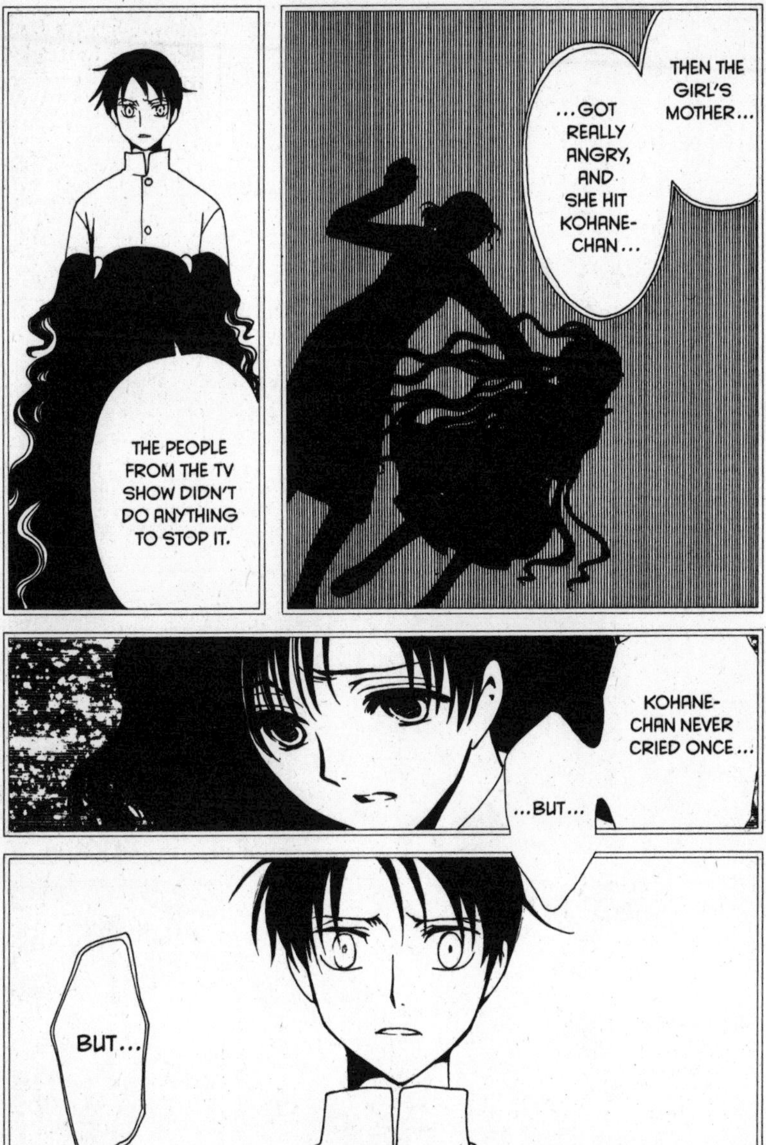
THEN THE GIRL'S MOTHER...
...GOT REALLY ANGRY, AND SHE HIT KOHANE-CHAN...
THE PEOPLE FROM THE TV SHOW DIDN'T DO ANYTHING TO STOP IT.
KOHANE-CHAN NEVER CRIED ONCE...
...BUT...
BUT...

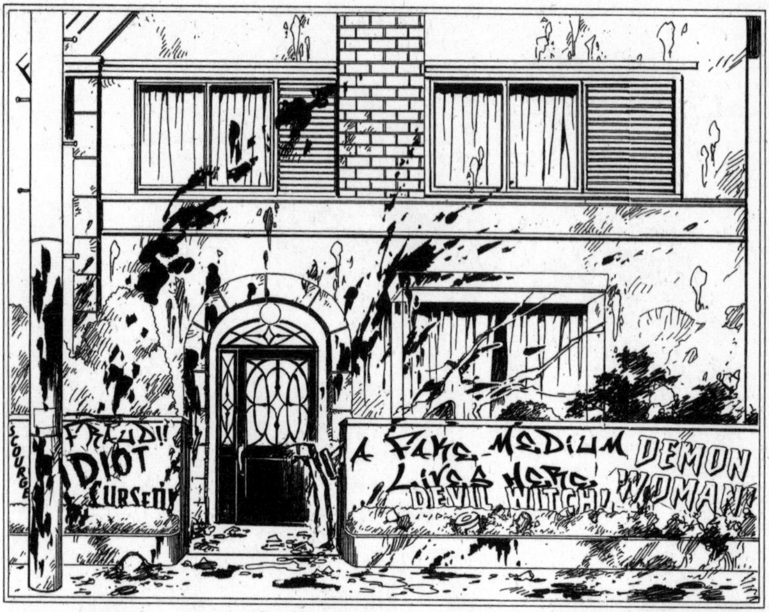
FRAUD!!
IDIOT
CURSED!!
SCOURGE
A FAKE MEDIUM LIVES HERE.
DEVIL WITCH!
DEMON WOMAN!!

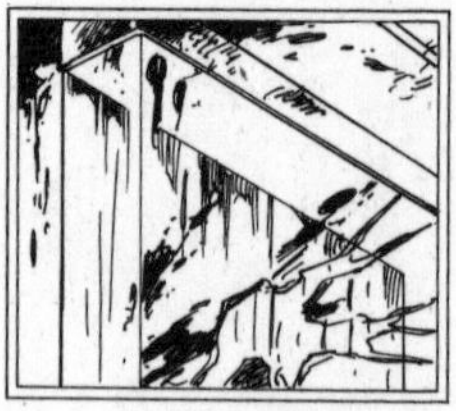

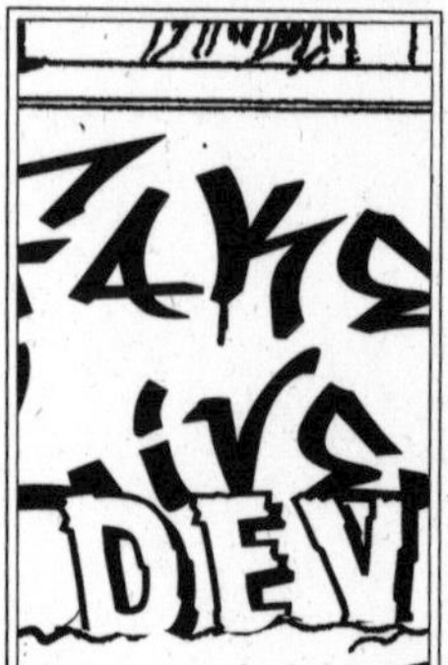
FAKE
DEV

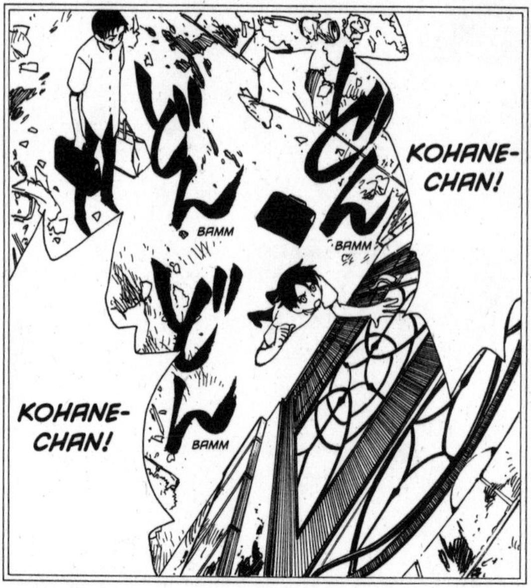
KOHANE-CHAN!
BAMM
BAMM
BAMM
KOHANE-CHAN!

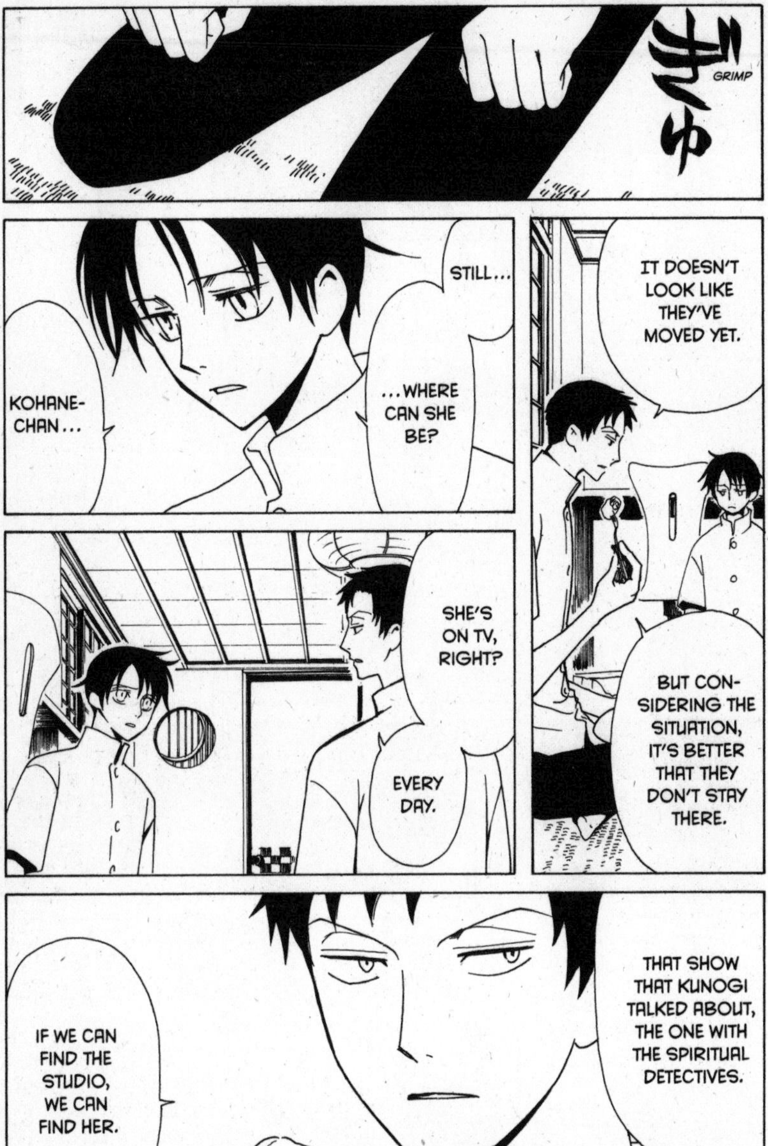
ぎゅ
GRIMP
IT DOESN'T LOOK LIKE THEY'VE MOVED YET.
BUT CON-SIDERING THE SITUATION, IT'S BETTER THAT THEY DON'T STAY THERE.
STILL...
...WHERE CAN SHE BE?
KOHANE-CHAN...
SHE'S ON TV, RIGHT?
EVERY DAY.
THAT SHOW THAT KUNOGI TALKED ABOUT, THE ONE WITH THE SPIRITUAL DETECTIVES.
IF WE CAN FIND THE STUDIO, WE CAN FIND HER.

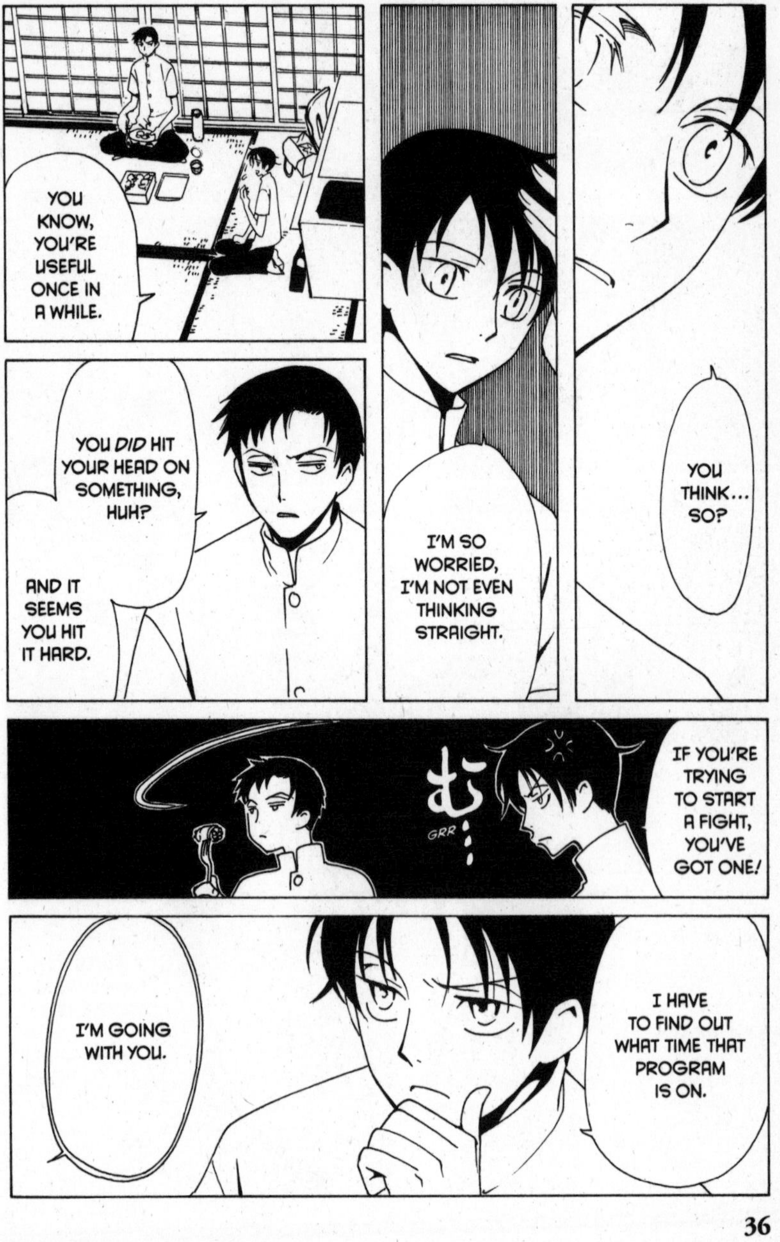
YOU THINK... SO?
I'M SO WORRIED, I'M NOT EVEN THINKING STRAIGHT.
YOU KNOW, YOU'RE USEFUL ONCE IN A WHILE.
YOU *DID* HIT YOUR HEAD ON SOMETHING, HUH?
AND IT SEEMS YOU HIT IT HARD.
IF YOU'RE TRYING TO START A FIGHT, YOU'VE GOT ONE!
む
GRR
I HAVE TO FIND OUT WHAT TIME THAT PROGRAM IS ON.
I'M GOING WITH YOU.

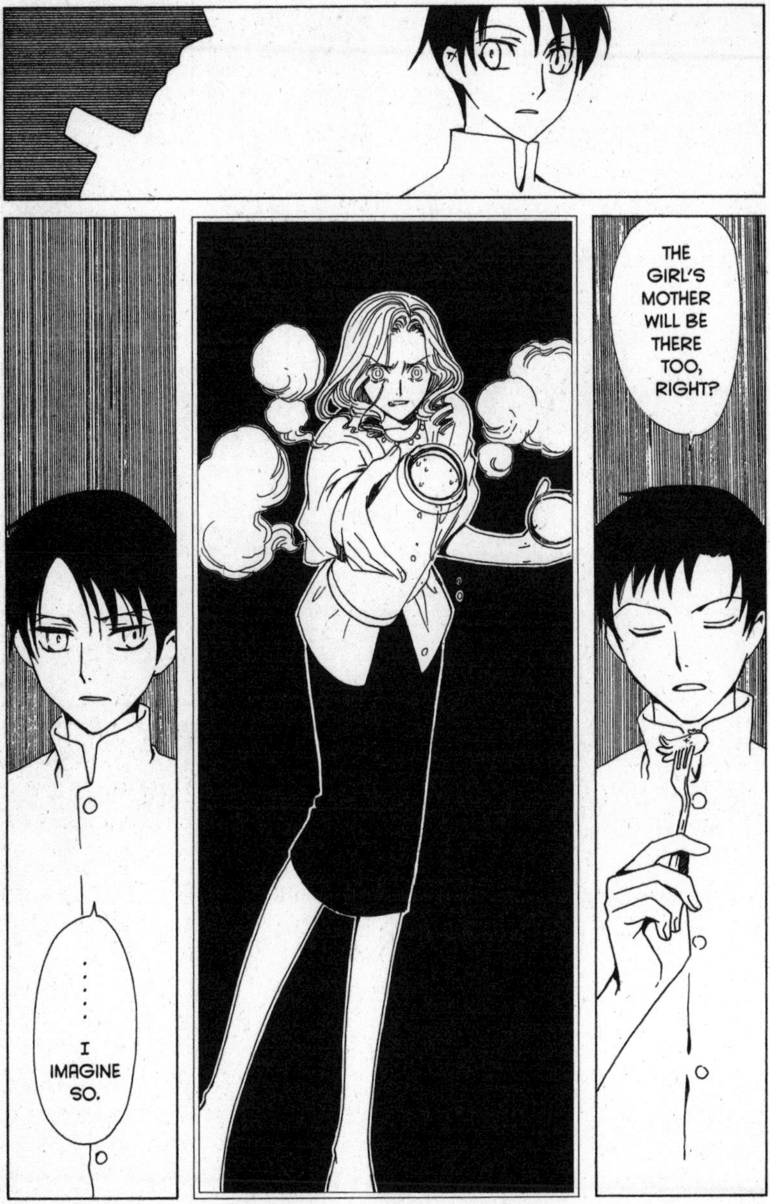
THE GIRL'S MOTHER WILL BE THERE TOO, RIGHT?
...... I IMAGINE SO.

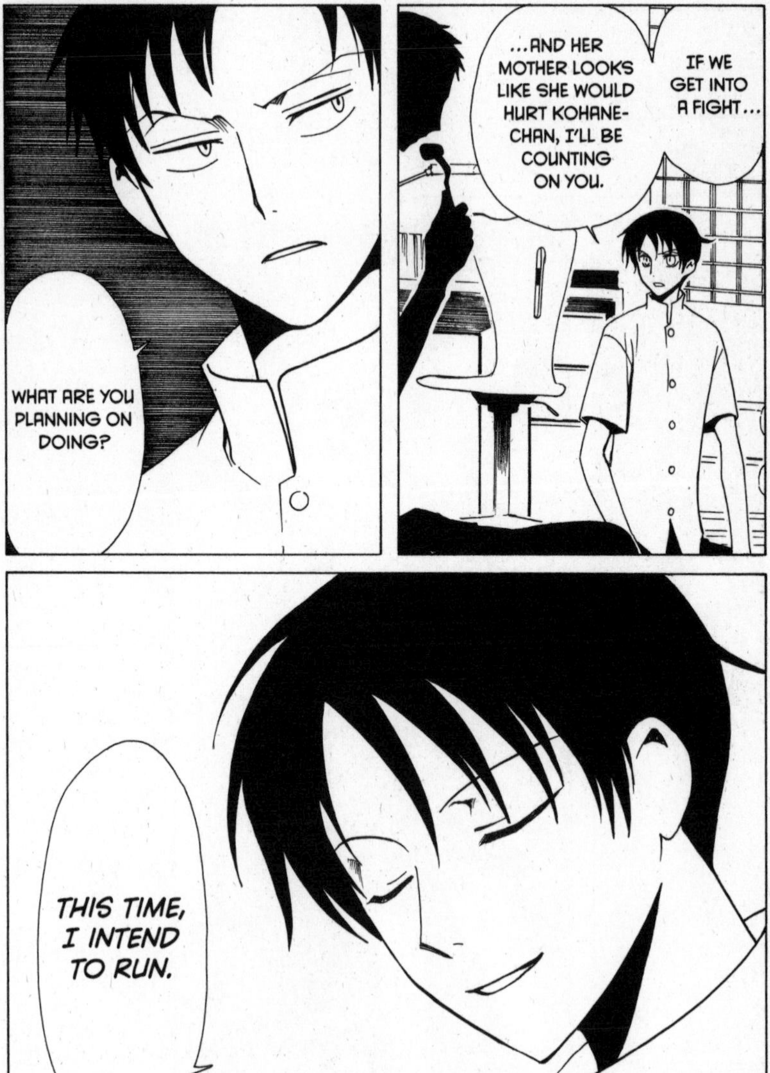
IF WE GET INTO A FIGHT...
...AND HER MOTHER LOOKS LIKE SHE WOULD HURT KOHANE-CHAN, I'LL BE COUNTING ON YOU.
WHAT ARE YOU PLANNING ON DOING?
THIS TIME, I INTEND TO RUN.

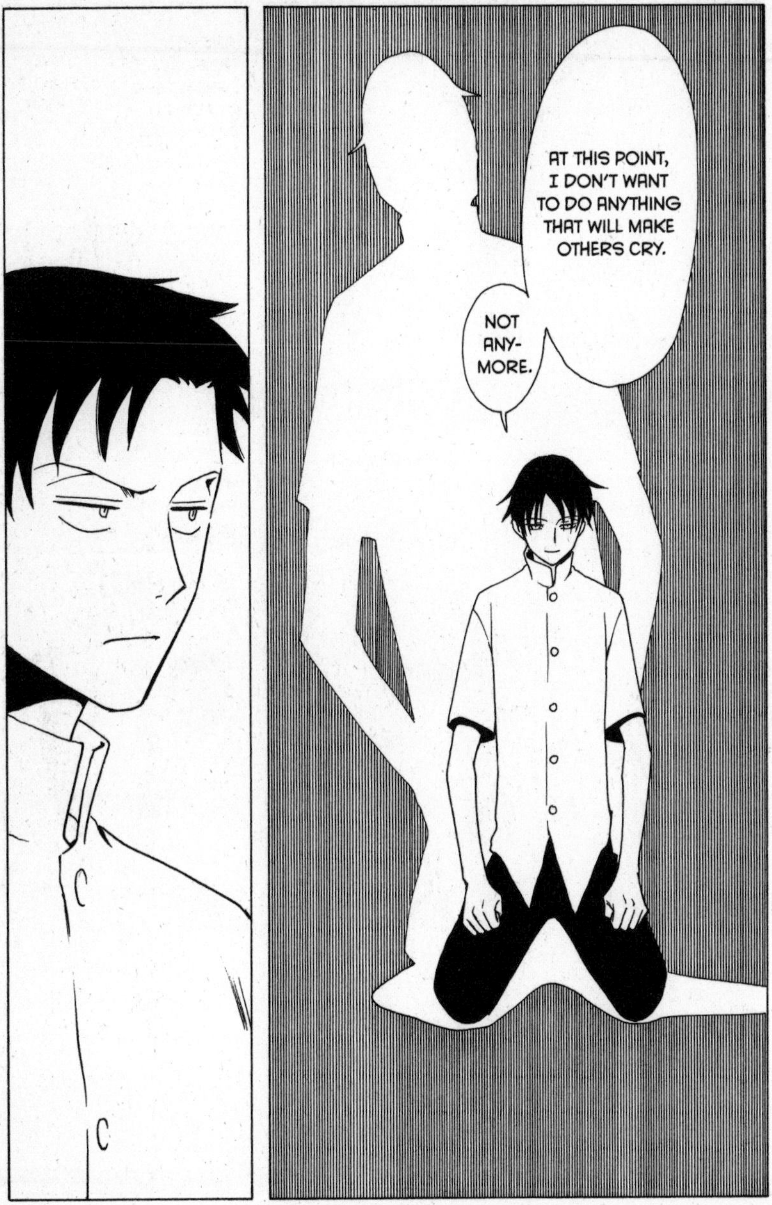
AT THIS POINT, I DON'T WANT TO DO ANYTHING THAT WILL MAKE OTHERS CRY.
NOT ANY-MORE.

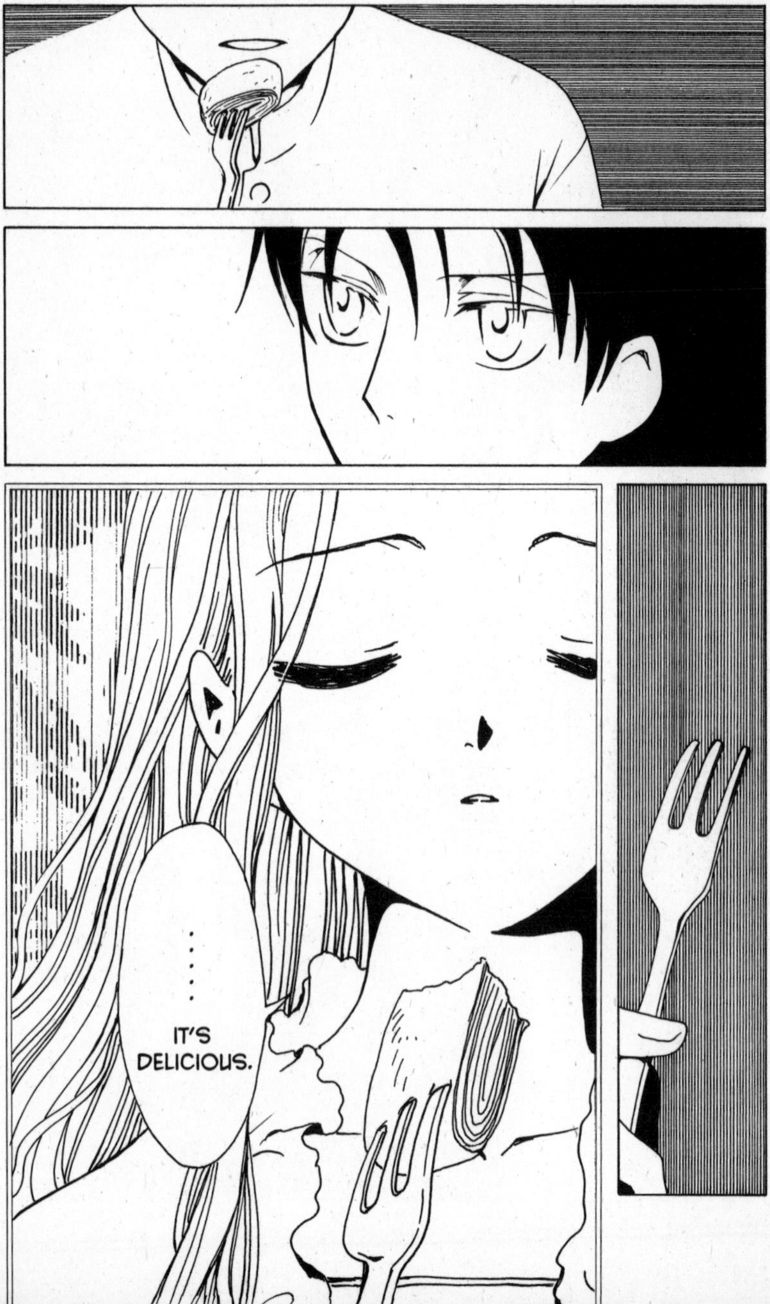
...... IT'S DELICIOUS.

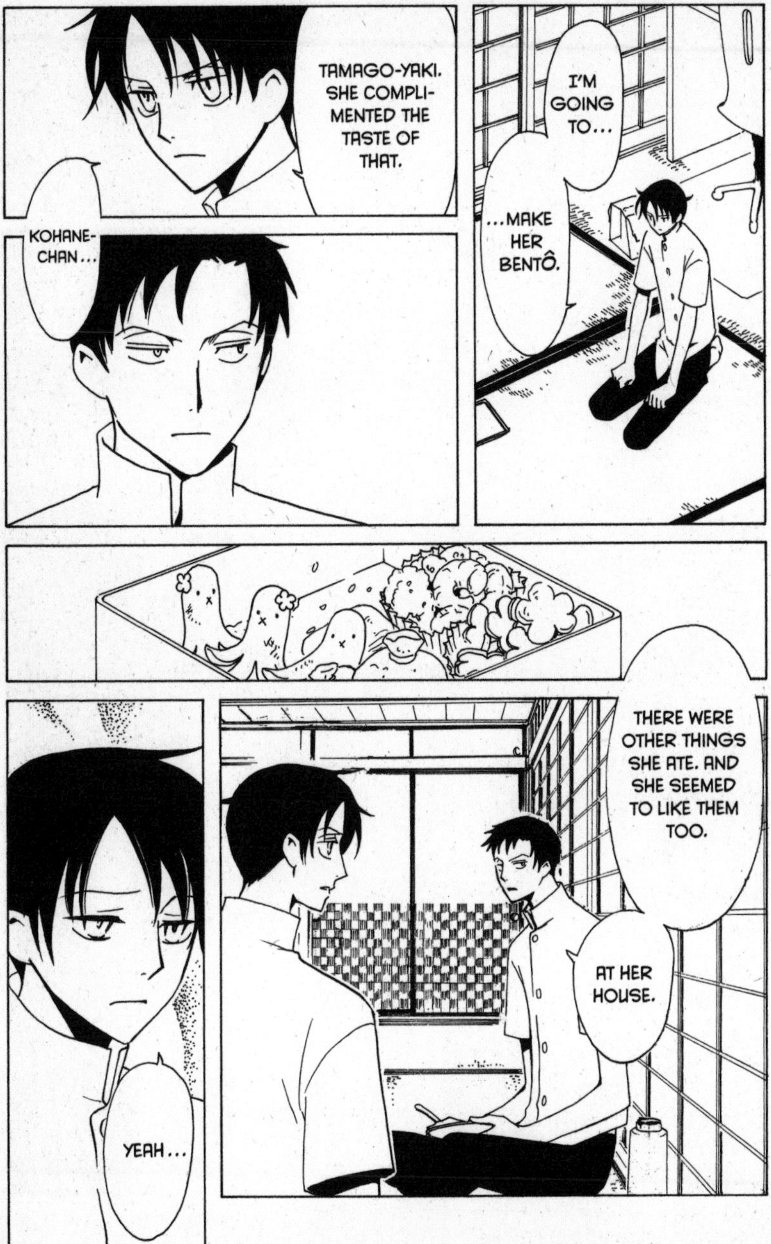
I'M GOING TO...
...MAKE HER BENTÔ.
TAMAGO-YAKI. SHE COMPLIMENTED THE TASTE OF THAT.
KOHANE-CHAN...
THERE WERE OTHER THINGS SHE ATE. AND SHE SEEMED TO LIKE THEM TOO.
AT HER HOUSE.
YEAH...

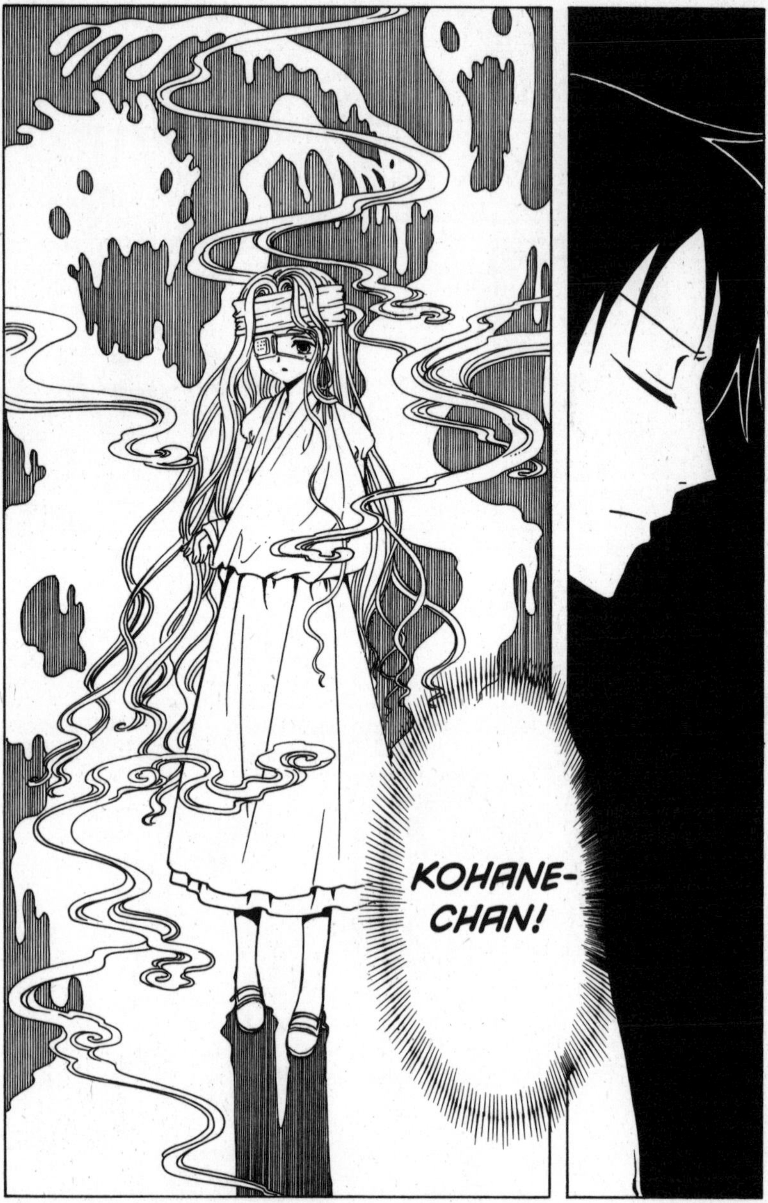
KOHANE-
CHAN!

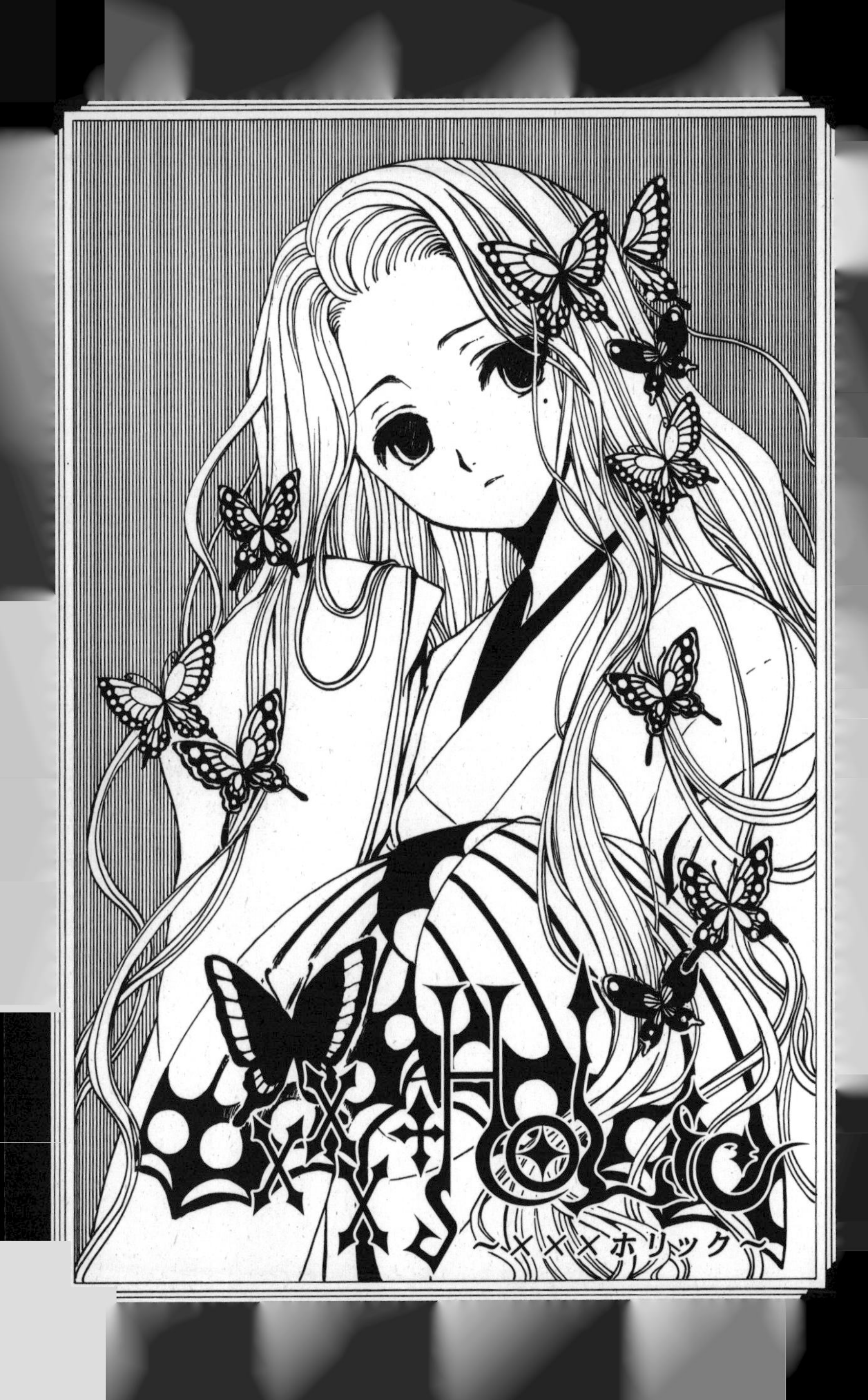
xxxHOLiC
〜×××ホリック〜

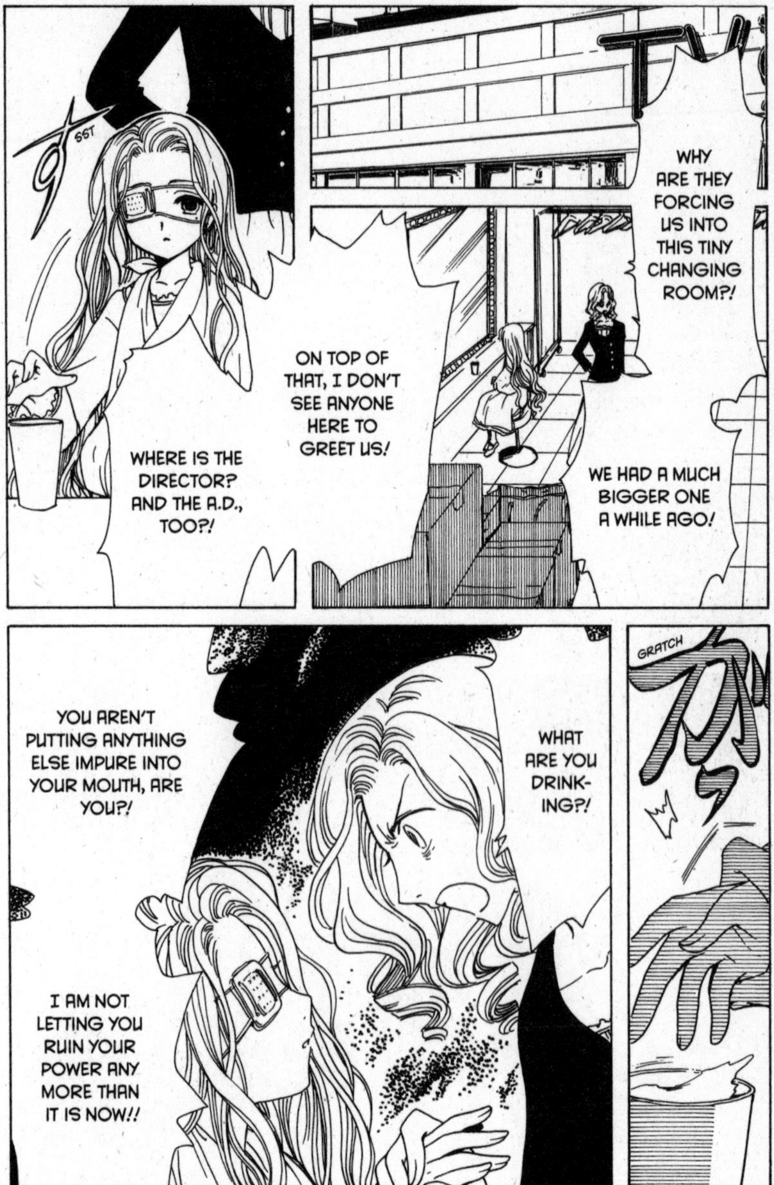
WHY ARE THEY FORCING US INTO THIS TINY CHANGING ROOM?!
WE HAD A MUCH BIGGER ONE A WHILE AGO!
ON TOP OF THAT, I DON'T SEE ANYONE HERE TO GREET US!
SST
WHERE IS THE DIRECTOR? AND THE A.D., TOO?!
GRATCH
WHAT ARE YOU DRINKING?!
YOU AREN'T PUTTING ANYTHING ELSE IMPURE INTO YOUR MOUTH, ARE YOU?!
I AM NOT LETTING YOU RUIN YOUR POWER ANY MORE THAN IT IS NOW!!

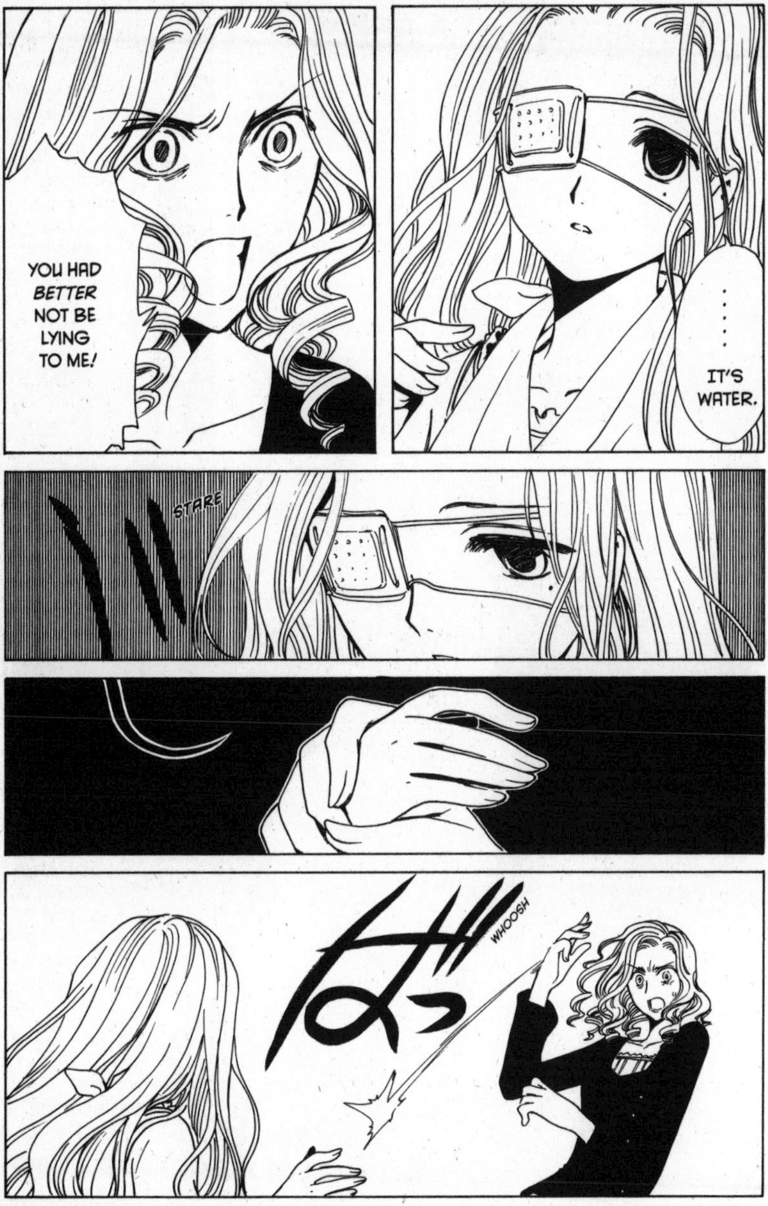
......
IT'S WATER.
YOU HAD *BETTER* NOT BE LYING TO ME!
STARE
WHOOSH

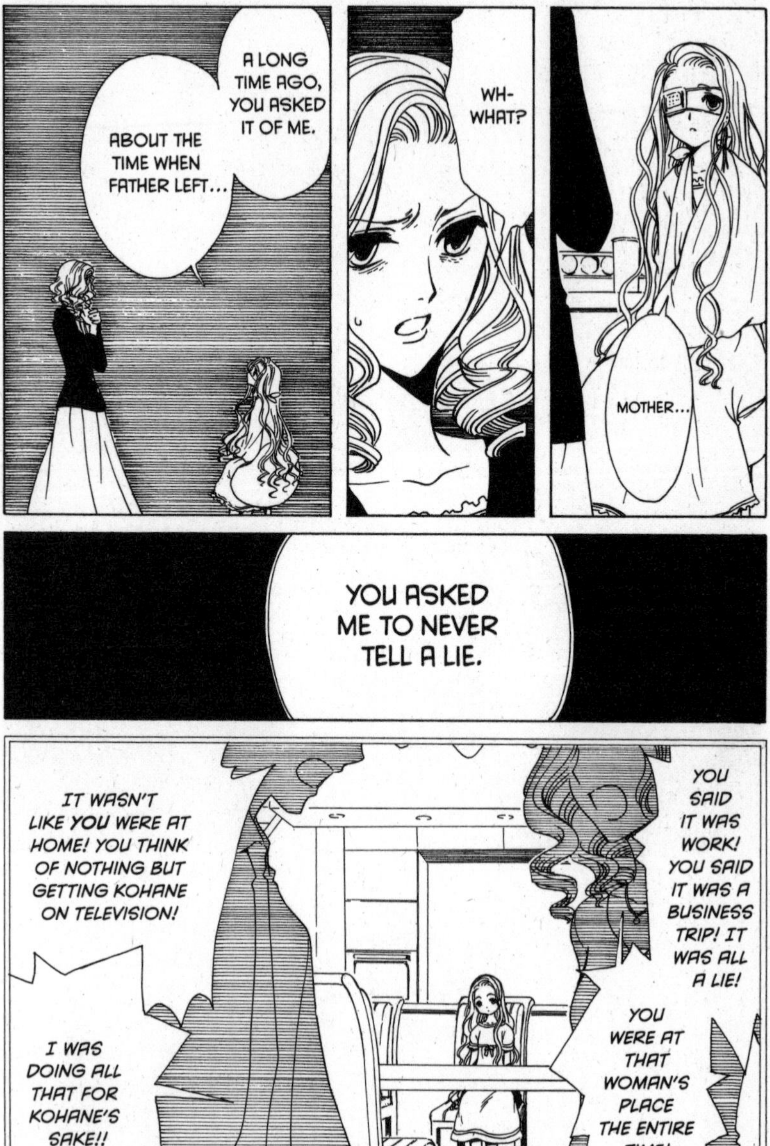
MOTHER...
WH- WHAT?
A LONG TIME AGO, YOU ASKED IT OF ME.
ABOUT THE TIME WHEN FATHER LEFT...
YOU ASKED ME TO NEVER TELL A LIE.
YOU SAID IT WAS WORK! YOU SAID IT WAS A BUSINESS TRIP! IT WAS ALL A LIE!
IT WASN'T LIKE *YOU* WERE AT HOME! YOU THINK OF NOTHING BUT GETTING KOHANE ON TELEVISION!
YOU WERE AT THAT WOMAN'S PLACE THE ENTIRE TIME!
I WAS DOING ALL THAT FOR KOHANE'S SAKE!!

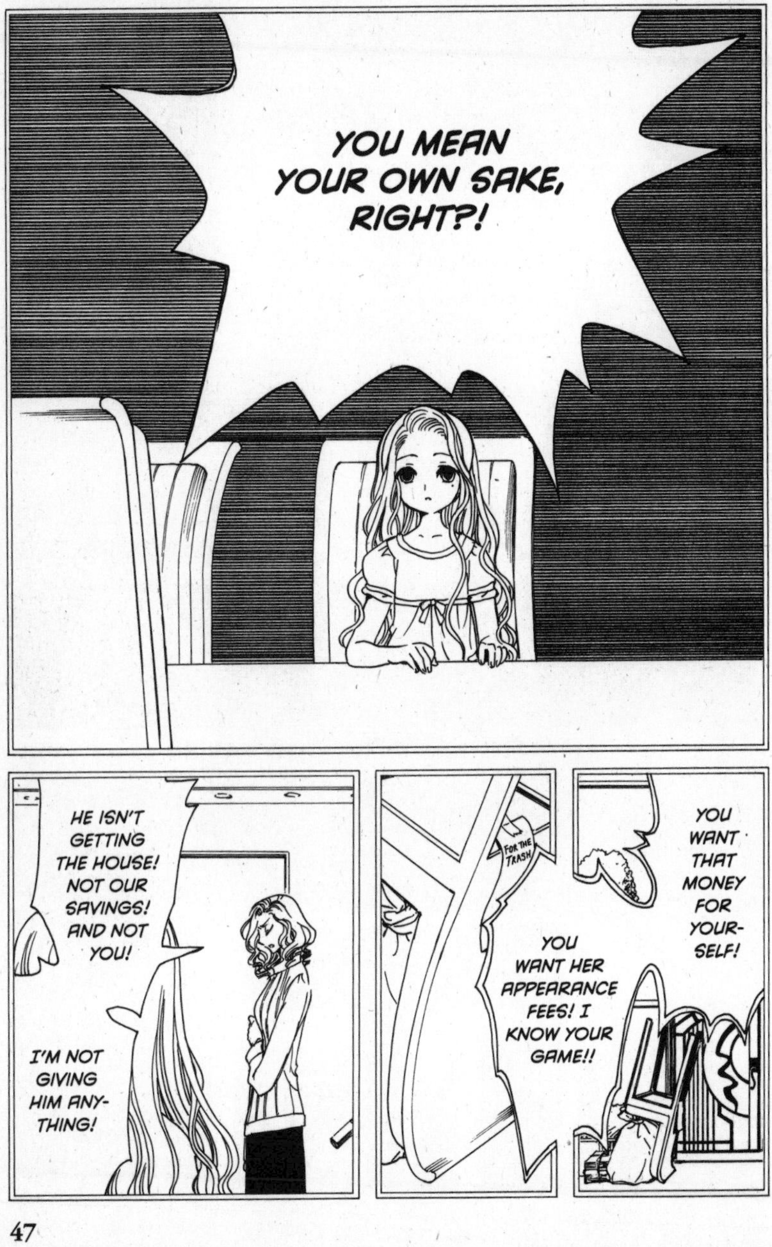
YOU MEAN YOUR OWN SAKE, RIGHT?!
YOU WANT THAT MONEY FOR YOUR-SELF!
FOR THE TRASH
YOU WANT HER APPEARANCE FEES! I KNOW YOUR GAME!!
HE ISN'T GETTING THE HOUSE! NOT OUR SAVINGS! AND NOT YOU!
I'M NOT GIVING HIM ANY-THING!

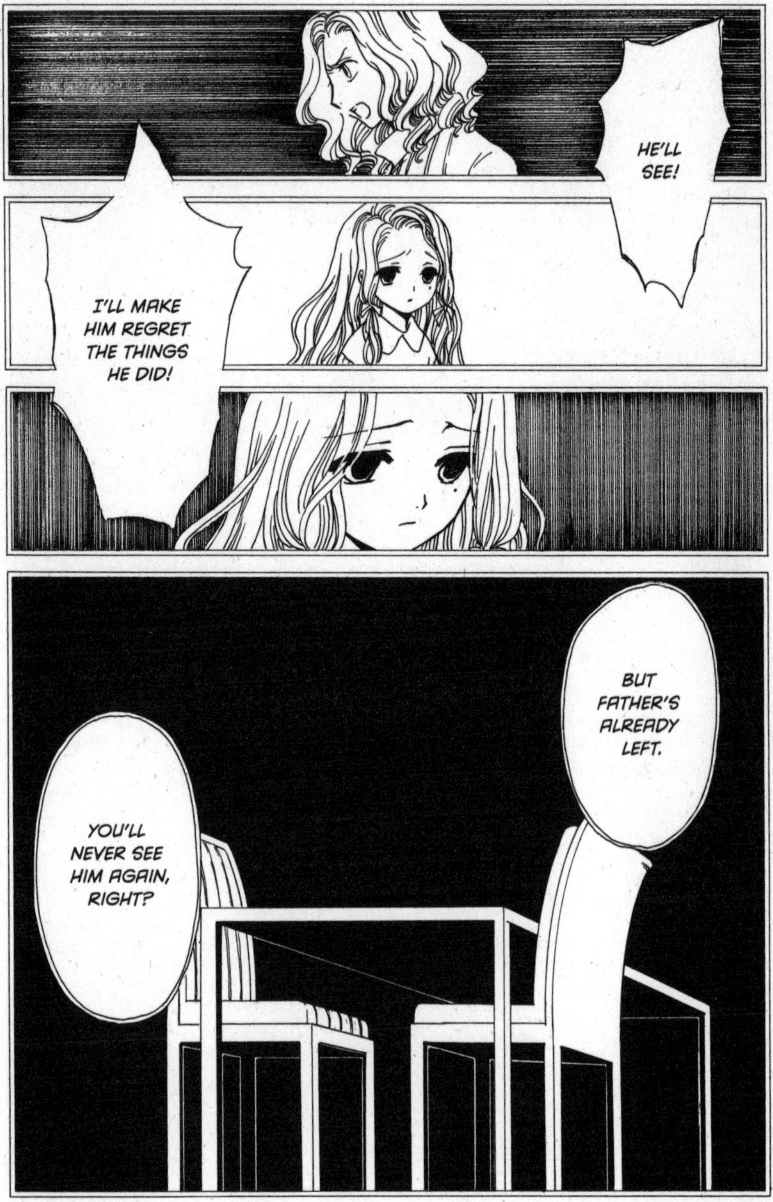
HE'LL SEE!
I'LL MAKE HIM REGRET THE THINGS HE DID!
BUT FATHER'S ALREADY LEFT.
YOU'LL NEVER SEE HIM AGAIN, RIGHT?

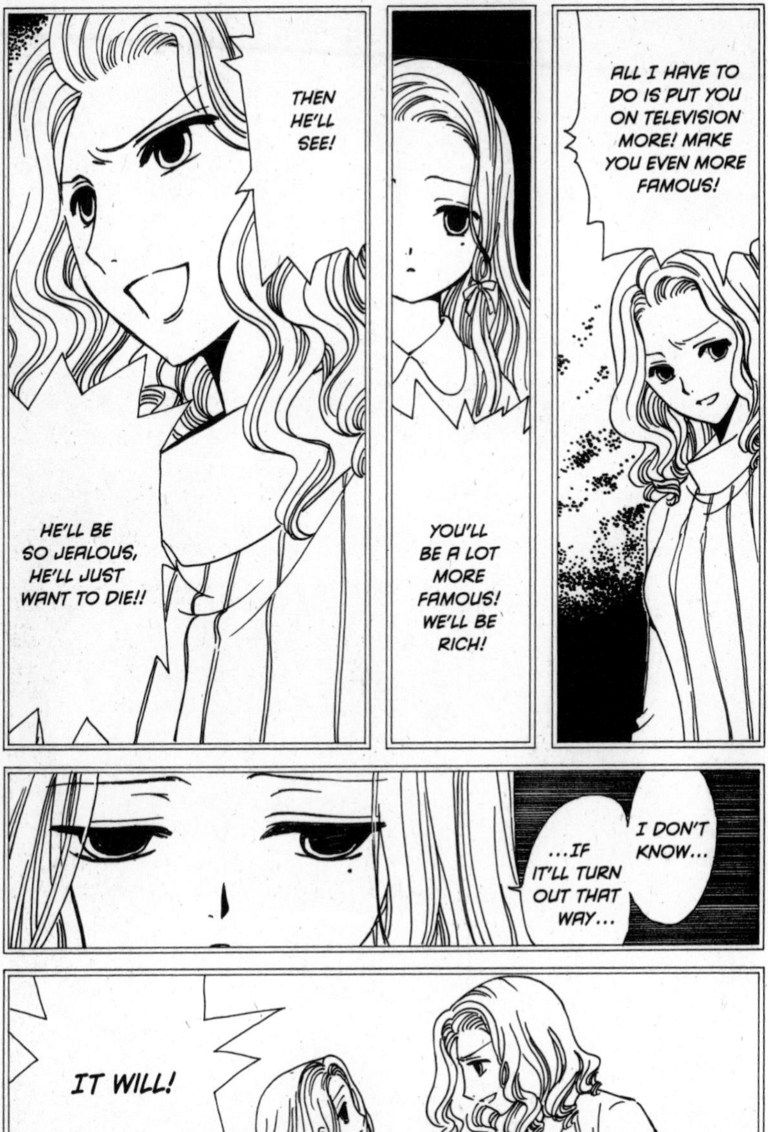
ALL I HAVE TO DO IS PUT YOU ON TELEVISION MORE! MAKE YOU EVEN MORE FAMOUS!
YOU'LL BE A LOT MORE FAMOUS! WE'LL BE RICH!
THEN HE'LL SEE!
HE'LL BE SO JEALOUS, HE'LL JUST WANT TO DIE!!
I DON'T KNOW...
...IF IT'LL TURN OUT THAT WAY...
IT WILL!

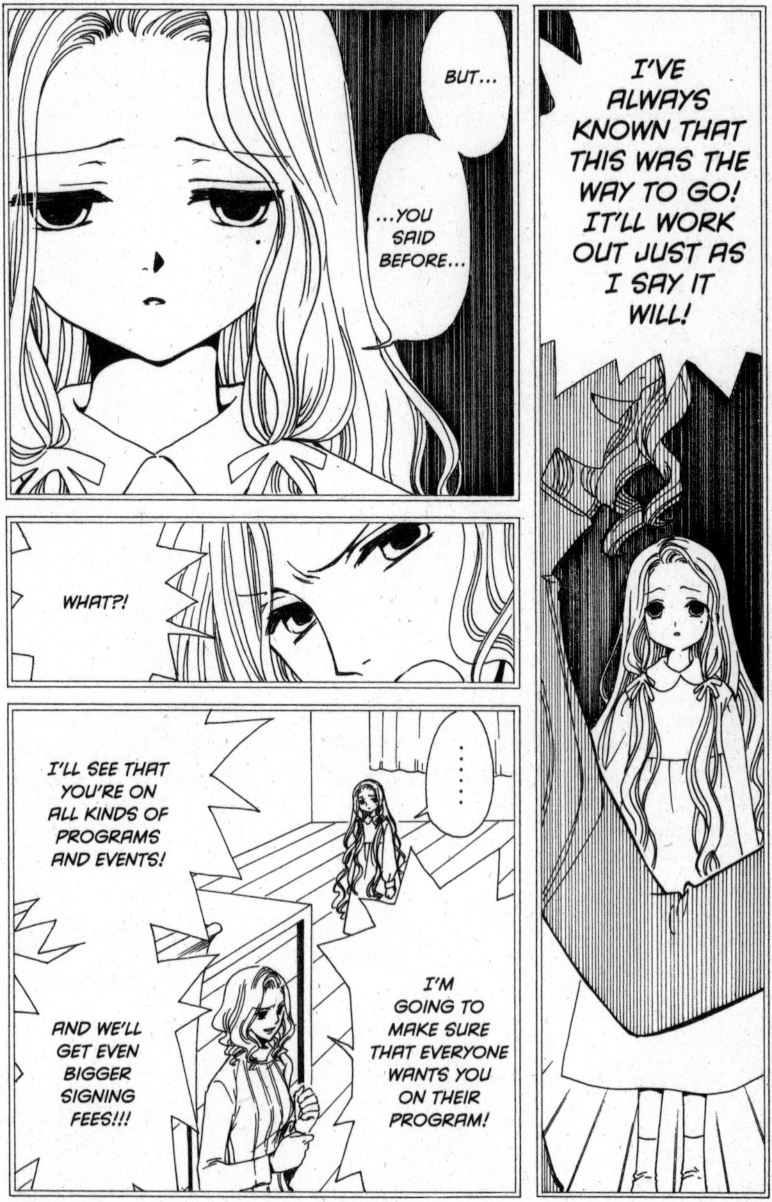
I'VE ALWAYS KNOWN THAT THIS WAS THE WAY TO GO! IT'LL WORK OUT JUST AS I SAY IT WILL!
BUT...
...YOU SAID BEFORE...
WHAT?!
......
I'LL SEE THAT YOU'RE ON ALL KINDS OF PROGRAMS AND EVENTS!
I'M GOING TO MAKE SURE THAT EVERYONE WANTS YOU ON THEIR PROGRAM!
AND WE'LL GET EVEN BIGGER SIGNING FEES!!!

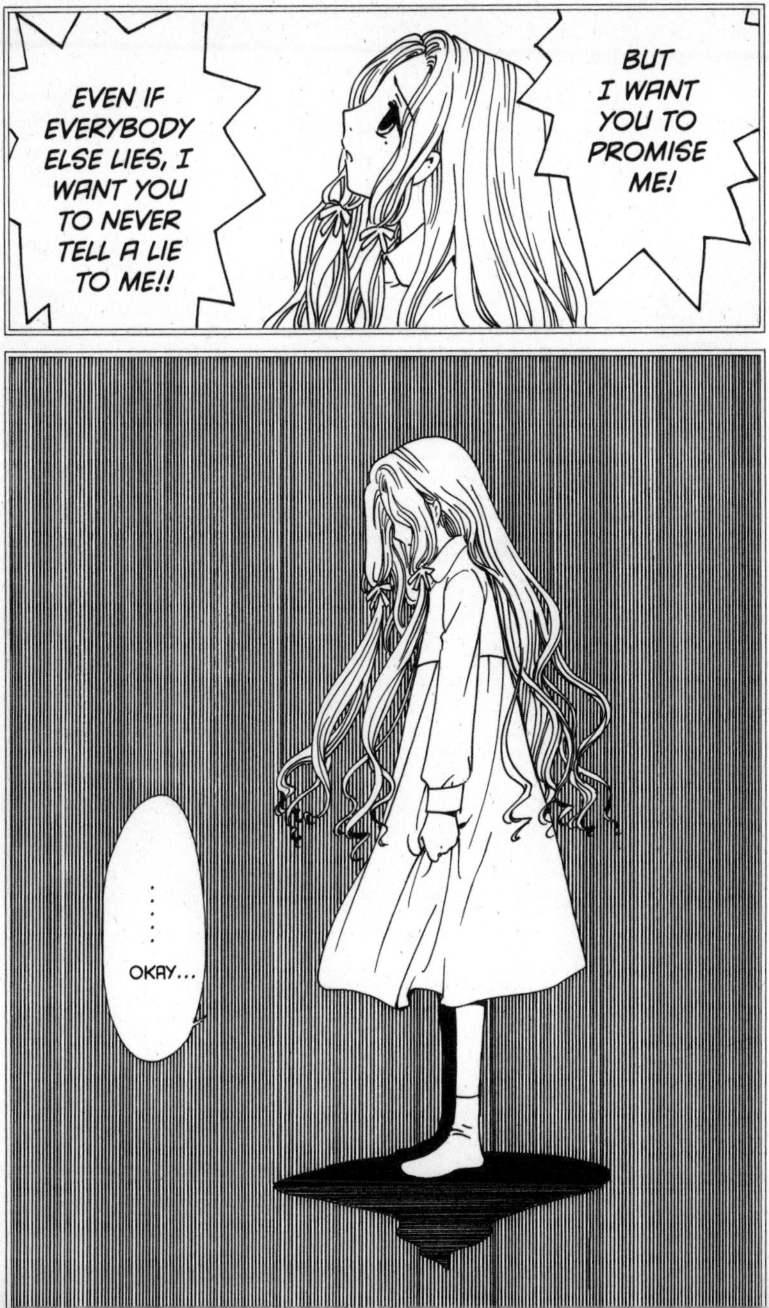
BUT I WANT YOU TO PROMISE ME!
EVEN IF EVERYBODY ELSE LIES, I WANT YOU TO NEVER TELL A LIE TO ME!!
...... OKAY...

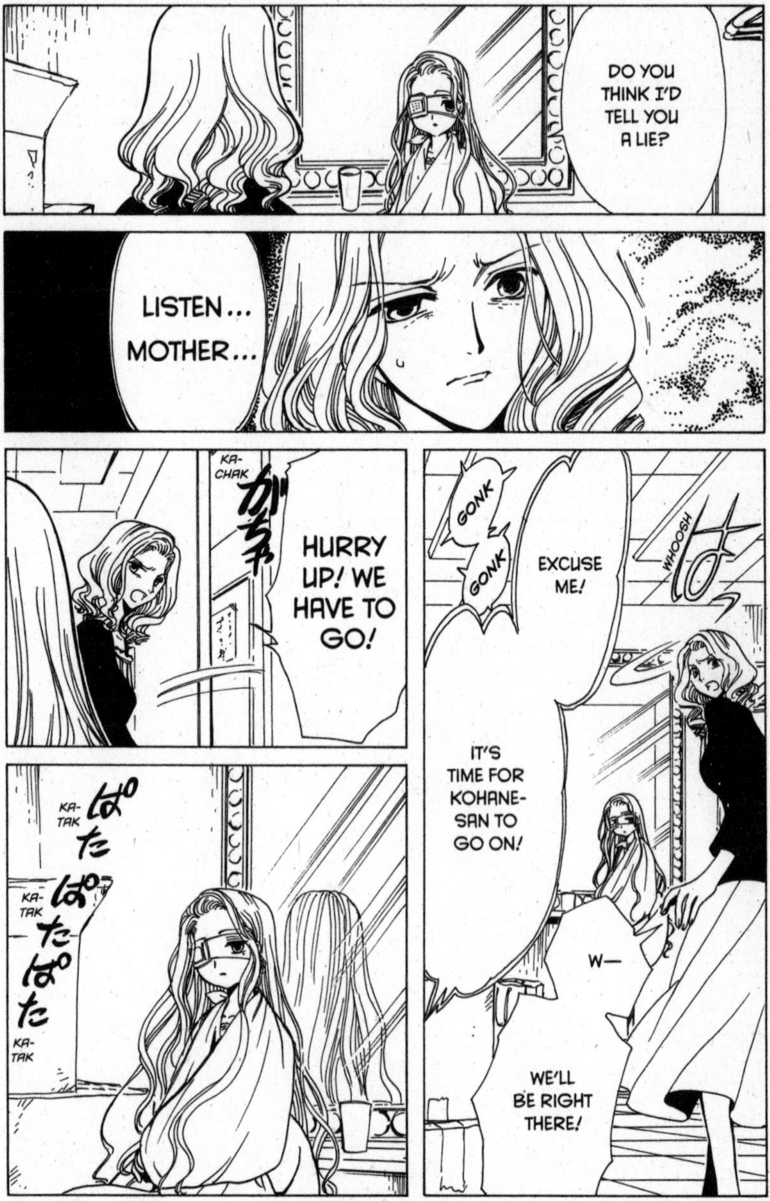
DO YOU THINK I'D TELL YOU A LIE?
LISTEN... MOTHER...
GONK
GONK
EXCUSE ME!
WHOOSH
IT'S TIME FOR KOHANE-SAN TO GO ON!
W—
WE'LL BE RIGHT THERE!
KA-CHAK
HURRY UP! WE HAVE TO GO!
KA-TAK
KA-TAK
KA-TAK

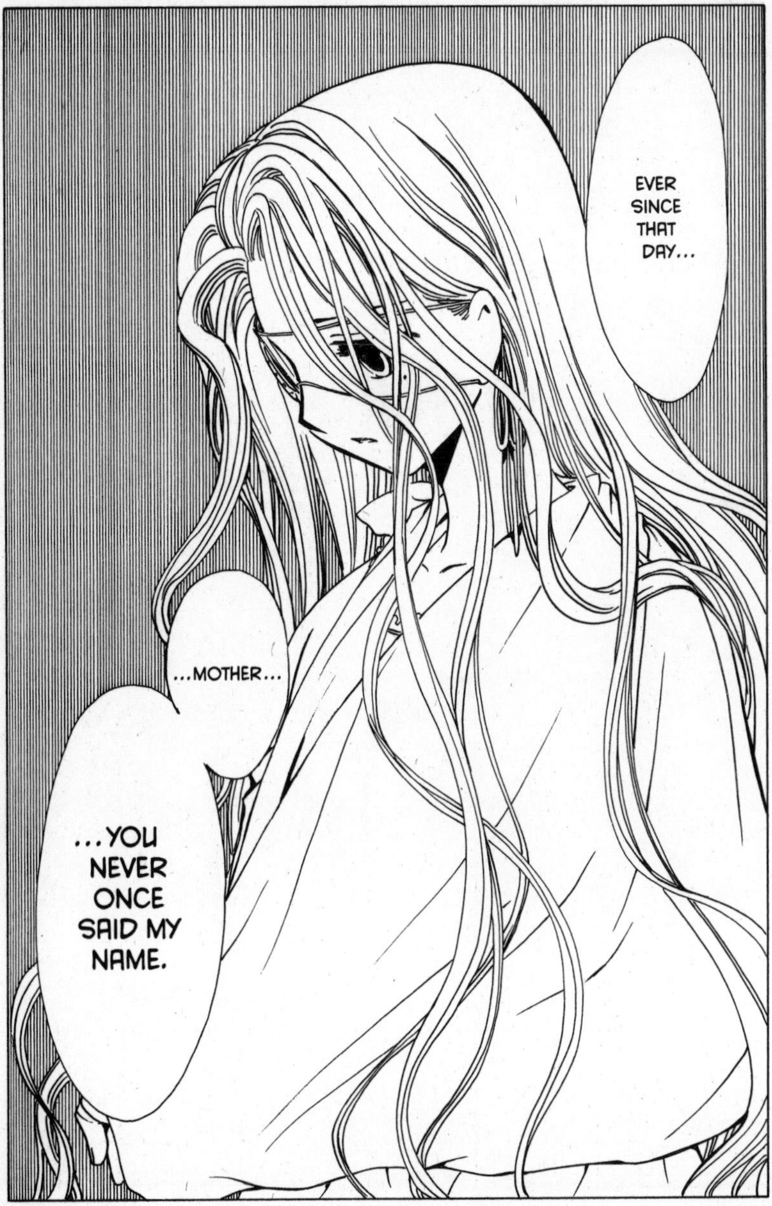
EVER SINCE THAT DAY...
...MOTHER...
...YOU NEVER ONCE SAID MY NAME.

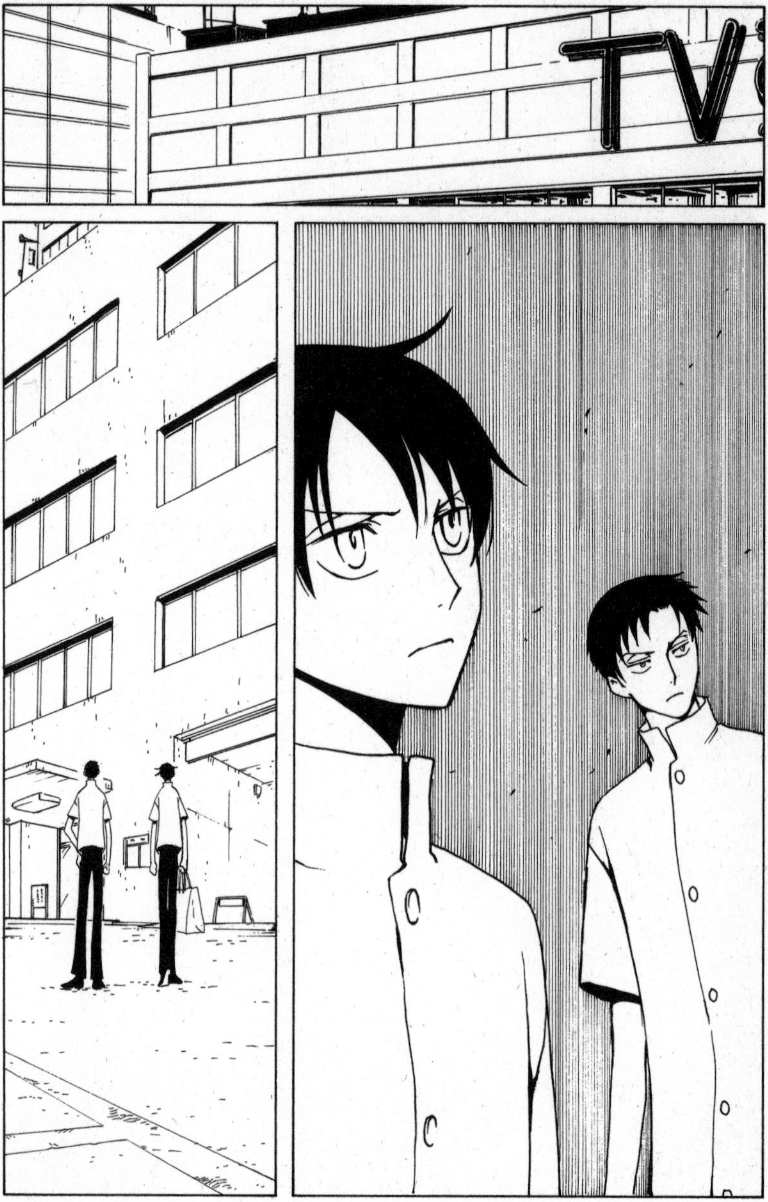
TV

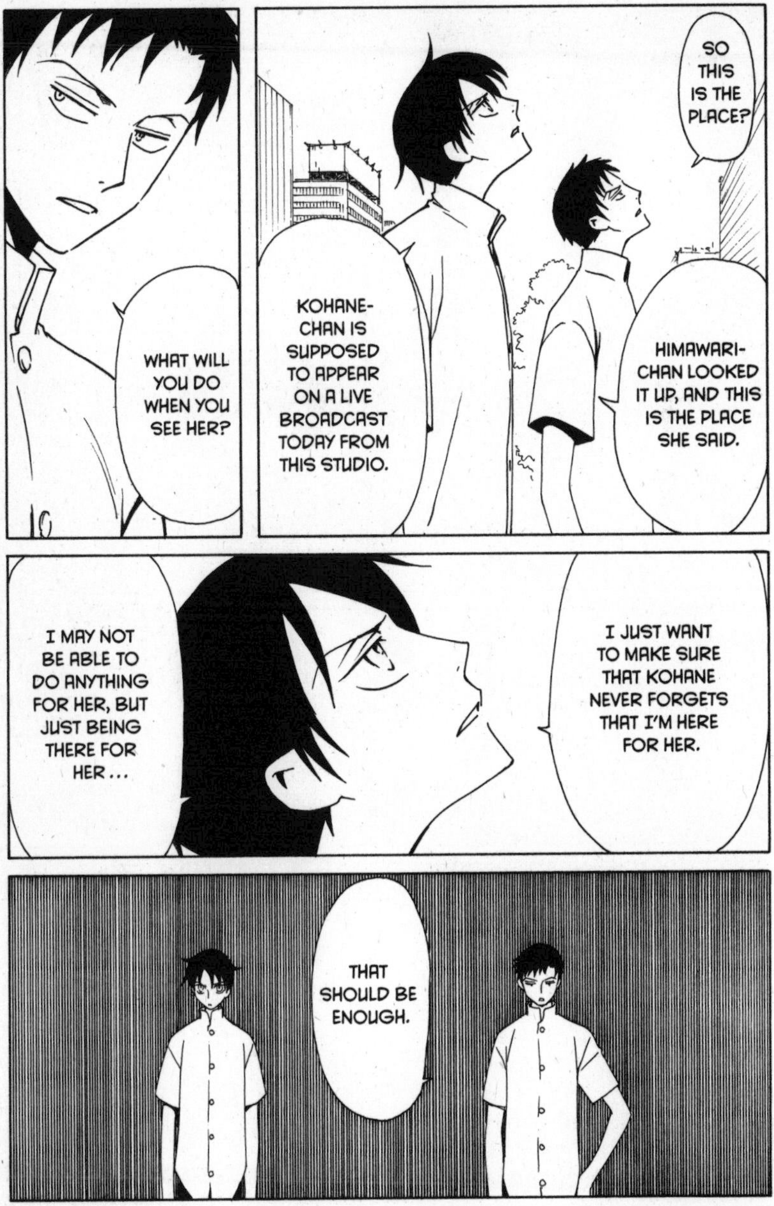
SO THIS IS THE PLACE?
HIMAWARI-CHAN LOOKED IT UP, AND THIS IS THE PLACE SHE SAID.
KOHANE-CHAN IS SUPPOSED TO APPEAR ON A LIVE BROADCAST TODAY FROM THIS STUDIO.
WHAT WILL YOU DO WHEN YOU SEE HER?
I JUST WANT TO MAKE SURE THAT KOHANE NEVER FORGETS THAT I'M HERE FOR HER.
I MAY NOT BE ABLE TO DO ANYTHING FOR HER, BUT JUST BEING THERE FOR HER...
THAT SHOULD BE ENOUGH.

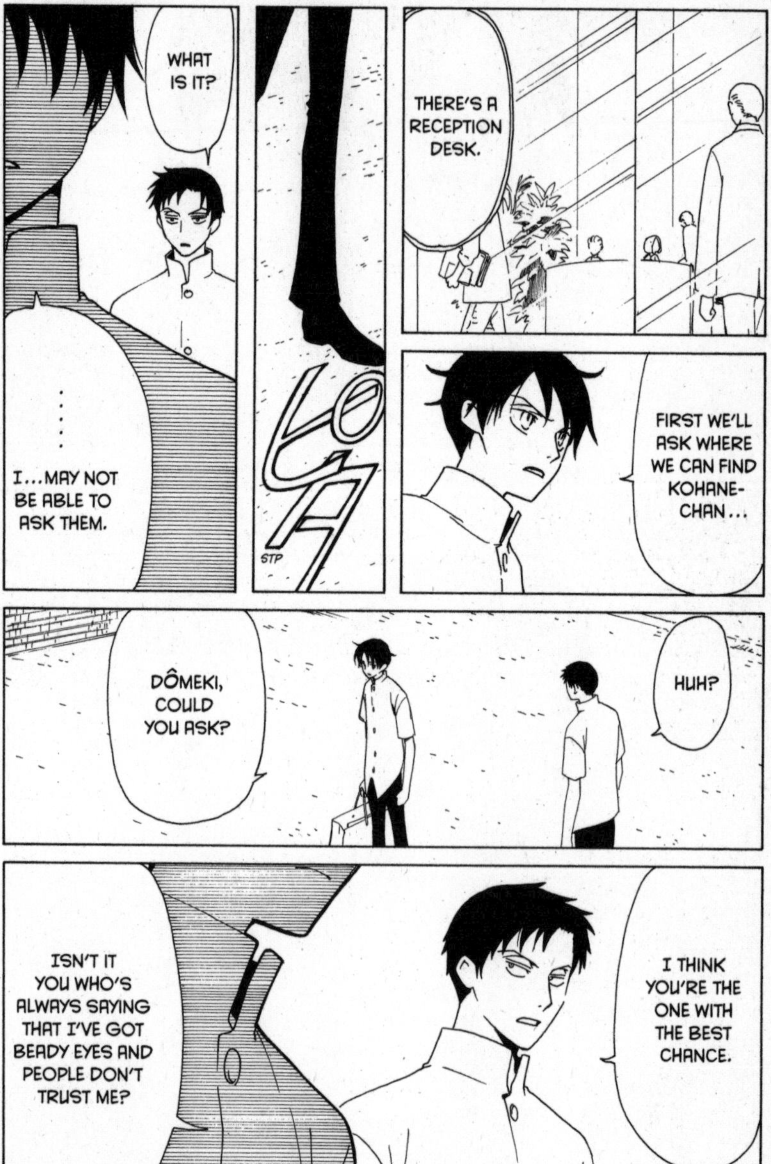
THERE'S A RECEPTION DESK.
FIRST WE'LL ASK WHERE WE CAN FIND KOHANE-CHAN...
STP
WHAT IS IT?
......
I...MAY NOT BE ABLE TO ASK THEM.
DÔMEKI, COULD YOU ASK?
HUH?
I THINK YOU'RE THE ONE WITH THE BEST CHANCE.
ISN'T IT YOU WHO'S ALWAYS SAYING THAT I'VE GOT BEADY EYES AND PEOPLE DON'T TRUST ME?

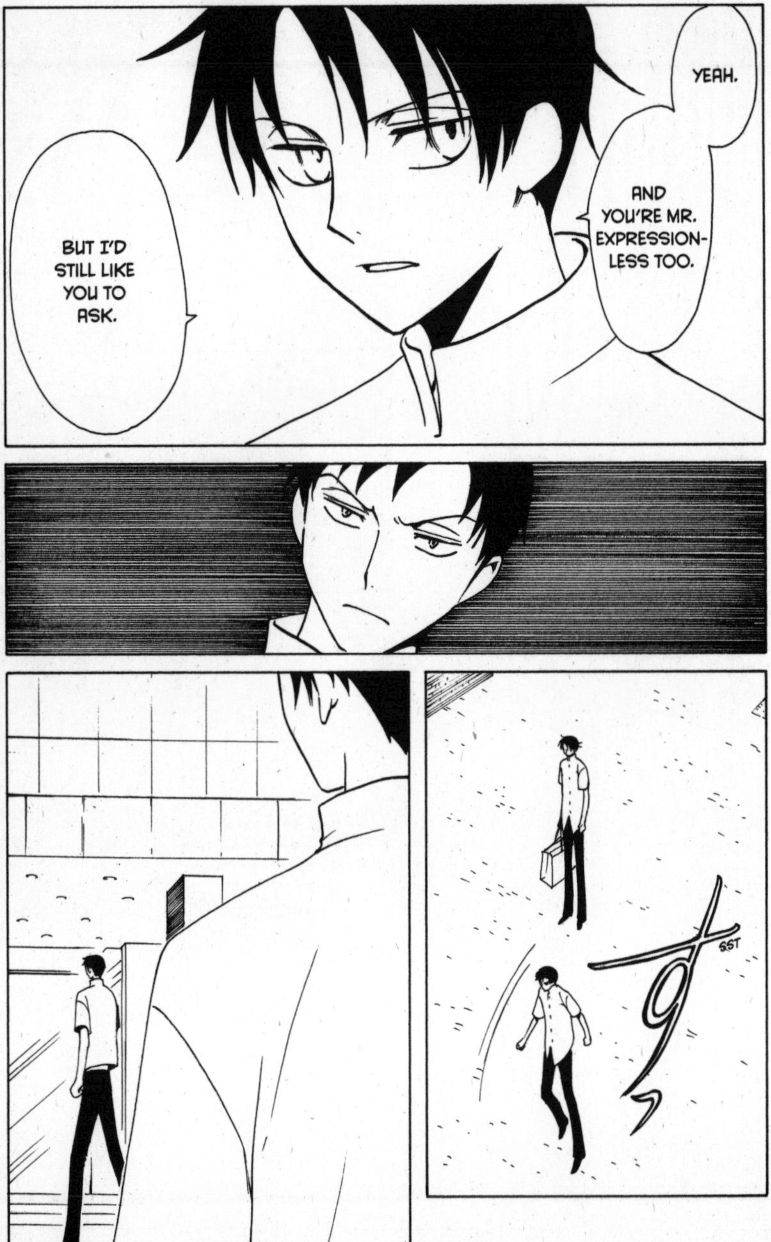
YEAH.
AND YOU'RE MR. EXPRESSION-LESS TOO.
BUT I'D STILL LIKE YOU TO ASK.
SST

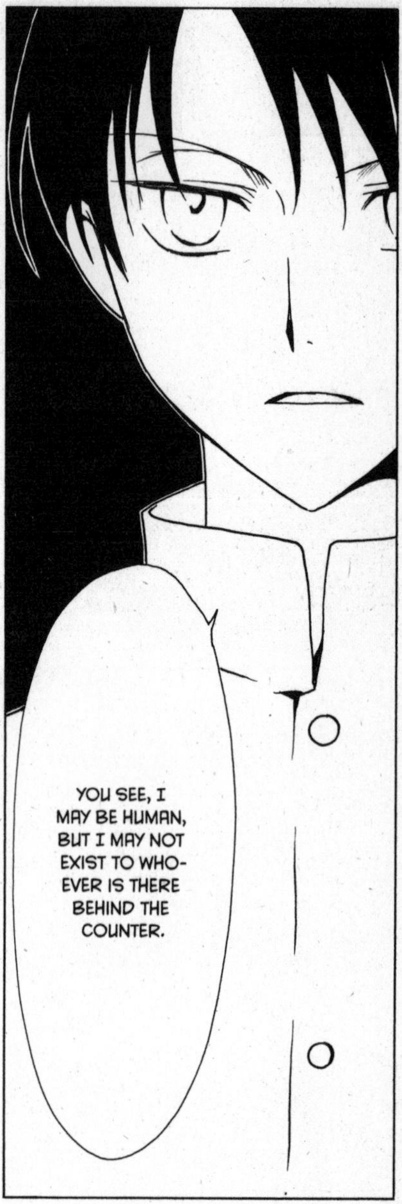
YOU SEE, I MAY BE HUMAN, BUT I MAY NOT EXIST TO WHO-EVER IS THERE BEHIND THE COUNTER.

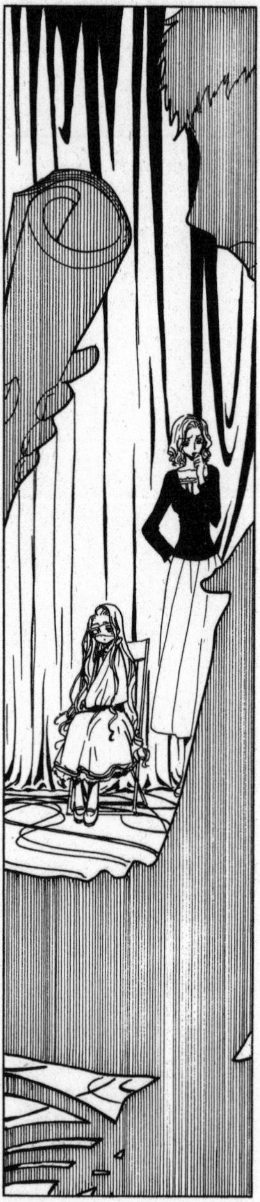

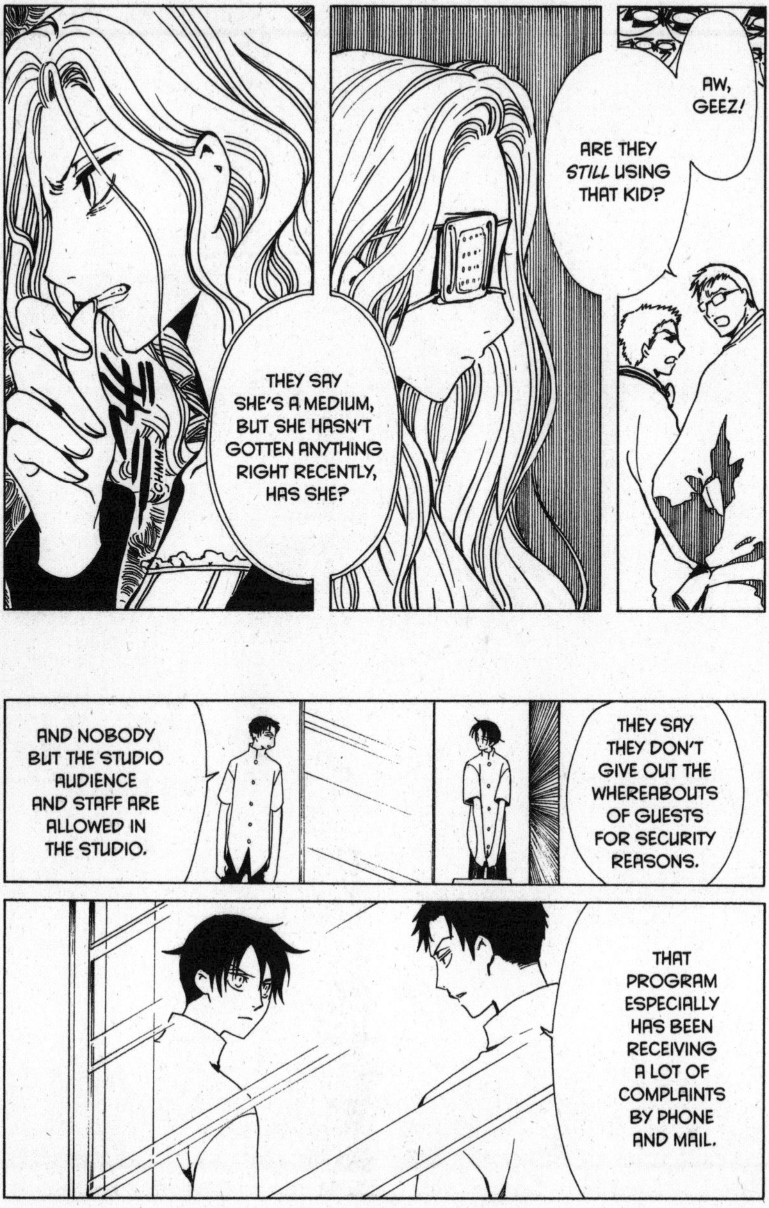
AW, GEEZ!
ARE THEY *STILL* USING THAT KID?
THEY SAY SHE'S A MEDIUM, BUT SHE HASN'T GOTTEN ANYTHING RIGHT RECENTLY, HAS SHE?
CHMM
THEY SAY THEY DON'T GIVE OUT THE WHEREABOUTS OF GUESTS FOR SECURITY REASONS.
AND NOBODY BUT THE STUDIO AUDIENCE AND STAFF ARE ALLOWED IN THE STUDIO.
THAT PROGRAM ESPECIALLY HAS BEEN RECEIVING A LOT OF COMPLAINTS BY PHONE AND MAIL.

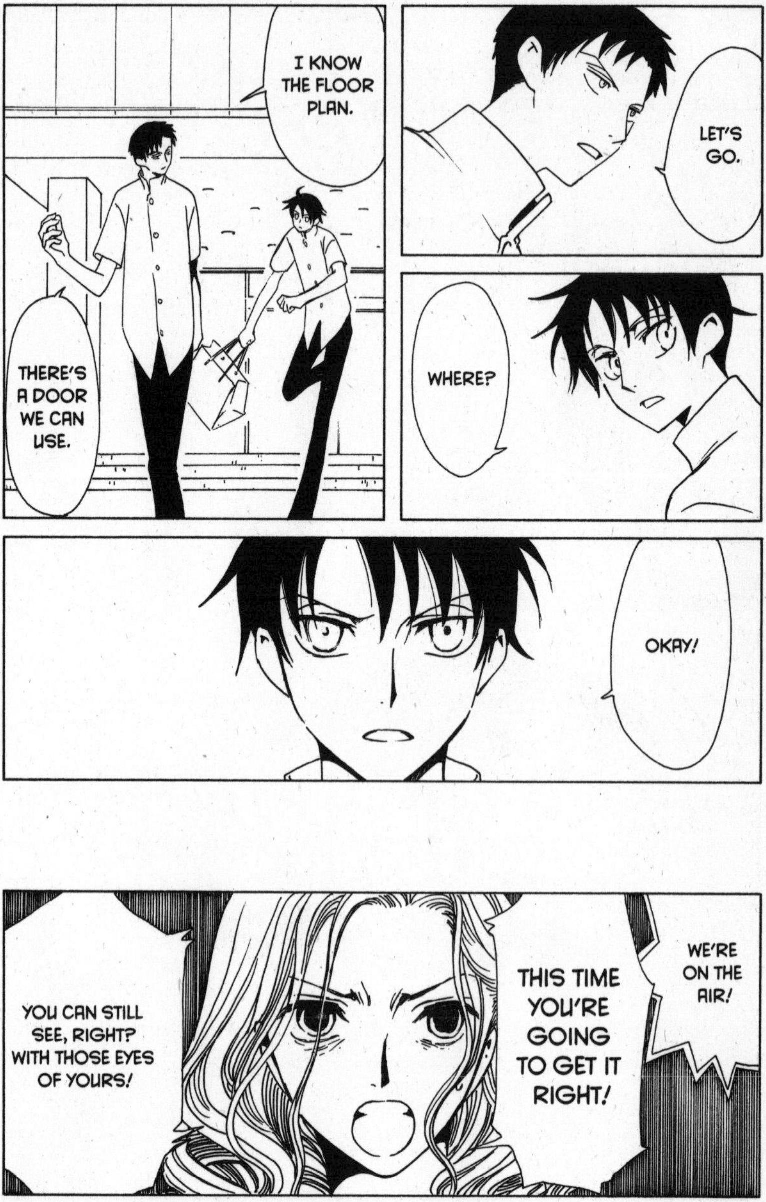
LET'S GO.
WHERE?
I KNOW THE FLOOR PLAN.
THERE'S A DOOR WE CAN USE.
OKAY!
WE'RE ON THE AIR!
THIS TIME YOU'RE GOING TO GET IT RIGHT!
YOU CAN STILL SEE, RIGHT? WITH THOSE EYES OF YOURS!

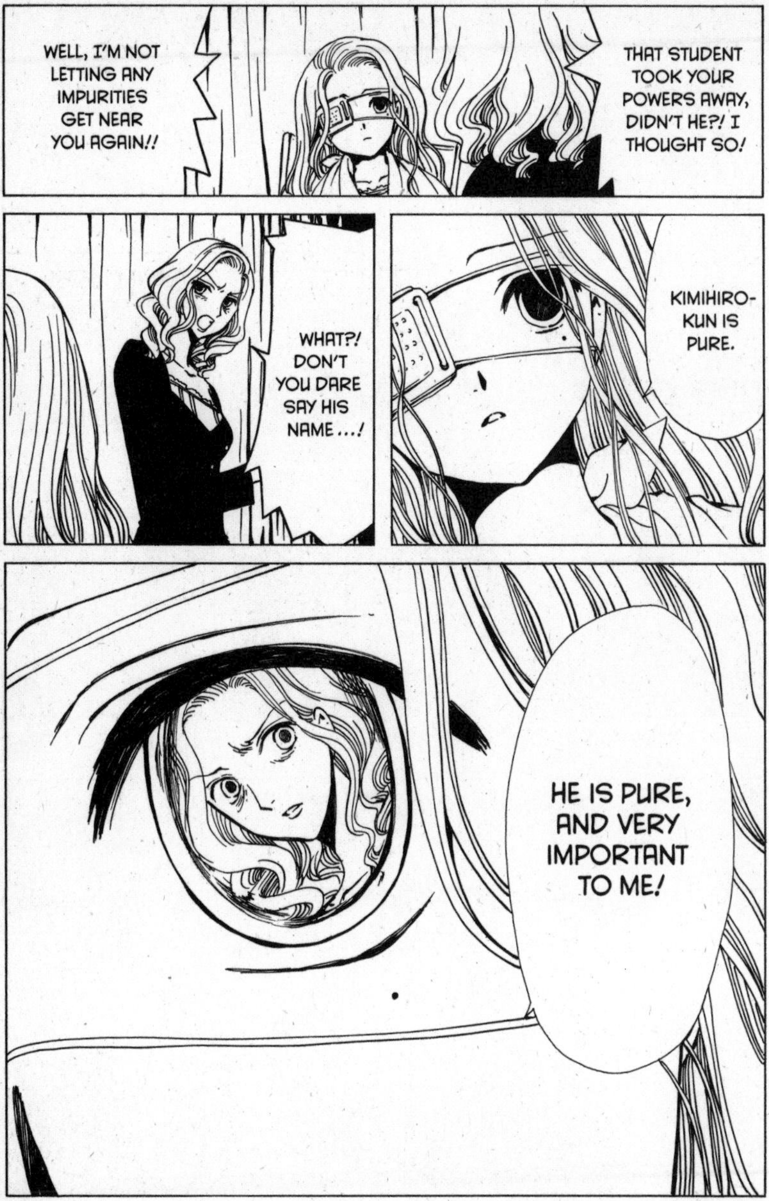
THAT STUDENT TOOK YOUR POWERS AWAY, DIDN'T HE?! I THOUGHT SO!
WELL, I'M NOT LETTING ANY IMPURITIES GET NEAR YOU AGAIN!!
KIMIHIRO-KUN IS PURE.
WHAT?! DON'T YOU DARE SAY HIS NAME...!
HE IS PURE, AND VERY IMPORTANT TO ME!

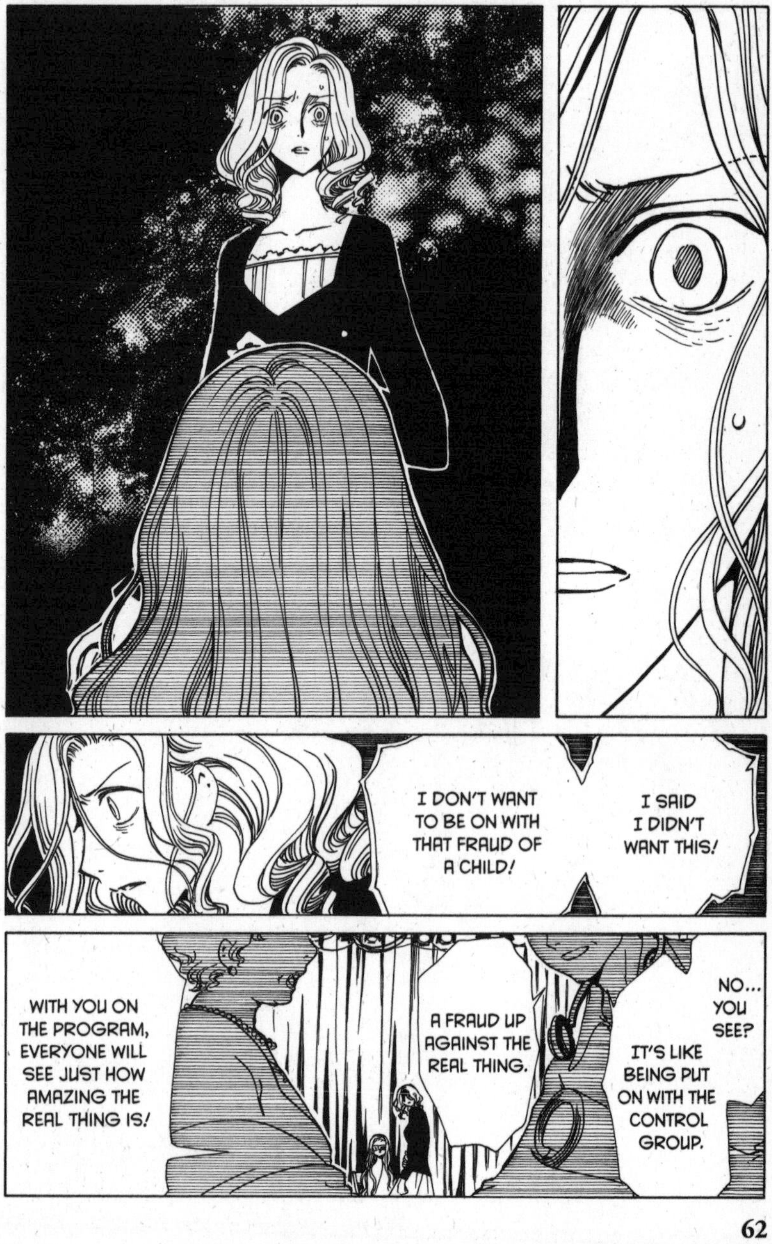
I SAID I DIDN'T WANT THIS!
I DON'T WANT TO BE ON WITH THAT FRAUD OF A CHILD!
NO... YOU SEE?
IT'S LIKE BEING PUT ON WITH THE CONTROL GROUP.
A FRAUD UP AGAINST THE REAL THING.
WITH YOU ON THE PROGRAM, EVERYONE WILL SEE JUST HOW AMAZING THE REAL THING IS!

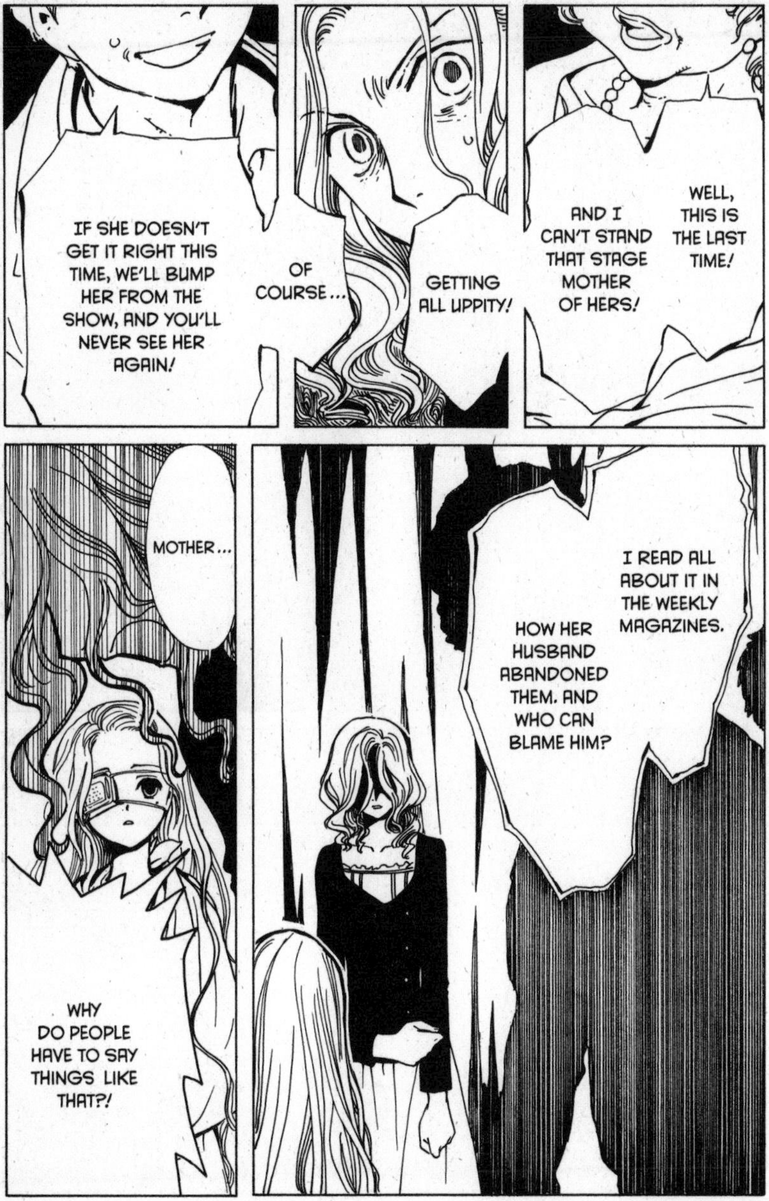
WELL, THIS IS THE LAST TIME!
AND I CAN'T STAND THAT STAGE MOTHER OF HERS!
GETTING ALL UPPITY!
OF COURSE...
IF SHE DOESN'T GET IT RIGHT THIS TIME, WE'LL BUMP HER FROM THE SHOW, AND YOU'LL NEVER SEE HER AGAIN!
I READ ALL ABOUT IT IN THE WEEKLY MAGAZINES.
HOW HER HUSBAND ABANDONED THEM. AND WHO CAN BLAME HIM?
MOTHER...
WHY DO PEOPLE HAVE TO SAY THINGS LIKE THAT?!

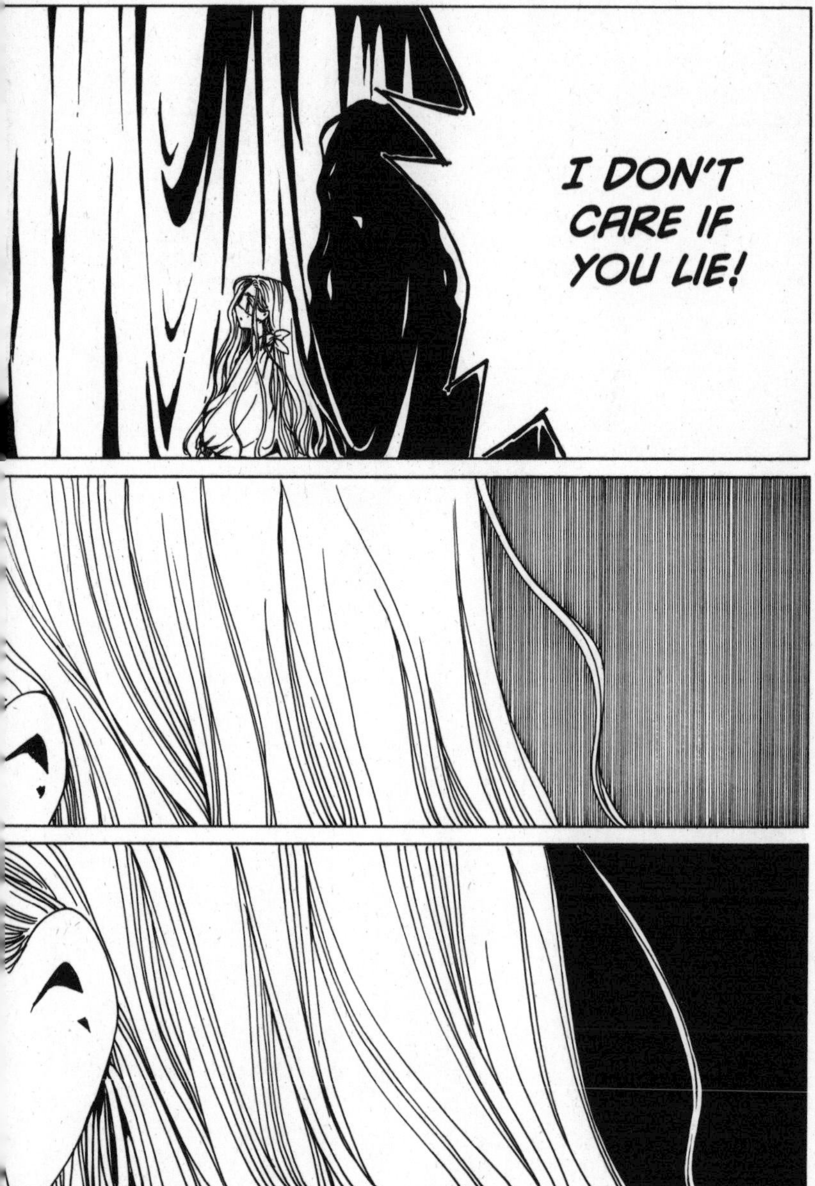
I DON'T CARE IF YOU LIE!

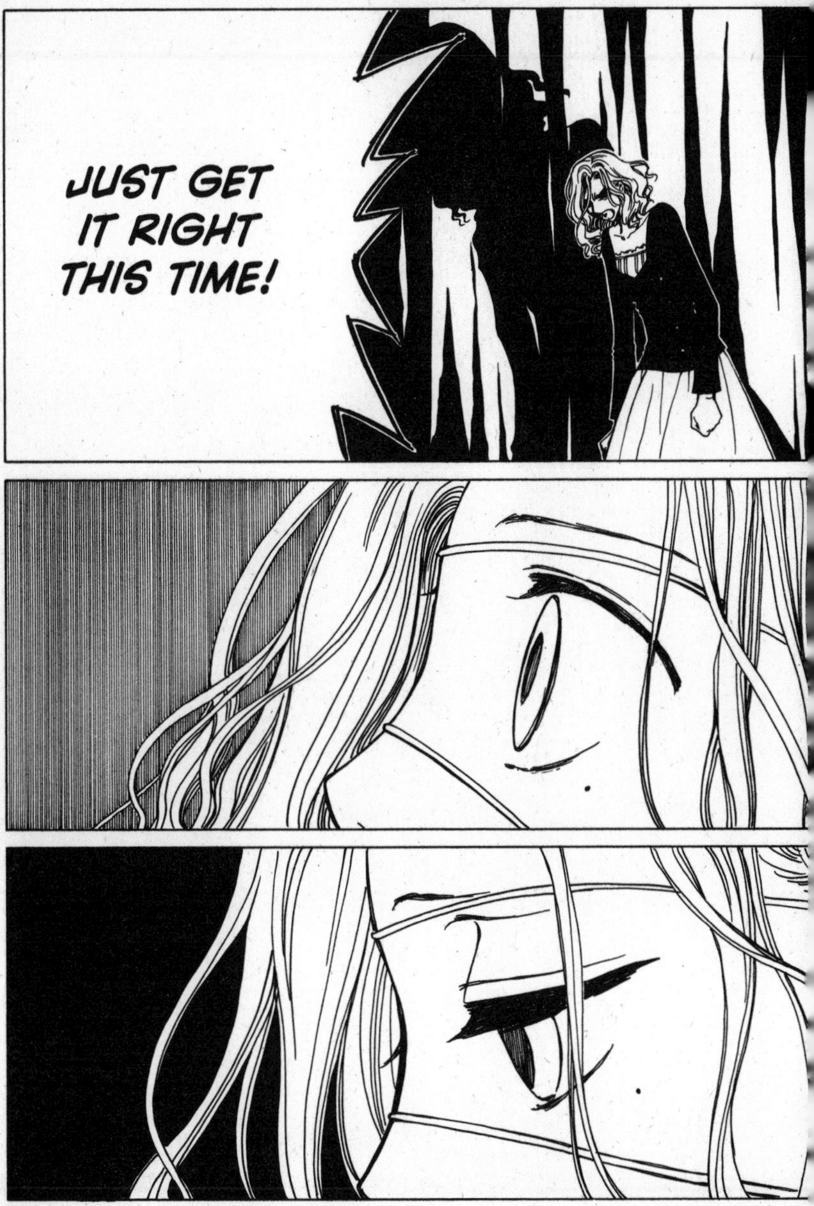
JUST GET
IT RIGHT
THIS TIME!

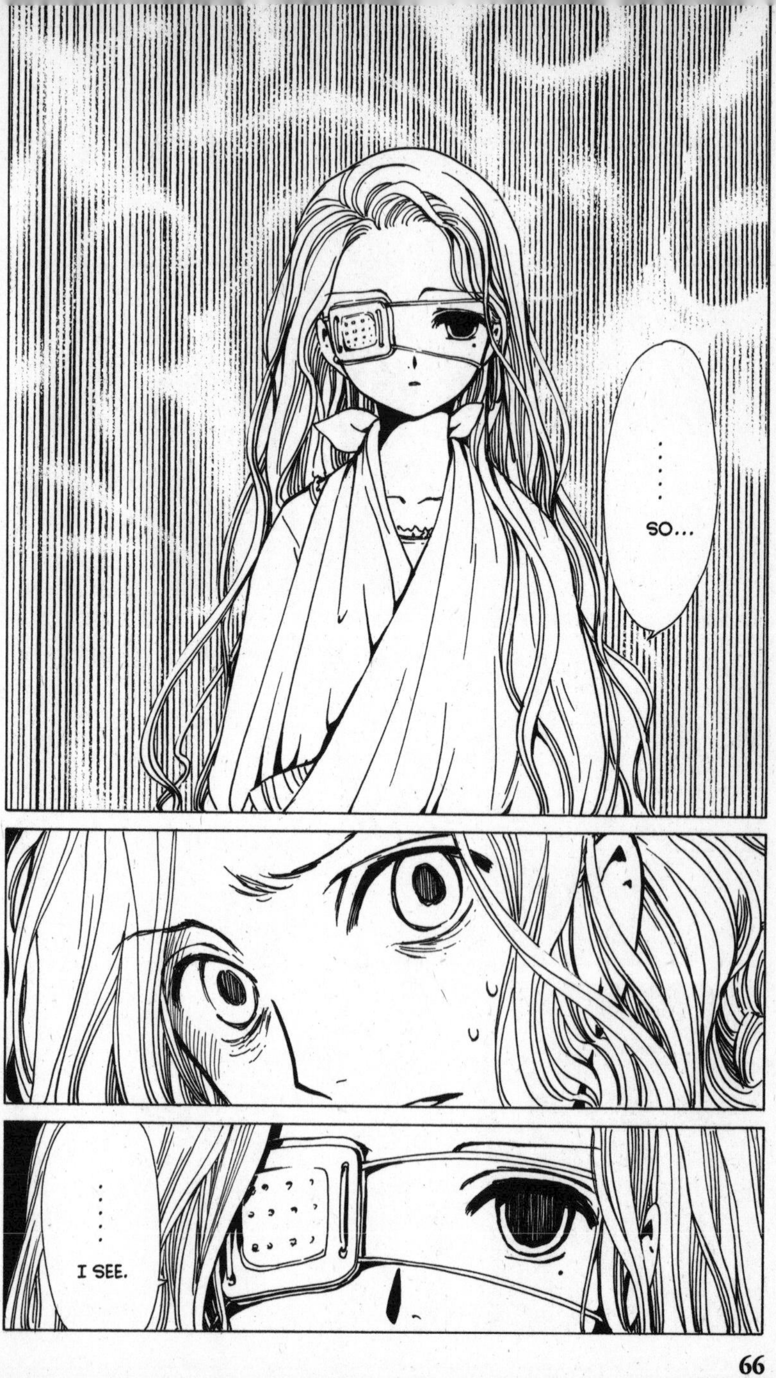
..... SO...
..... I SEE.

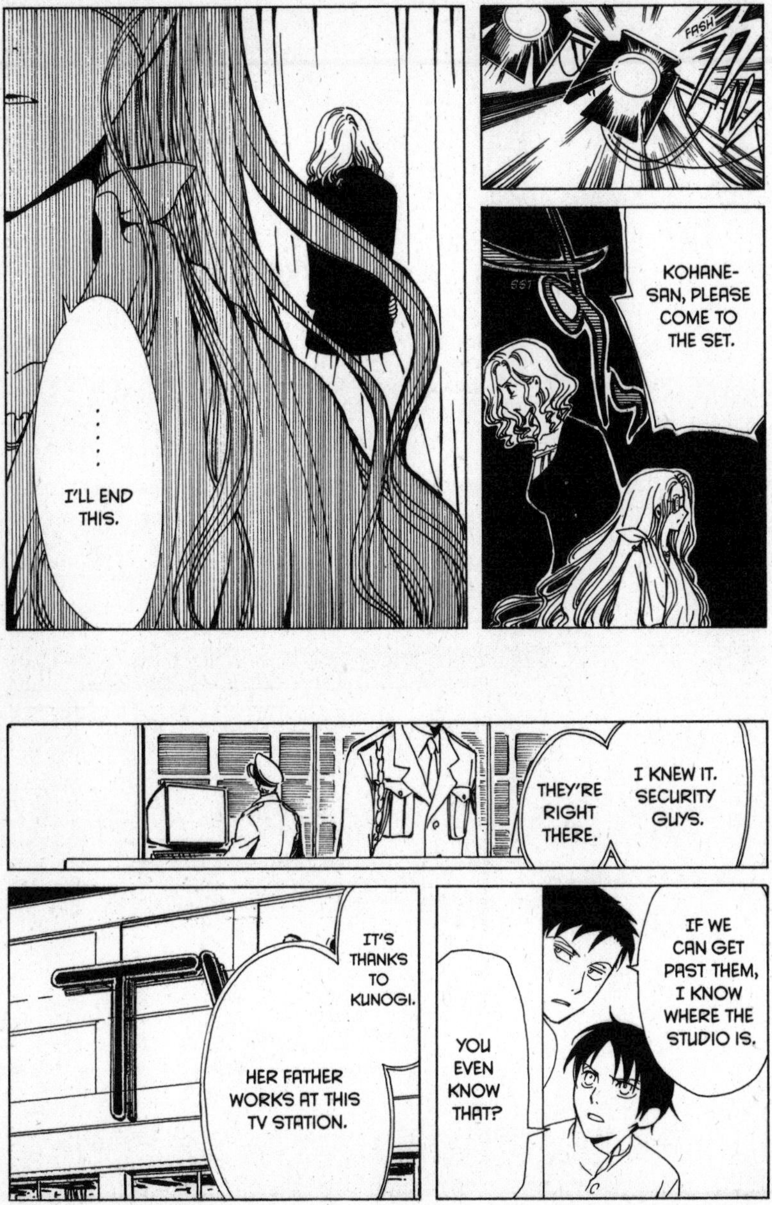
FASH
KOHANE-SAN, PLEASE COME TO THE SET.
..... I'LL END THIS.
I KNEW IT. SECURITY GUYS.
THEY'RE RIGHT THERE.
IF WE CAN GET PAST THEM, I KNOW WHERE THE STUDIO IS.
YOU EVEN KNOW THAT?
IT'S THANKS TO KUNOGI.
HER FATHER WORKS AT THIS TV STATION.

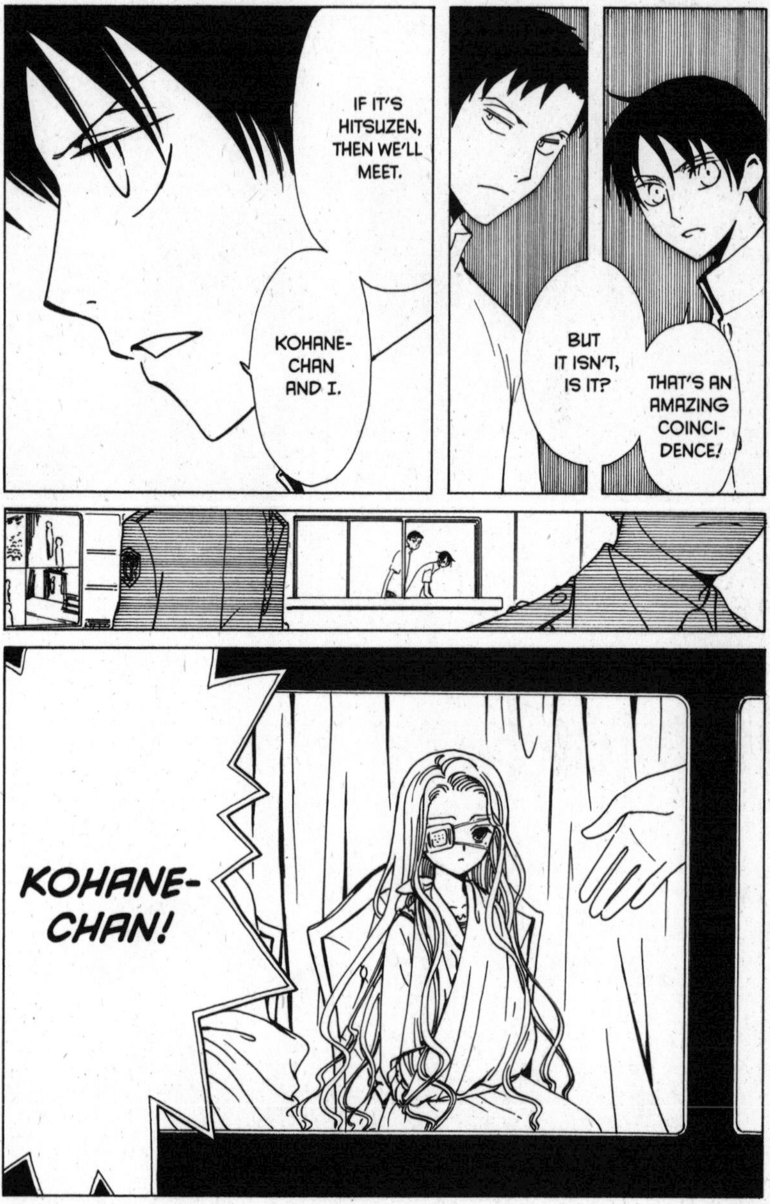
THAT'S AN AMAZING COINCIDENCE!
BUT IT ISN'T, IS IT?
IF IT'S HITSUZEN, THEN WE'LL MEET.
KOHANE-CHAN AND I.
KOHANE-CHAN!

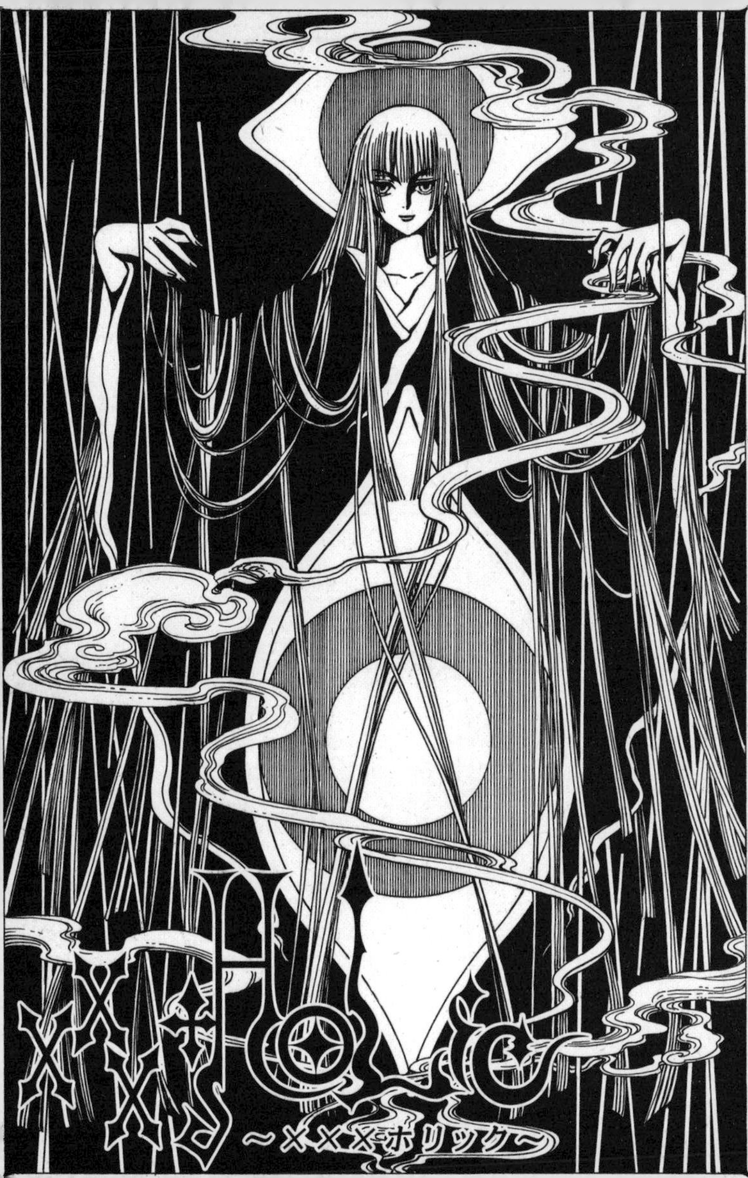
xxxHOLiC
〜×××ホリック〜

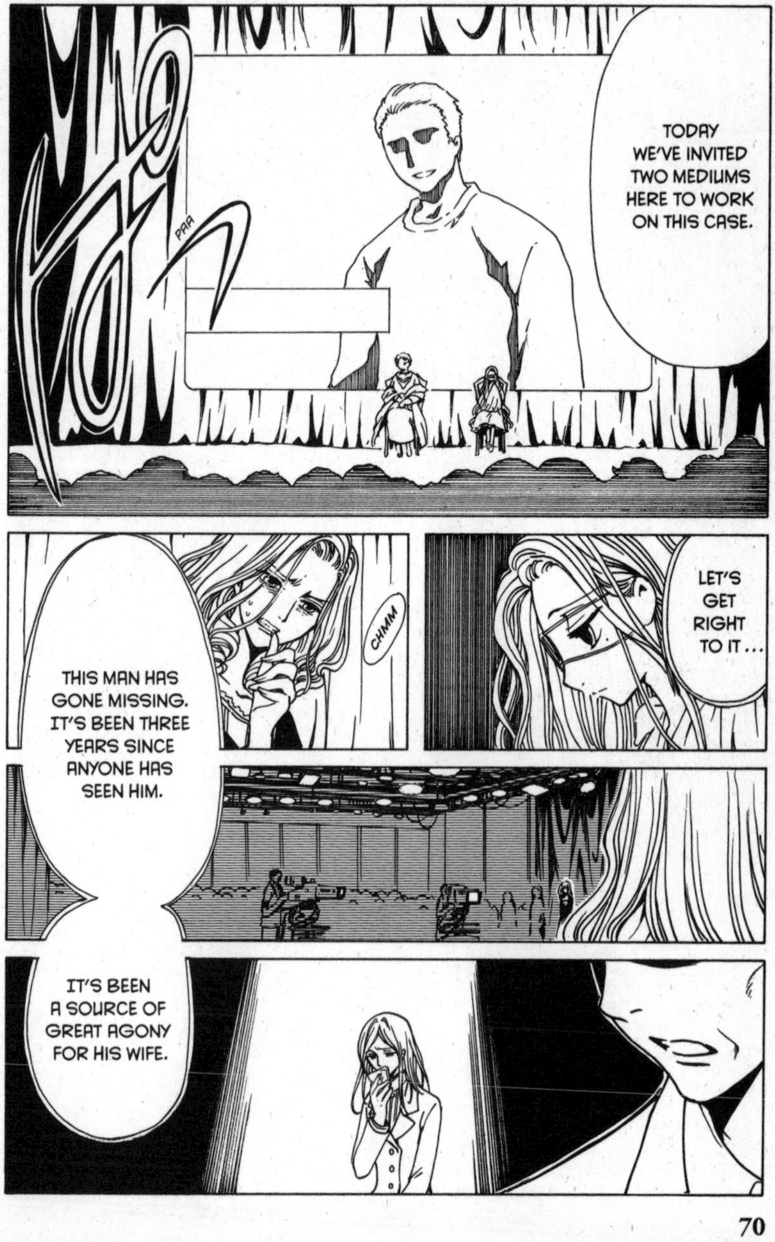
TODAY WE'VE INVITED TWO MEDIUMS HERE TO WORK ON THIS CASE.
PAA
LET'S GET RIGHT TO IT...
CHMM
THIS MAN HAS GONE MISSING. IT'S BEEN THREE YEARS SINCE ANYONE HAS SEEN HIM.
IT'S BEEN A SOURCE OF GREAT AGONY FOR HIS WIFE.

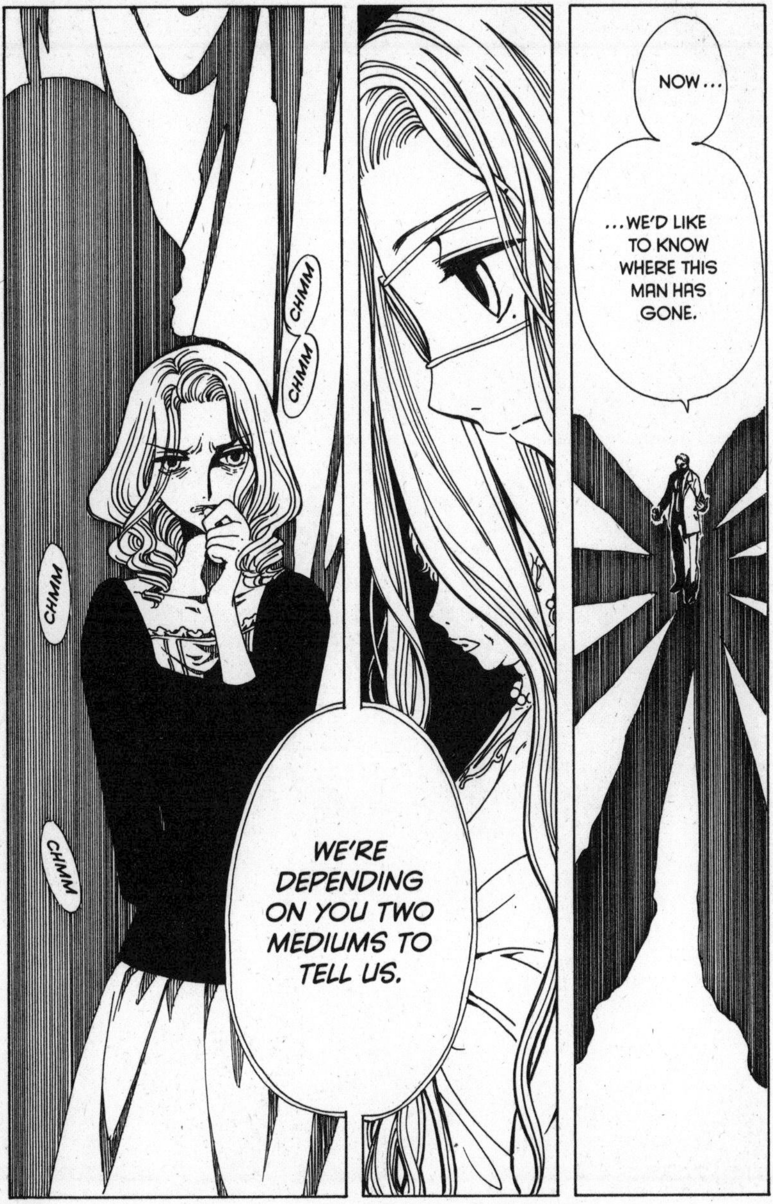
NOW...
...WE'D LIKE TO KNOW WHERE THIS MAN HAS GONE.
WE'RE DEPENDING ON YOU TWO MEDIUMS TO TELL US.
CHMM
CHMM
CHMM
CHMM

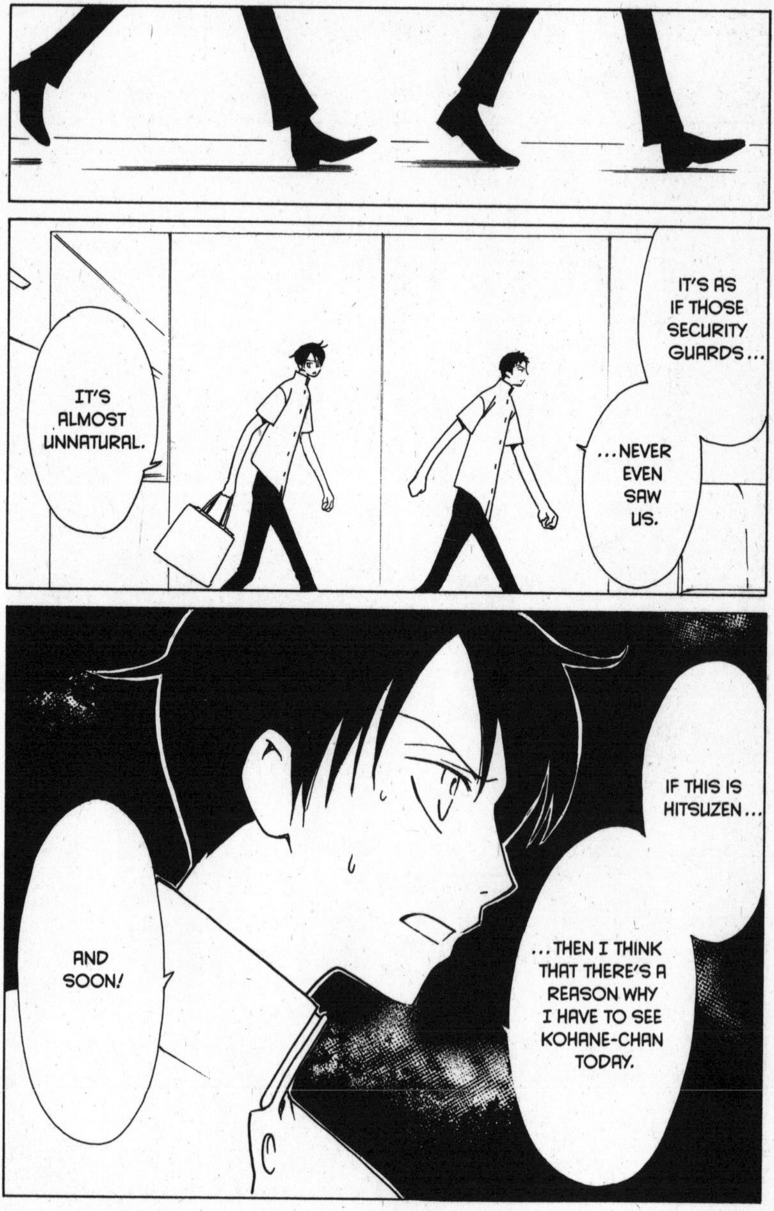
IT'S AS IF THOSE SECURITY GUARDS...
...NEVER EVEN SAW US.
IT'S ALMOST UNNATURAL.
IF THIS IS HITSUZEN...
...THEN I THINK THAT THERE'S A REASON WHY I HAVE TO SEE KOHANE-CHAN TODAY.
AND SOON!

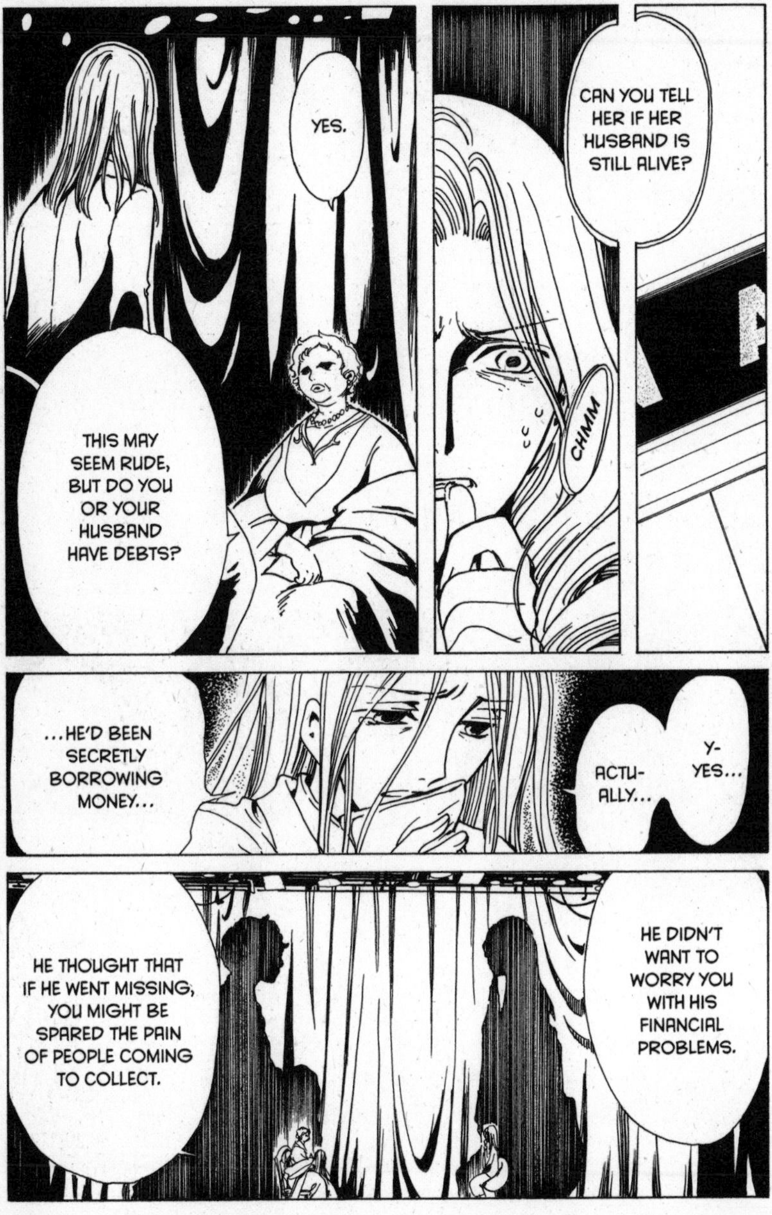
CAN YOU TELL HER IF HER HUSBAND IS STILL ALIVE?
CHMM
YES.
THIS MAY SEEM RUDE, BUT DO YOU OR YOUR HUSBAND HAVE DEBTS?
Y- YES...
ACTU- ALLY...
...HE'D BEEN SECRETLY BORROWING MONEY...
HE DIDN'T WANT TO WORRY YOU WITH HIS FINANCIAL PROBLEMS.
HE THOUGHT THAT IF HE WENT MISSING, YOU MIGHT BE SPARED THE PAIN OF PEOPLE COMING TO COLLECT.

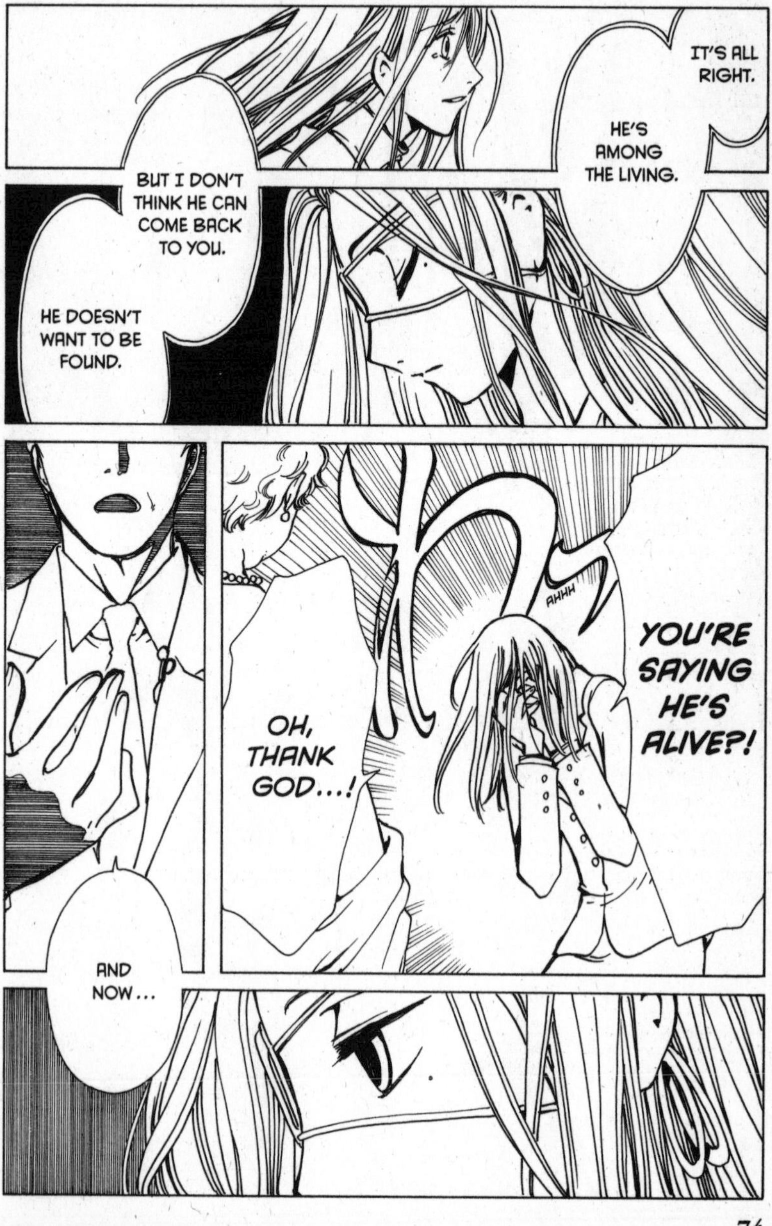
IT'S ALL RIGHT.
HE'S AMONG THE LIVING.
BUT I DON'T THINK HE CAN COME BACK TO YOU.
HE DOESN'T WANT TO BE FOUND.
YOU'RE SAYING HE'S ALIVE?!
AHHH
OH, THANK GOD...!
AND NOW...

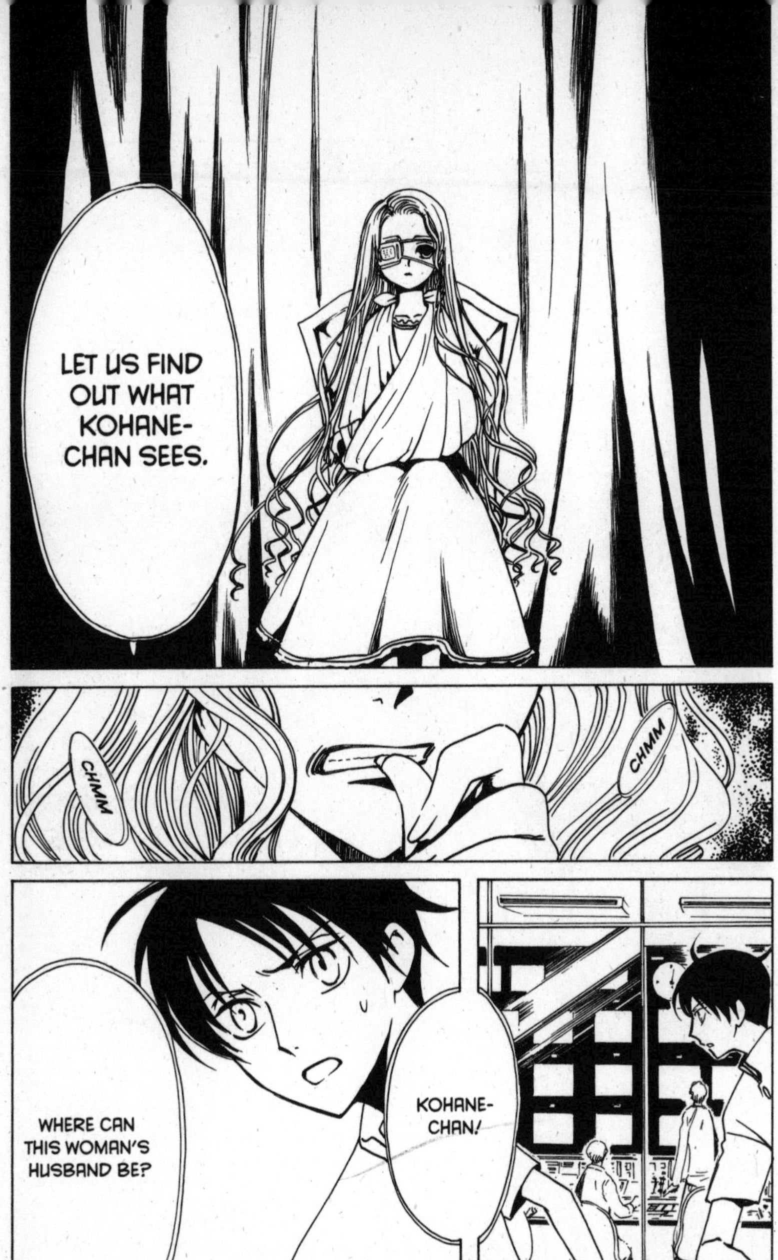
LET US FIND OUT WHAT KOHANE-CHAN SEES.
CHMM
CHMM
KOHANE-CHAN!
WHERE CAN THIS WOMAN'S HUSBAND BE?

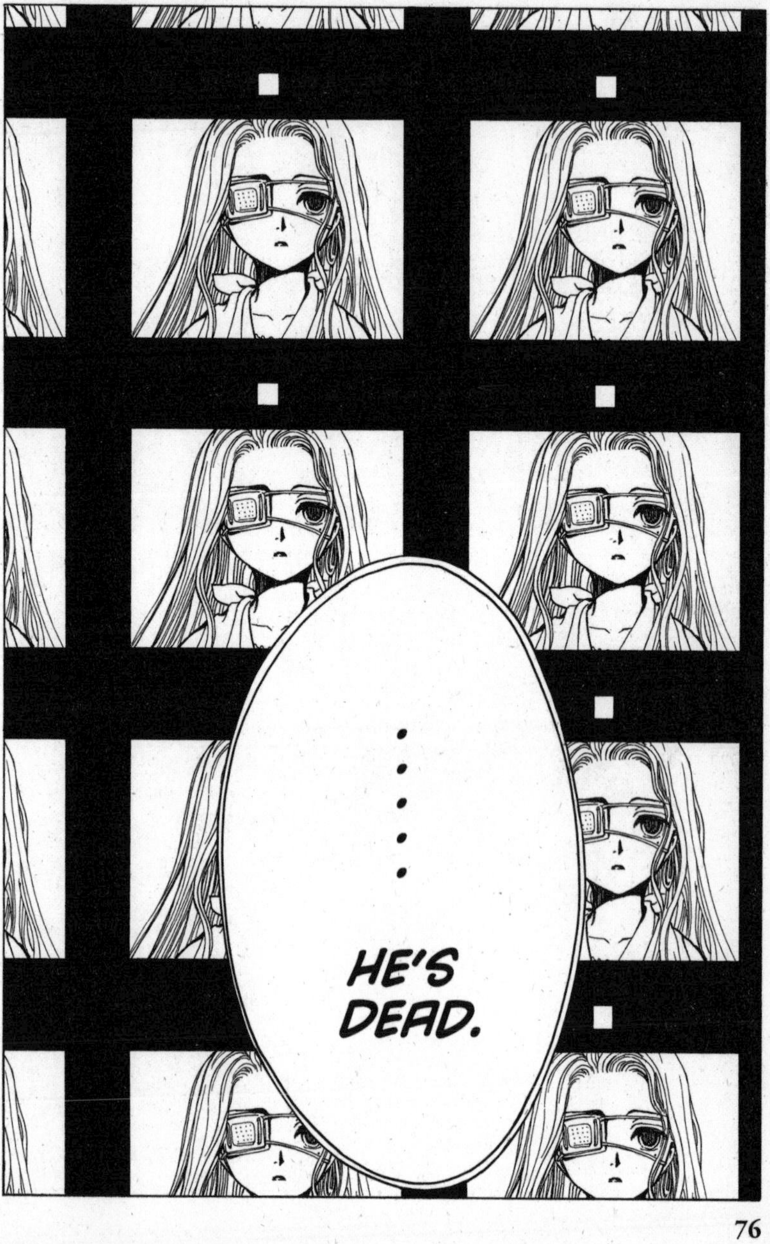
.....
HE'S DEAD.

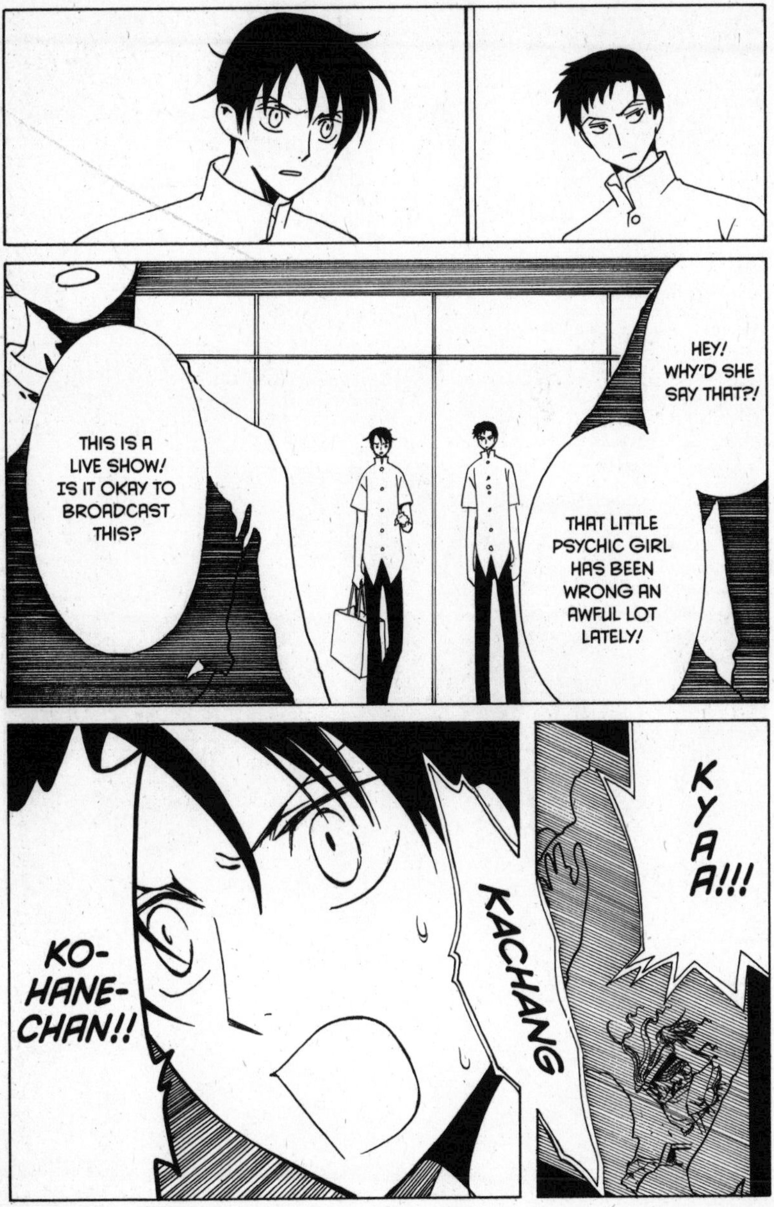
HEY! WHY'D SHE SAY THAT?!
THAT LITTLE PSYCHIC GIRL HAS BEEN WRONG AN AWFUL LOT LATELY!
THIS IS A LIVE SHOW! IS IT OKAY TO BROADCAST THIS?
KYAA!!!
KACHANG
KO-HANE-CHAN!!

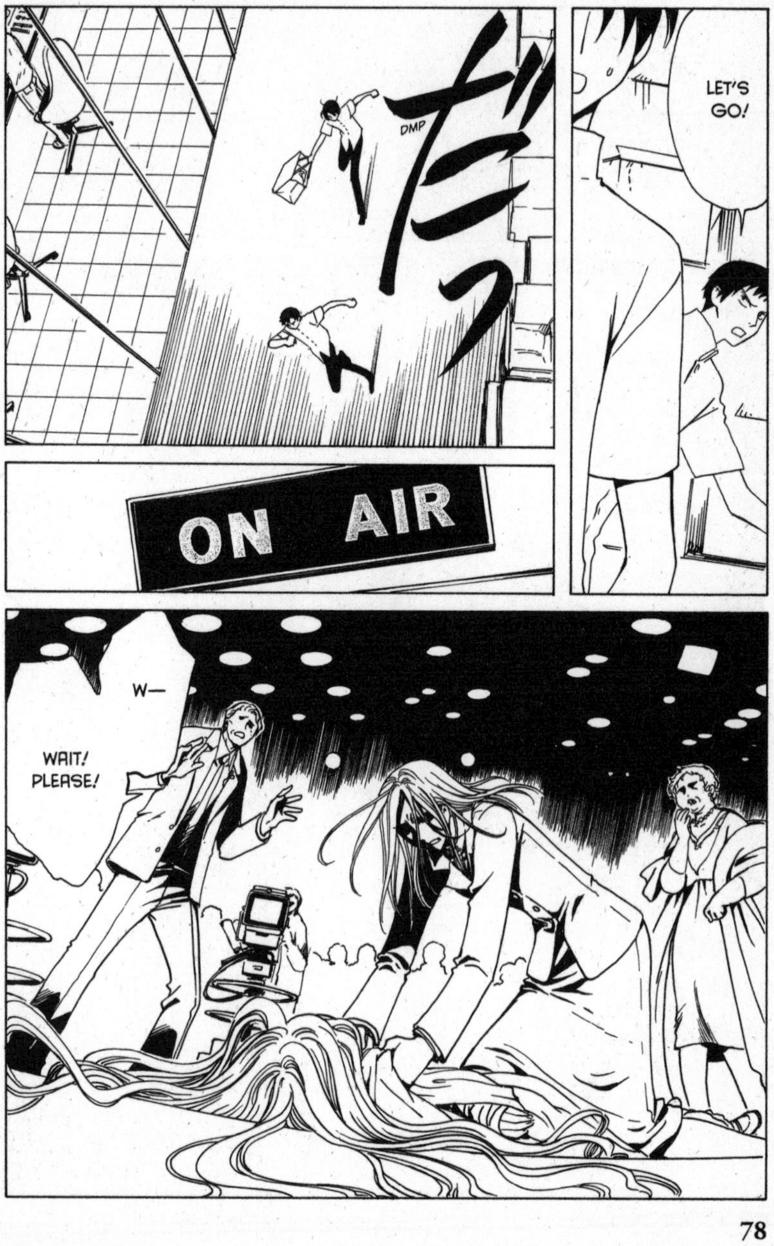
LET'S GO!
DMP
だっ
ON AIR
W—
WAIT! PLEASE!

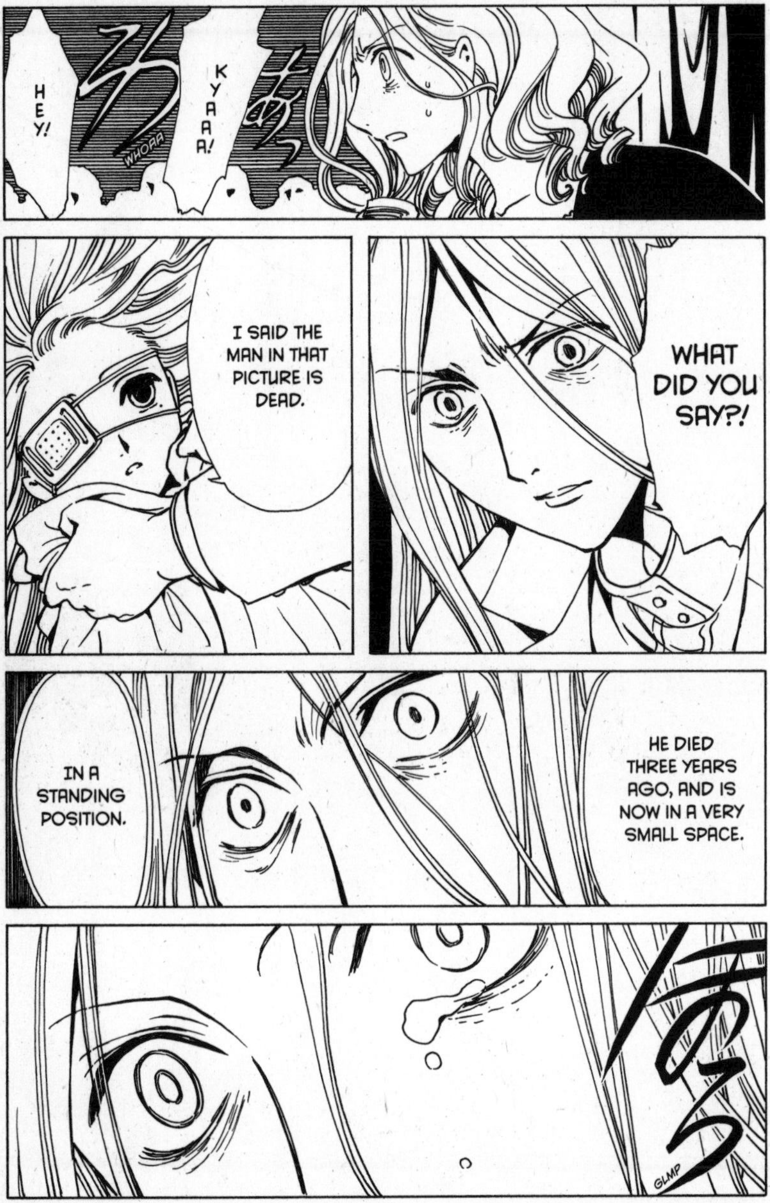
KYAAA!
WHOAA
HEY!
WHAT DID YOU SAY?!
I SAID THE MAN IN THAT PICTURE IS DEAD.
HE DIED THREE YEARS AGO, AND IS NOW IN A VERY SMALL SPACE.
IN A STANDING POSITION.
GLMP

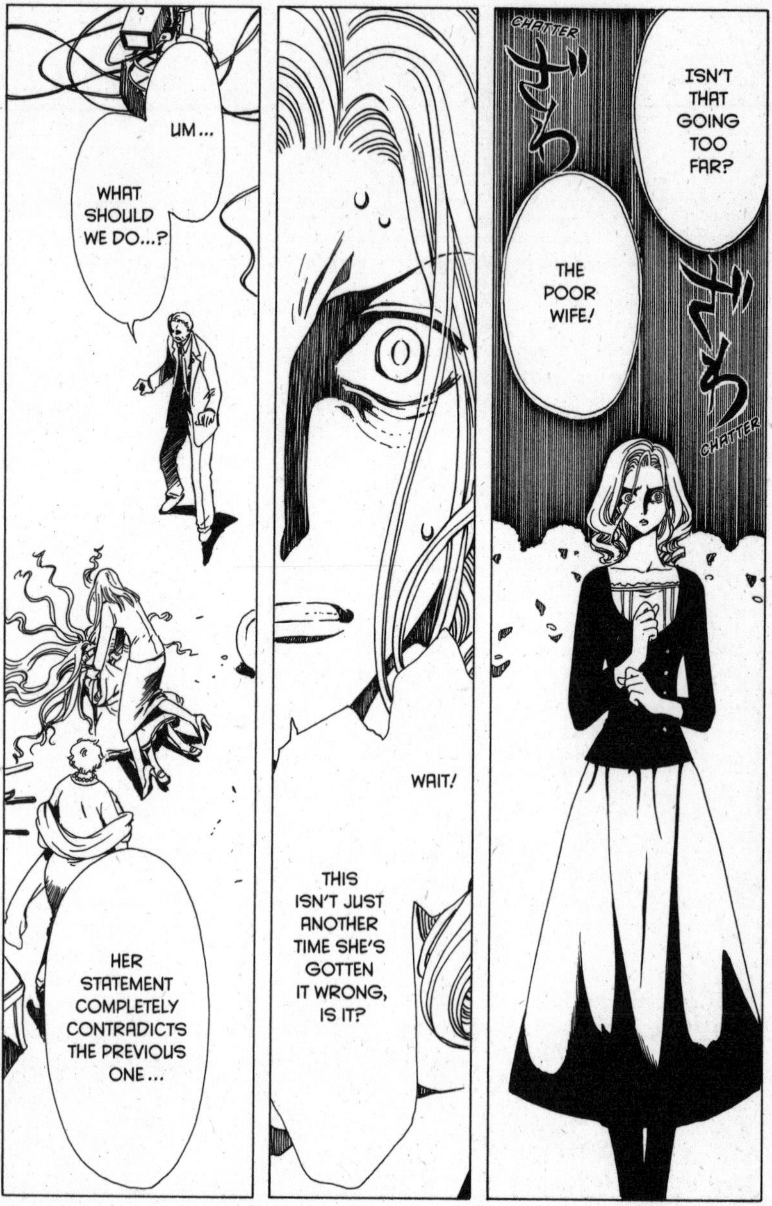
ISN'T THAT GOING TOO FAR?
CHATTER
ざわ
THE POOR WIFE!
ざわ
CHATTER
WAIT!
THIS ISN'T JUST ANOTHER TIME SHE'S GOTTEN IT WRONG, IS IT?
UM...
WHAT SHOULD WE DO...?
HER STATEMENT COMPLETELY CONTRADICTS THE PREVIOUS ONE...

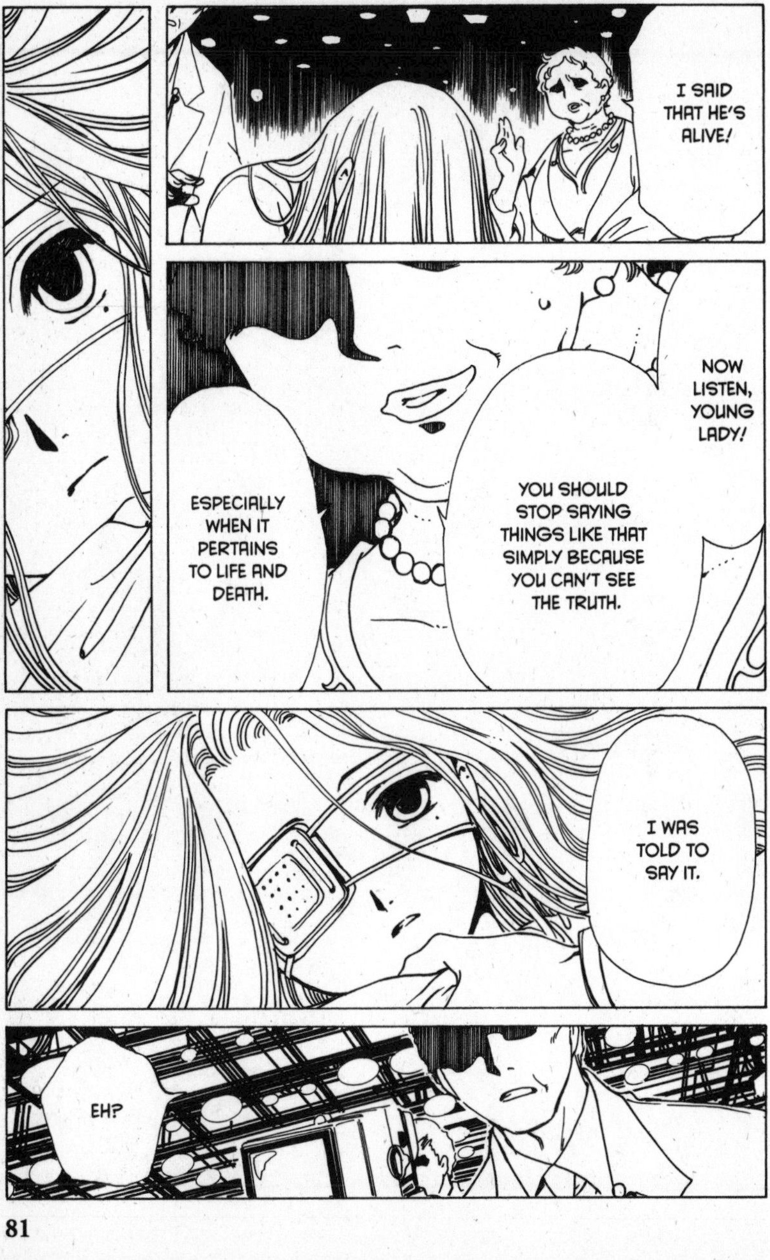
I SAID THAT HE'S ALIVE!
NOW LISTEN, YOUNG LADY!
YOU SHOULD STOP SAYING THINGS LIKE THAT SIMPLY BECAUSE YOU CAN'T SEE THE TRUTH.
ESPECIALLY WHEN IT PERTAINS TO LIFE AND DEATH.
I WAS TOLD TO SAY IT.
EH?

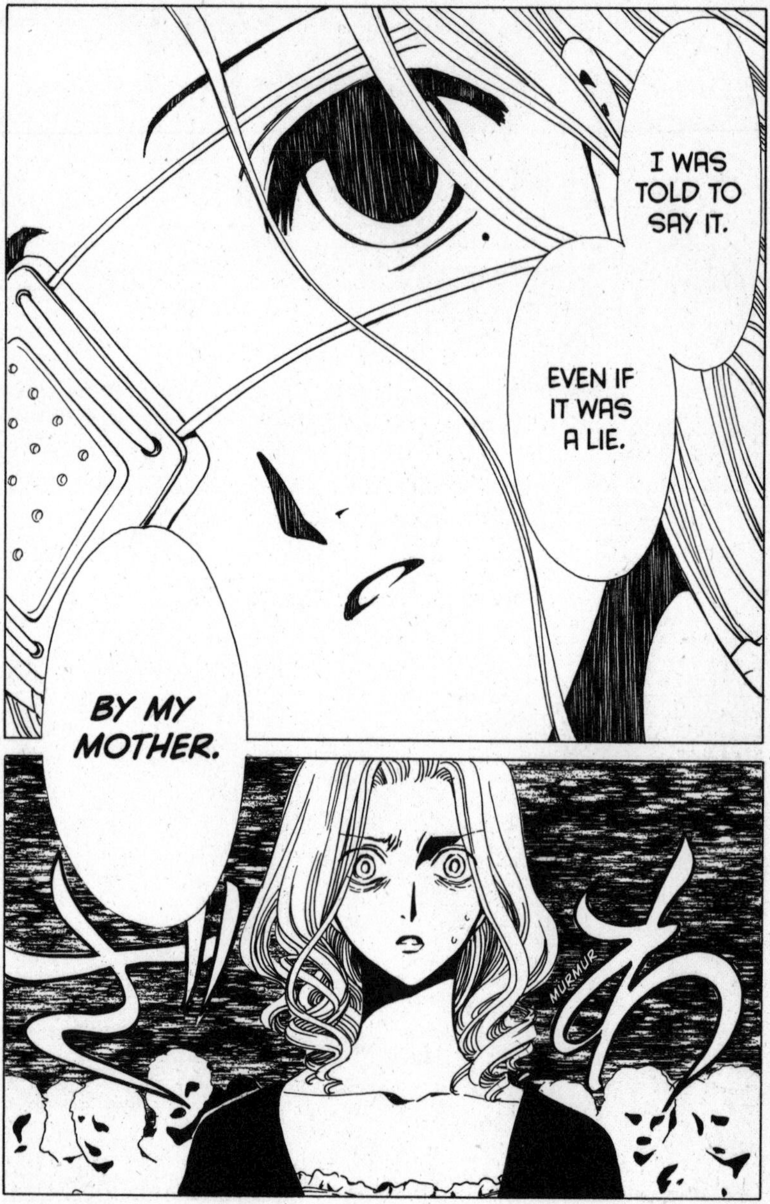
I WAS TOLD TO SAY IT.
EVEN IF IT WAS A LIE.
BY MY MOTHER.
MURMUR

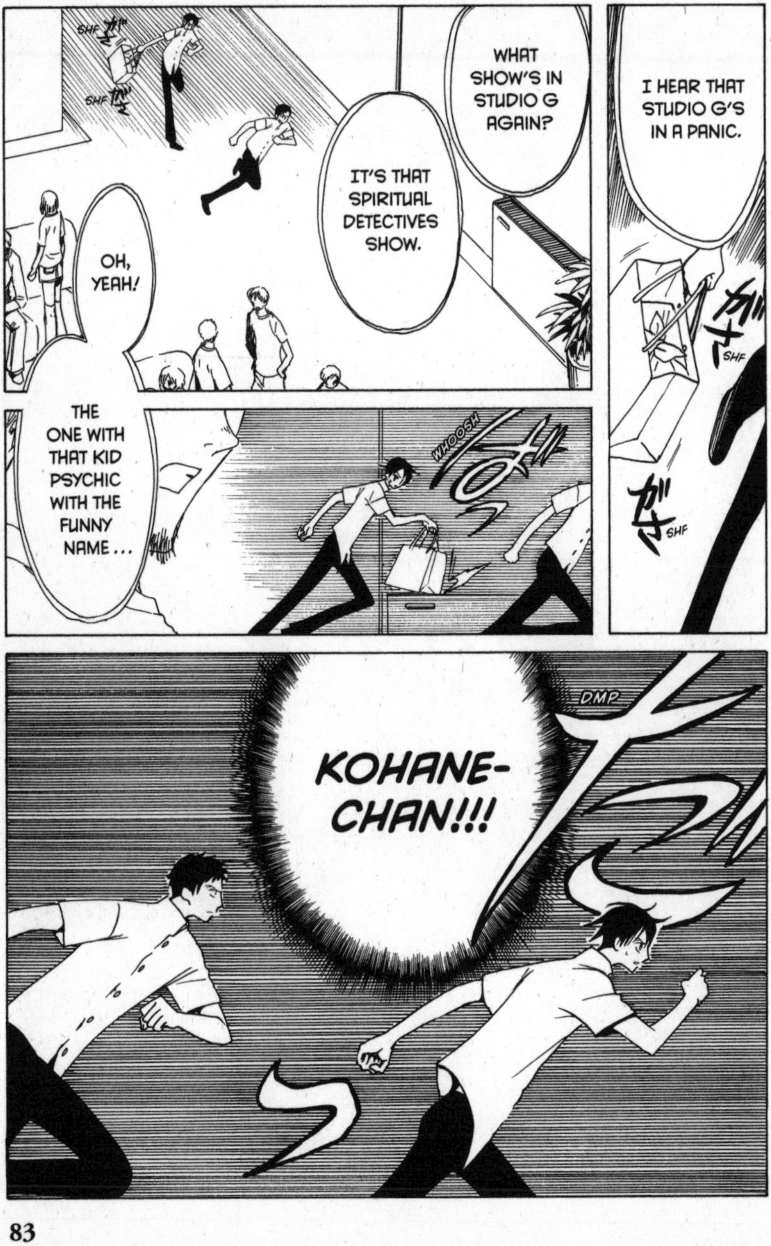
I HEAR THAT STUDIO G'S IN A PANIC.
SHF
SHF
WHAT SHOW'S IN STUDIO G AGAIN?
IT'S THAT SPIRITUAL DETECTIVES SHOW.
SHF
SHF
OH, YEAH!
WHOOSH
THE ONE WITH THAT KID PSYCHIC WITH THE FUNNY NAME...
DMP
KOHANE-CHAN!!!

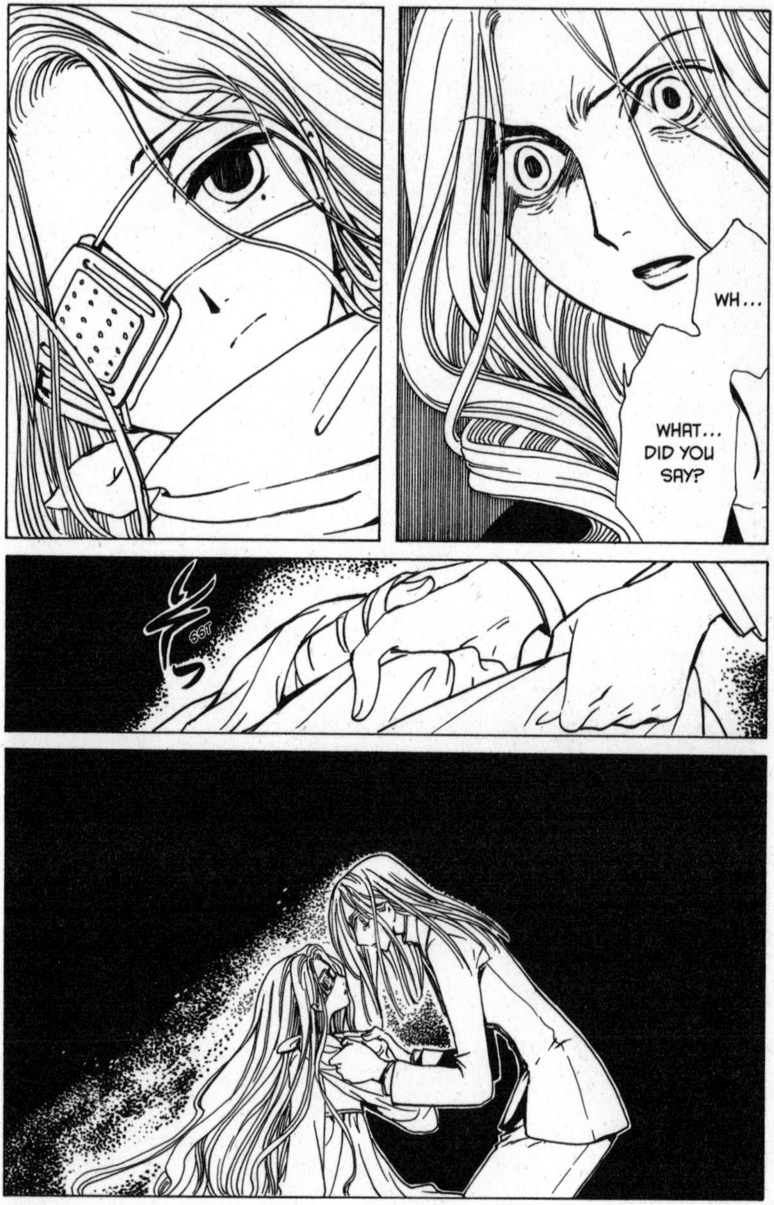
WH...
WHAT... DID YOU SAY?
SST

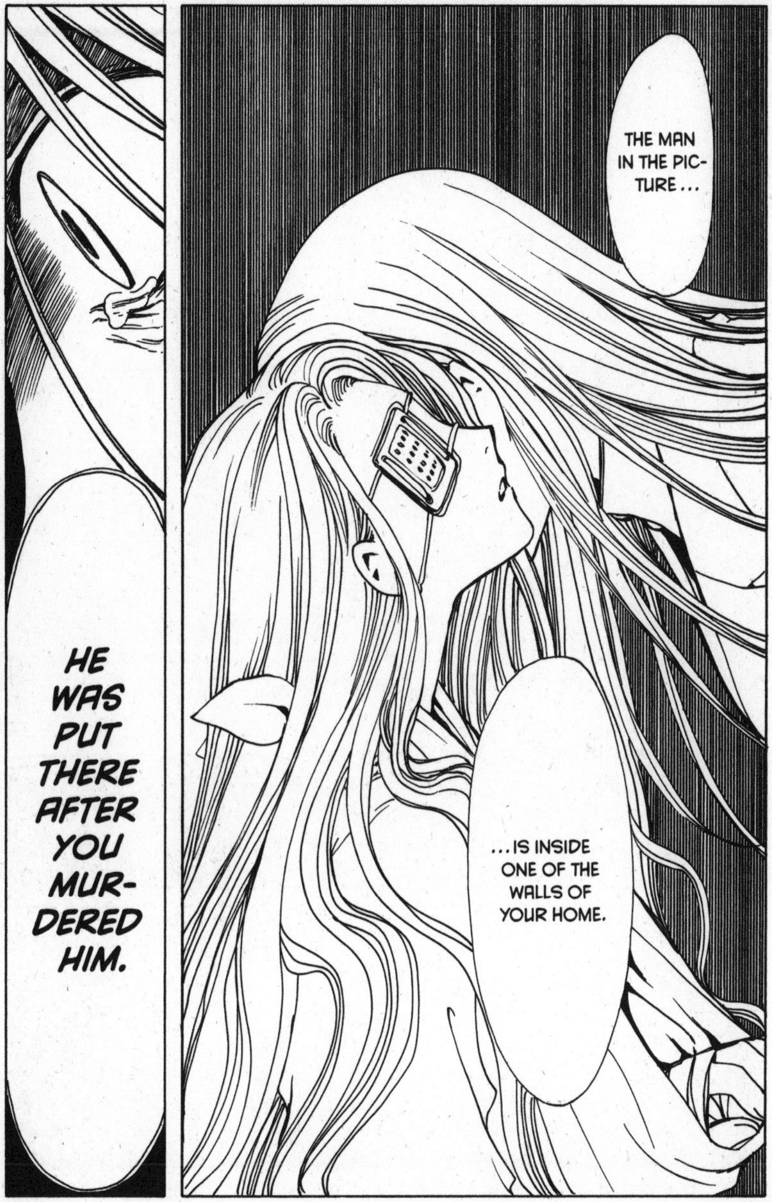
THE MAN IN THE PIC-TURE...
...IS INSIDE ONE OF THE WALLS OF YOUR HOME.
HE WAS PUT THERE AFTER YOU MUR-DERED HIM.

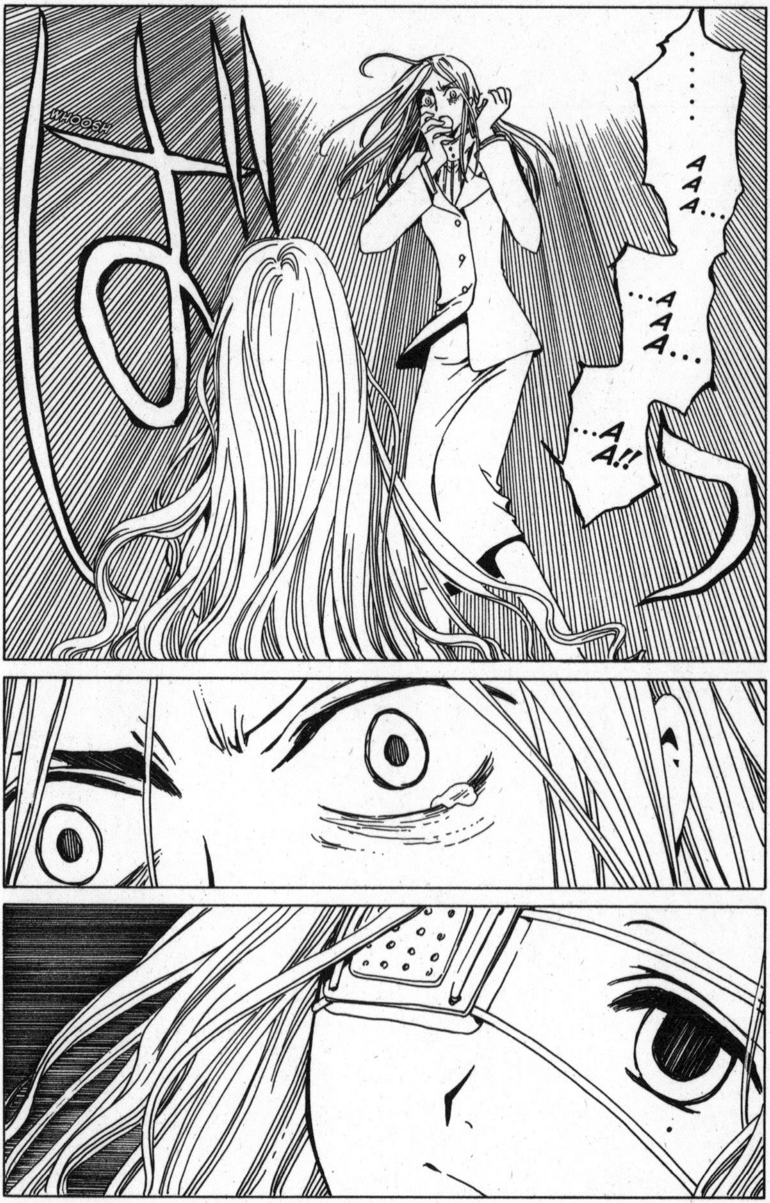
......AAA......AAA......AA!!
WHOOSH

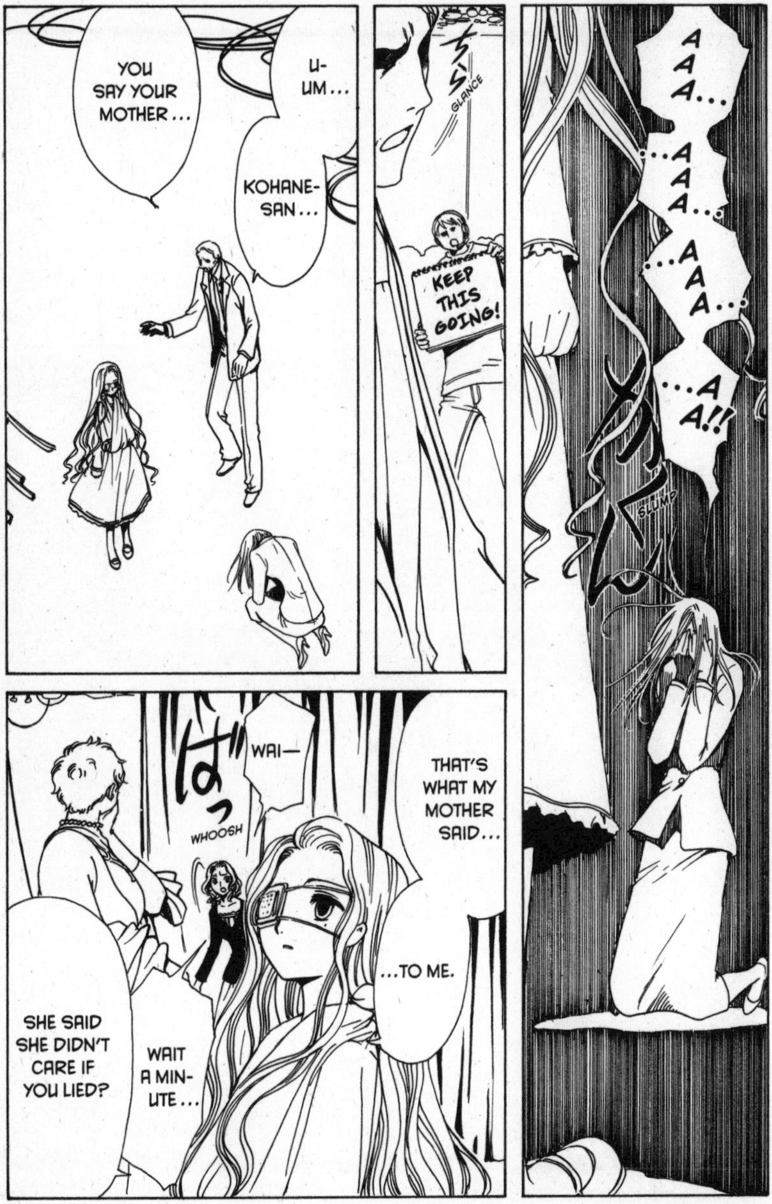
AAA… …AAA… …AAA… …AA!!
SLUMP
GLANCE
KEEP THIS GOING!
U-UM…
KOHANE-SAN…
YOU SAY YOUR MOTHER…
THAT'S WHAT MY MOTHER SAID…
…TO ME.
WAI—
WHOOSH
WAIT A MIN-UTE…
SHE SAID SHE DIDN'T CARE IF YOU LIED?

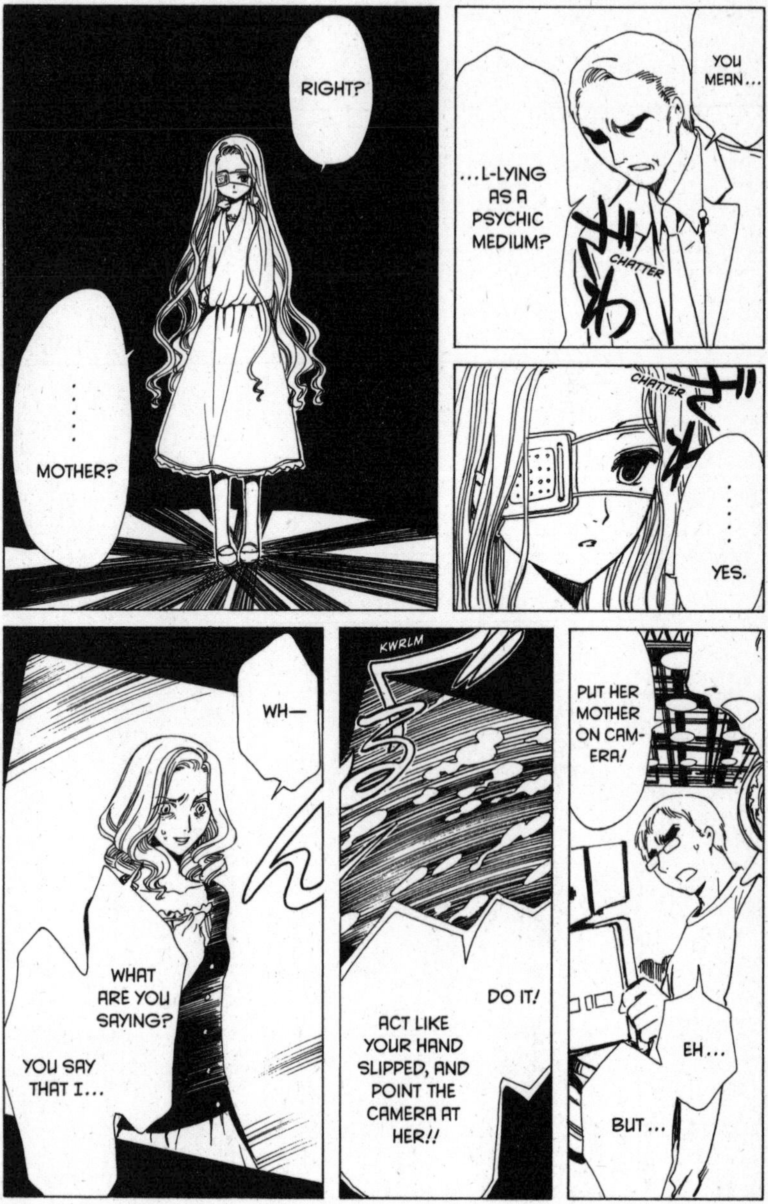
YOU MEAN...
...L-LYING AS A PSYCHIC MEDIUM?
CHATTER
CHATTER
...... YES.
RIGHT?
...... MOTHER?
PUT HER MOTHER ON CAM-ERA!
EH...
BUT...
KWRLM
DO IT!
ACT LIKE YOUR HAND SLIPPED, AND POINT THE CAMERA AT HER!!
WH—
WHAT ARE YOU SAYING?
YOU SAY THAT I...

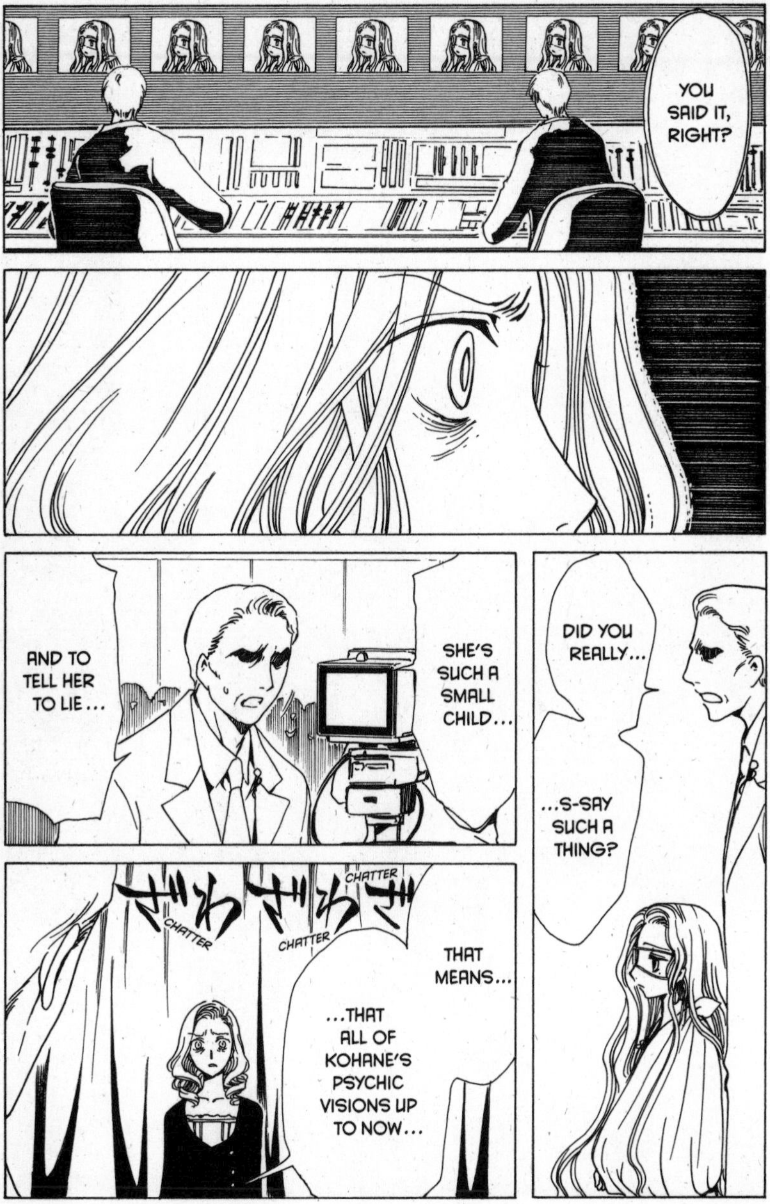
YOU SAID IT, RIGHT?
DID YOU REALLY...
...S-SAY SUCH A THING?
SHE'S SUCH A SMALL CHILD...
AND TO TELL HER TO LIE...
CHATTER
CHATTER
CHATTER
THAT MEANS...
...THAT ALL OF KOHANE'S PSYCHIC VISIONS UP TO NOW...

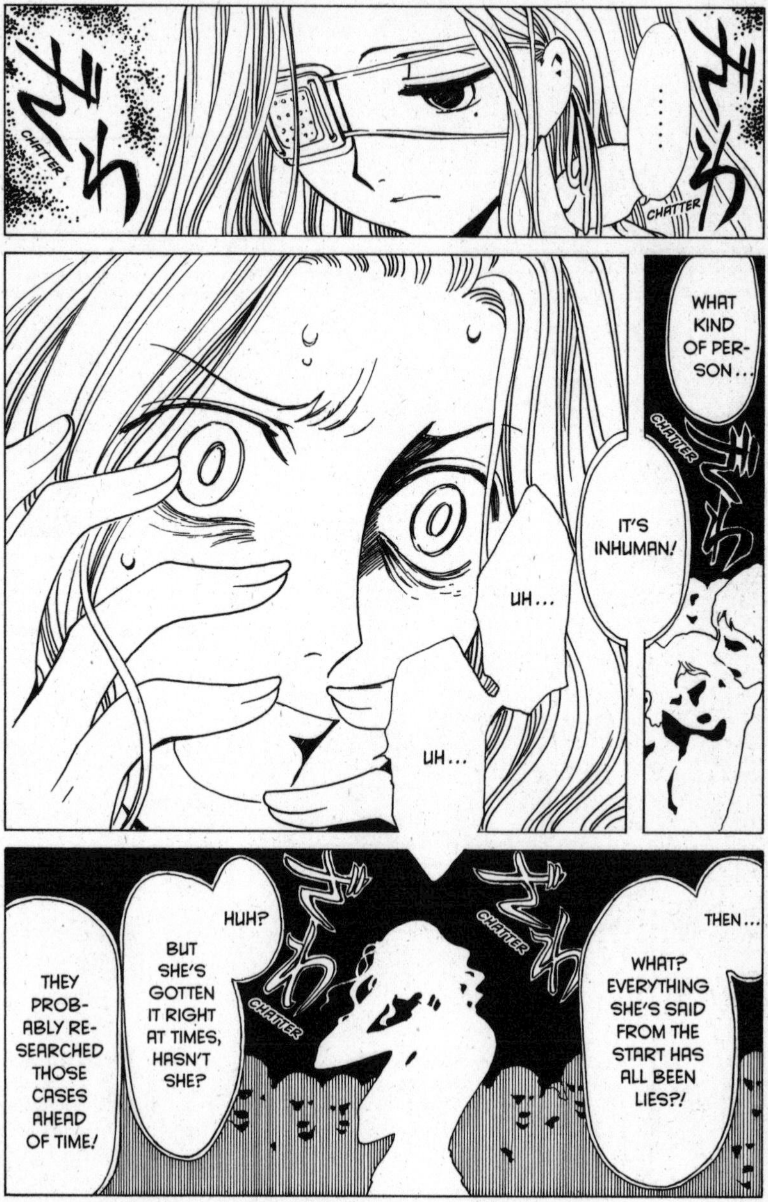
CHATTER
......
CHATTER
WHAT KIND OF PERSON...
CHATTER
IT'S INHUMAN!
UH...
UH...
THEN...
WHAT? EVERYTHING SHE'S SAID FROM THE START HAS ALL BEEN LIES?!
CHATTER
HUH?
BUT SHE'S GOTTEN IT RIGHT AT TIMES, HASN'T SHE?
CHATTER
THEY PROBABLY RESEARCHED THOSE CASES AHEAD OF TIME!

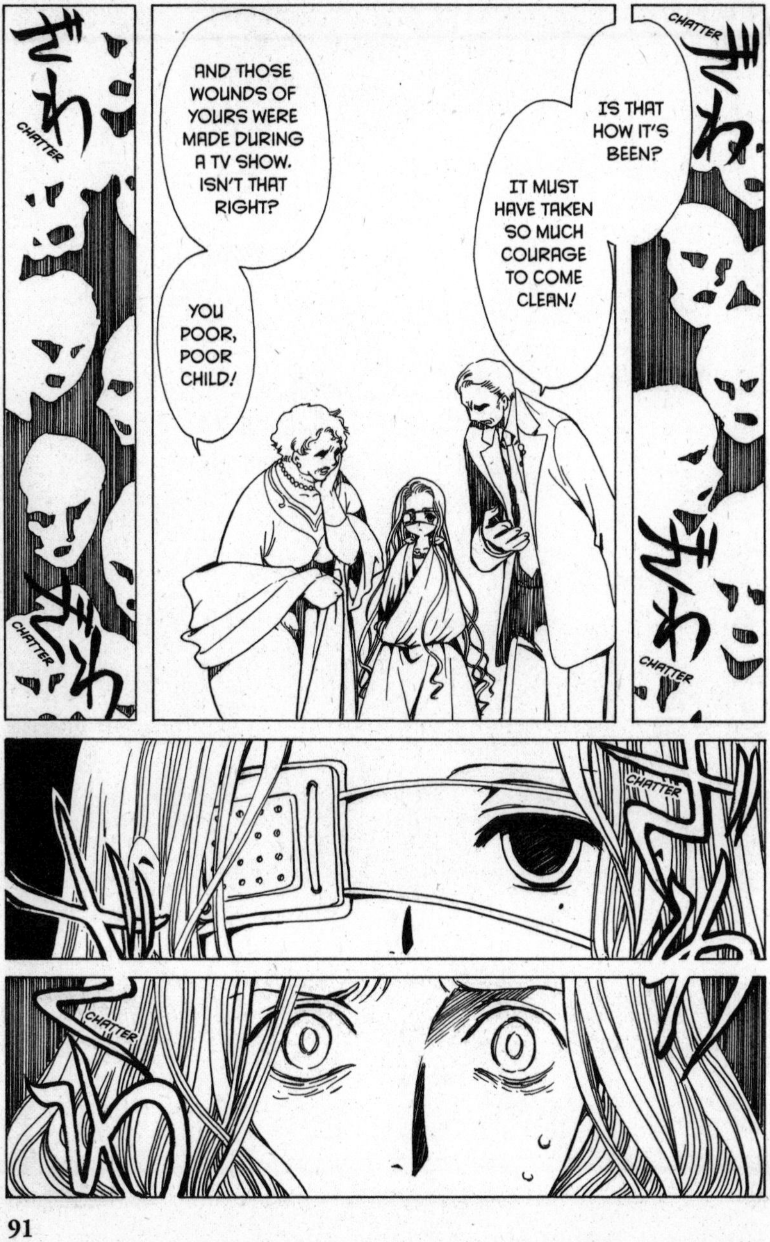
CHATTER
CHATTER
IS THAT HOW IT'S BEEN?
IT MUST HAVE TAKEN SO MUCH COURAGE TO COME CLEAN!
AND THOSE WOUNDS OF YOURS WERE MADE DURING A TV SHOW. ISN'T THAT RIGHT?
YOU POOR, POOR CHILD!
CHATTER
CHATTER
CHATTER
CHATTER

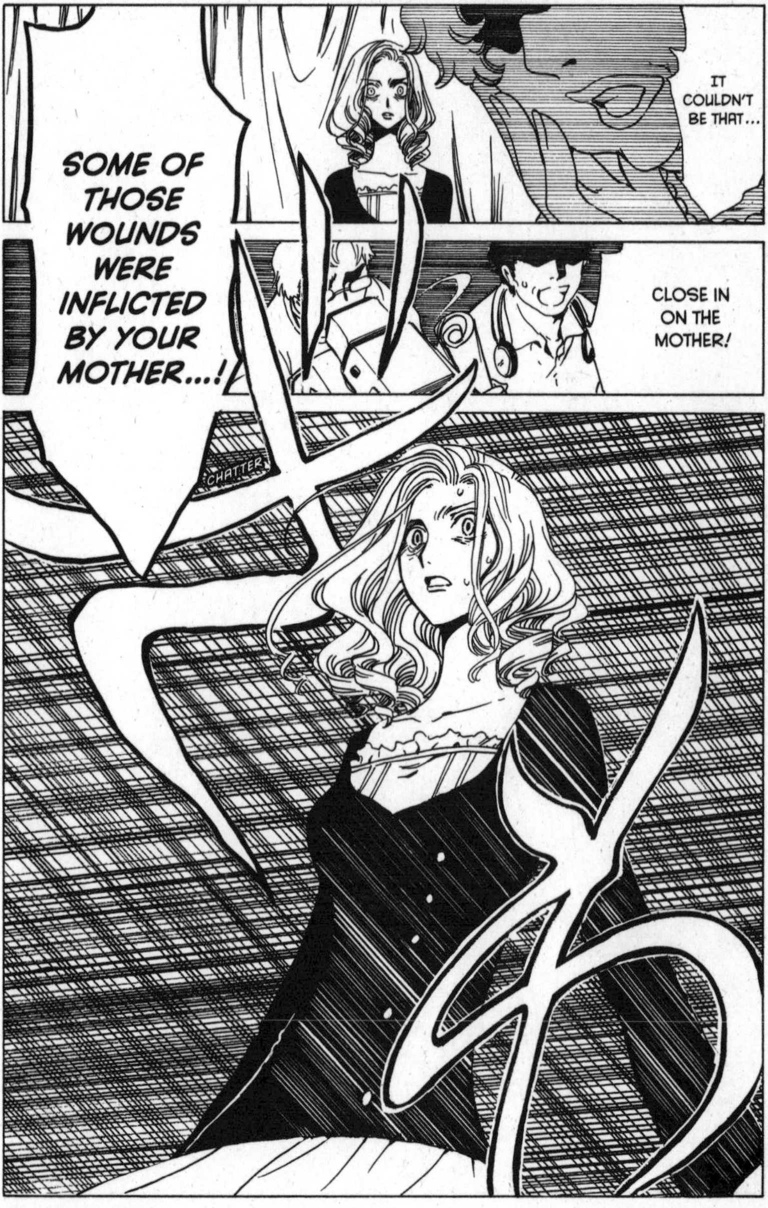
IT COULDN'T BE THAT...
SOME OF THOSE WOUNDS WERE INFLICTED BY YOUR MOTHER...!
CLOSE IN ON THE MOTHER!
CHATTER

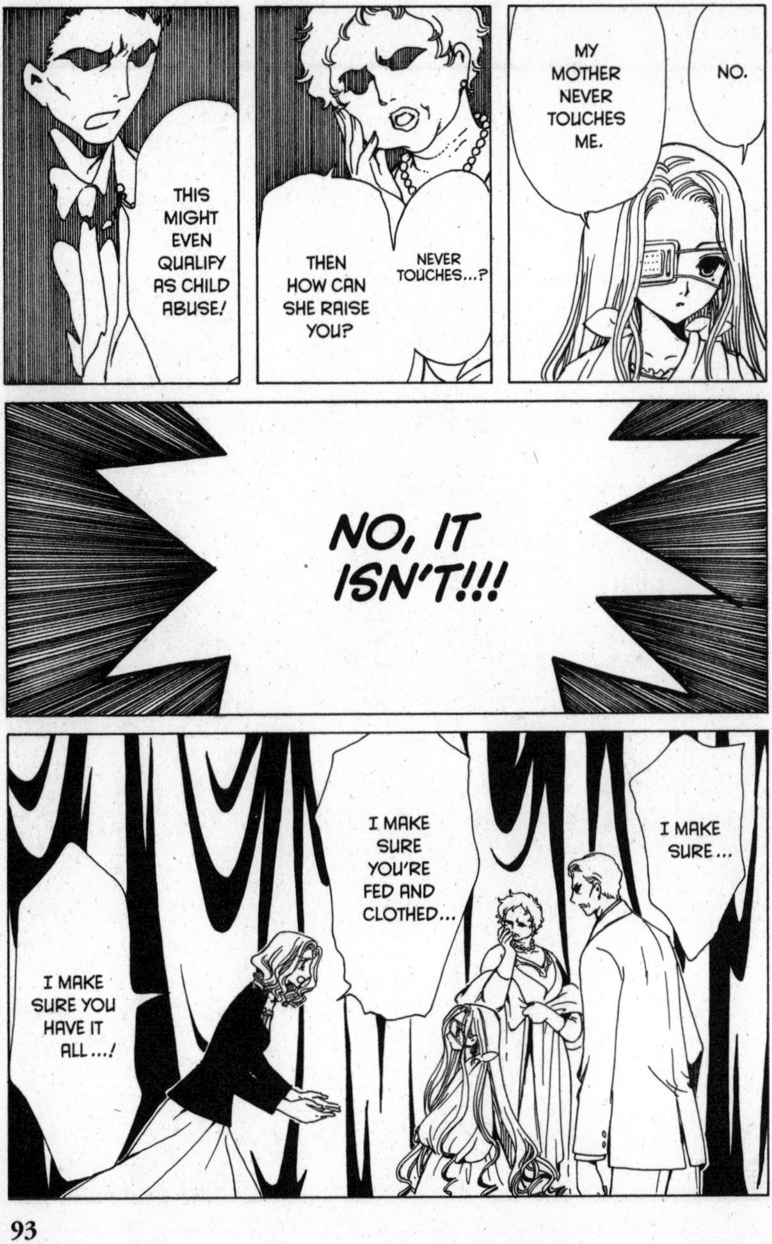
NO.
MY MOTHER NEVER TOUCHES ME.
NEVER TOUCHES...?
THEN HOW CAN SHE RAISE YOU?
THIS MIGHT EVEN QUALIFY AS CHILD ABUSE!
NO, IT ISN'T!!!
I MAKE SURE...
I MAKE SURE YOU'RE FED AND CLOTHED...
I MAKE SURE YOU HAVE IT ALL...!

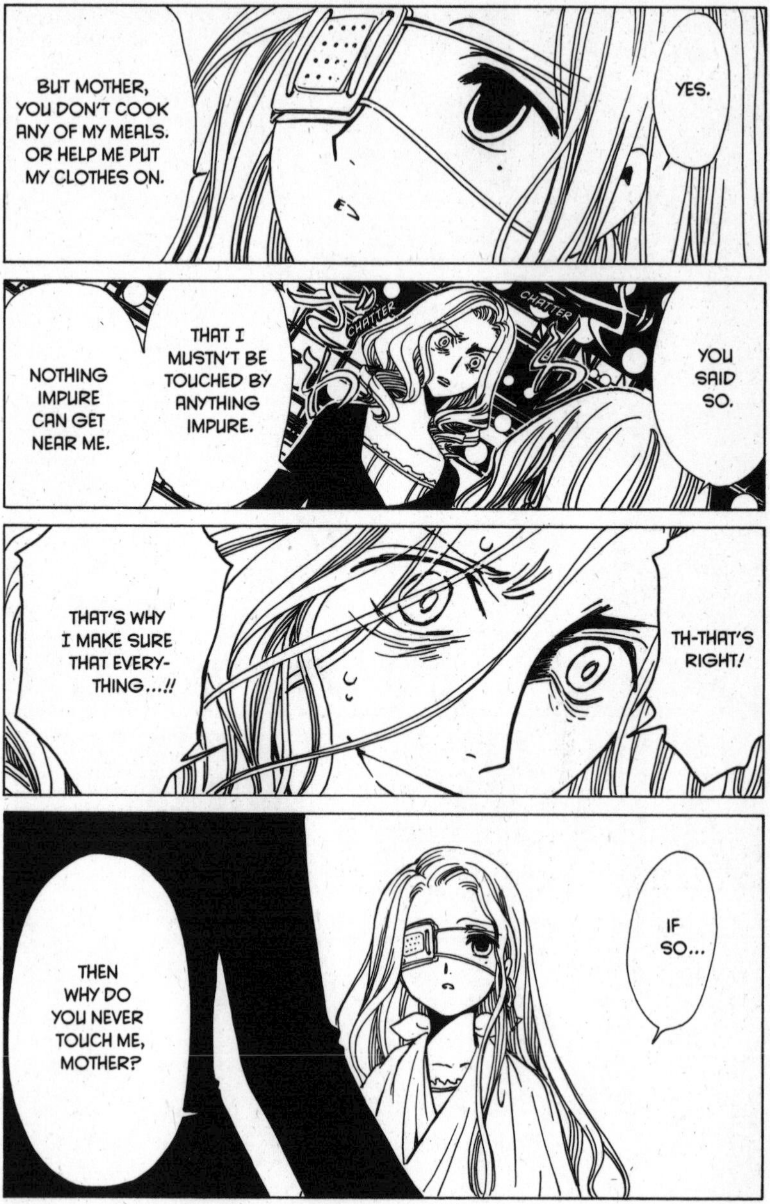
YES.
BUT MOTHER, YOU DON'T COOK ANY OF MY MEALS. OR HELP ME PUT MY CLOTHES ON.
YOU SAID SO.
CHATTER
CHATTER
THAT I MUSTN'T BE TOUCHED BY ANYTHING IMPURE.
NOTHING IMPURE CAN GET NEAR ME.
TH-THAT'S RIGHT!
THAT'S WHY I MAKE SURE THAT EVERY-THING...!!
IF SO...
THEN WHY DO YOU NEVER TOUCH ME, MOTHER?

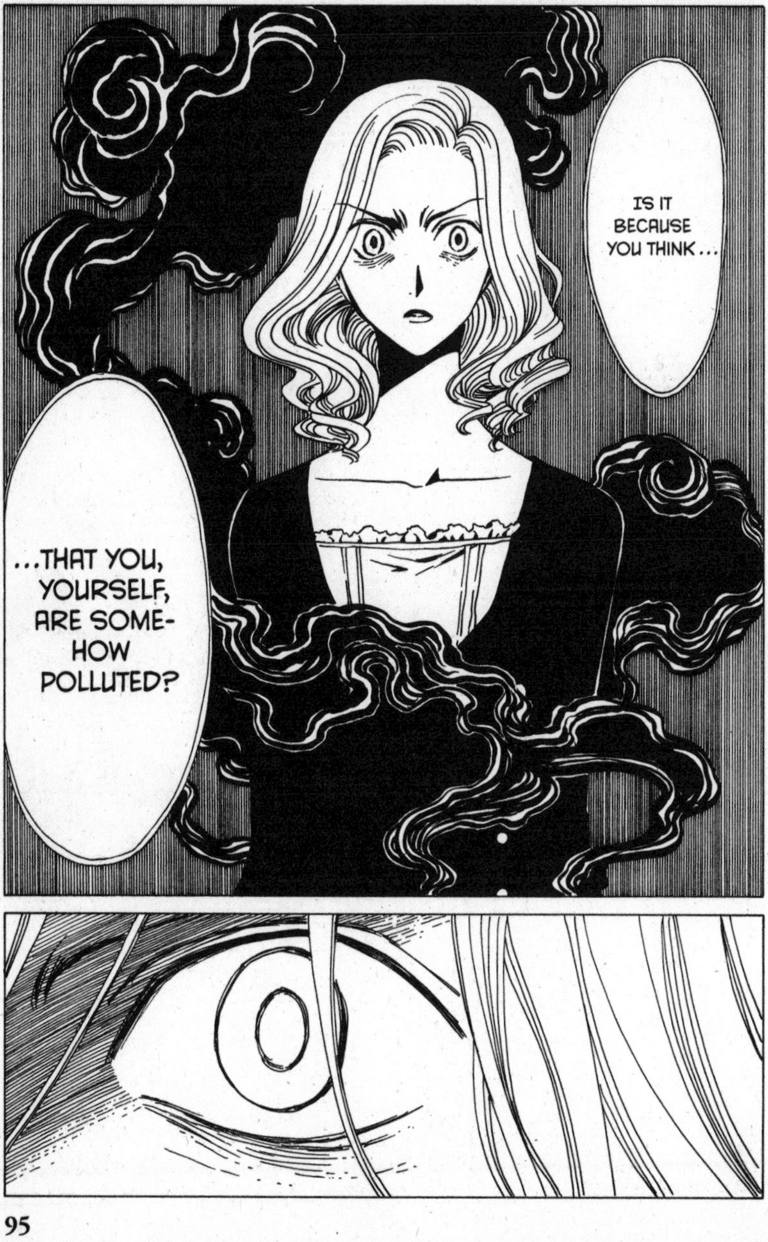
IS IT BECAUSE YOU THINK...
...THAT YOU, YOURSELF, ARE SOME-HOW POLLUTED?

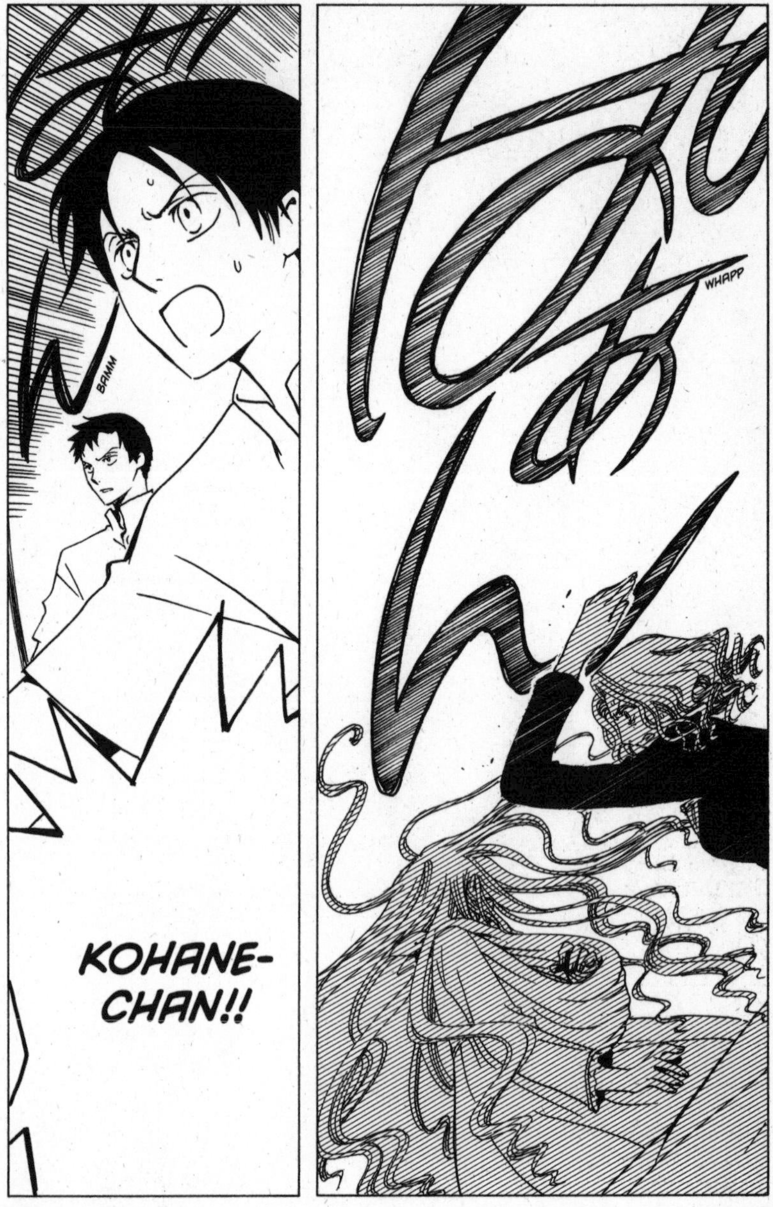
WHAPP
BAMM
KOHANE-CHAN!!

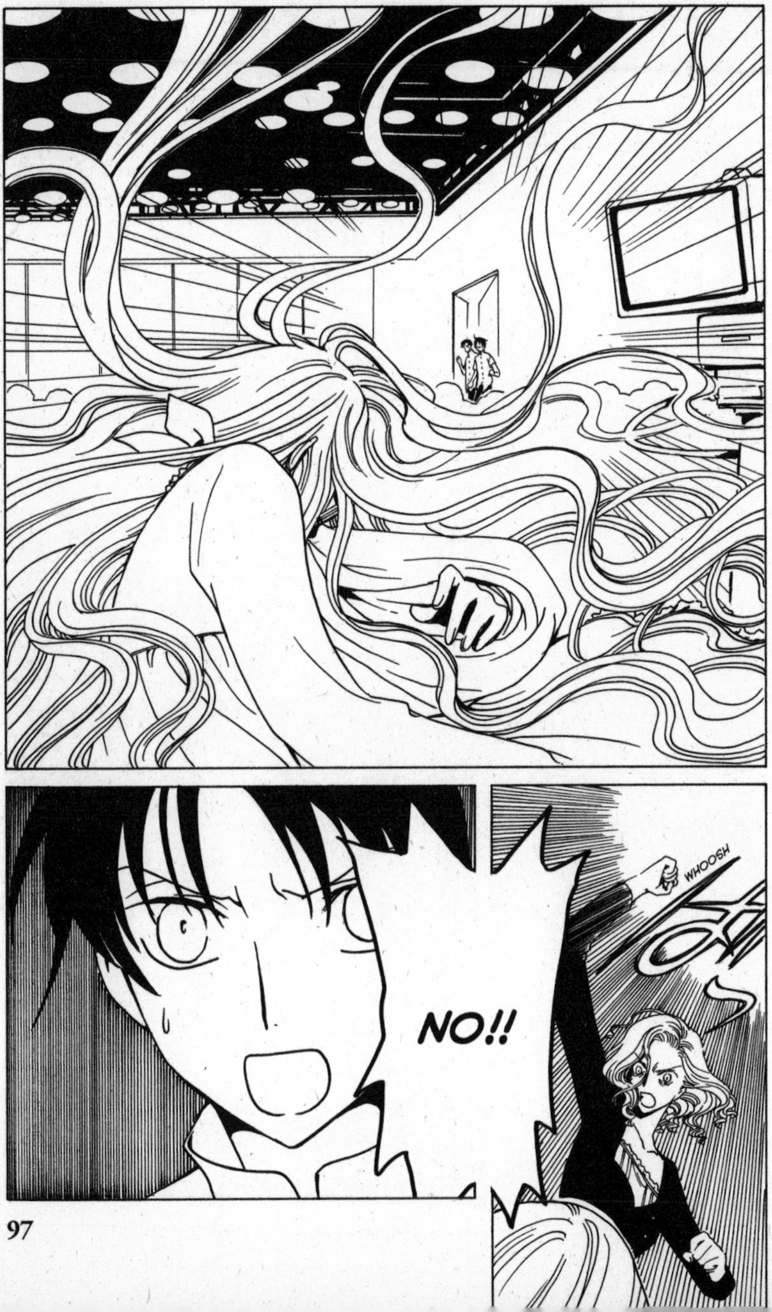
WHOOSH
NO!!

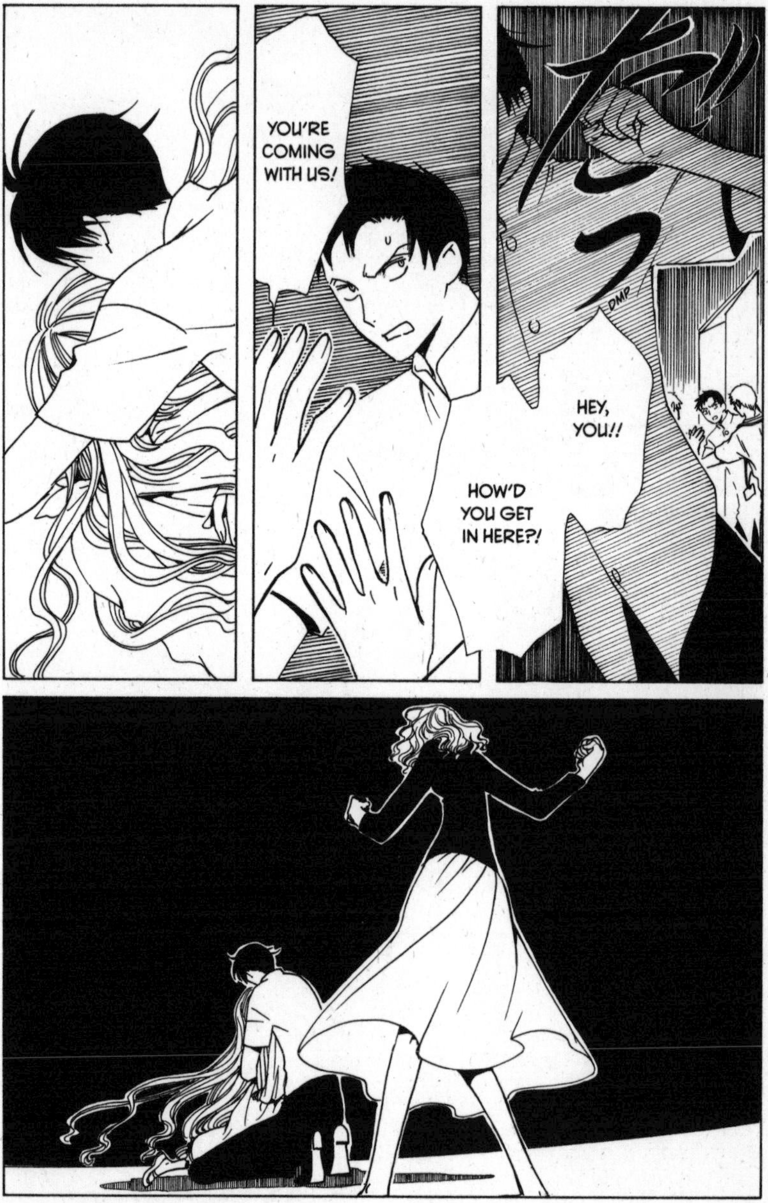
DMP
HEY, YOU!!
HOW'D YOU GET IN HERE?!
YOU'RE COMING WITH US!

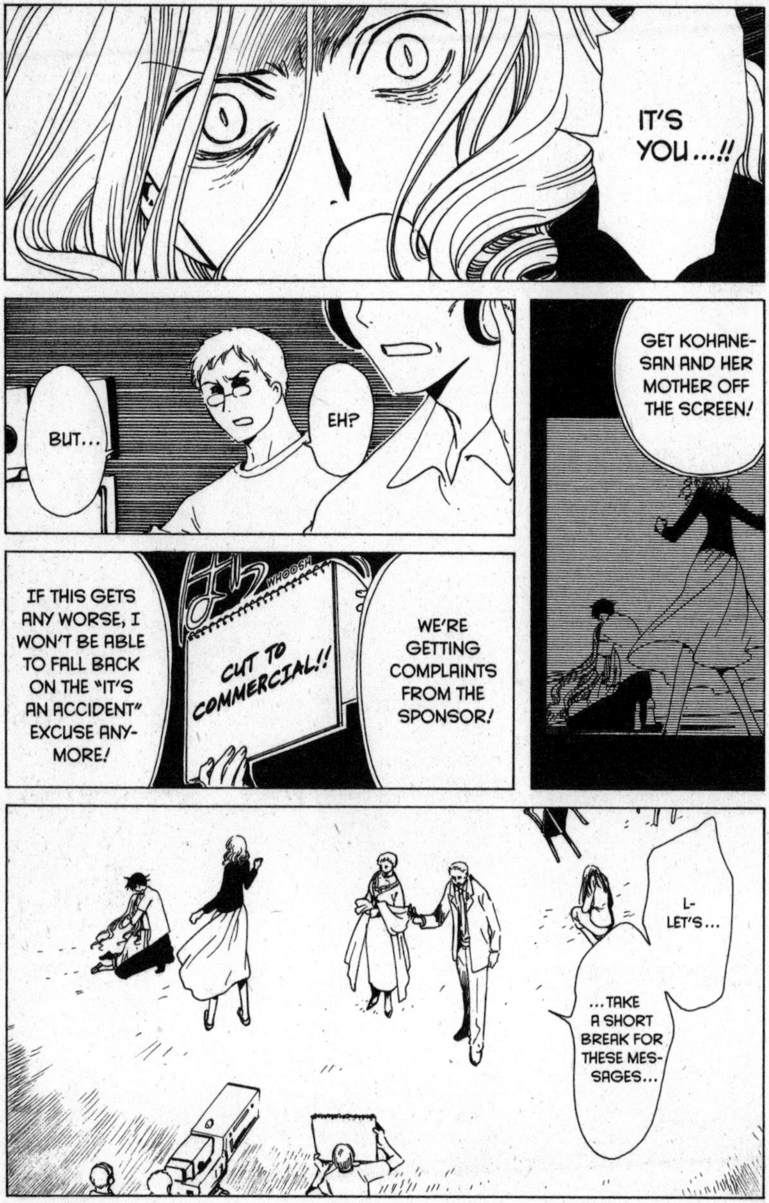
IT'S YOU...!!
GET KOHANE-SAN AND HER MOTHER OFF THE SCREEN!
EH?
BUT...
WE'RE GETTING COMPLAINTS FROM THE SPONSOR!
WHOOSH
CUT TO COMMERCIAL!!
IF THIS GETS ANY WORSE, I WON'T BE ABLE TO FALL BACK ON THE "IT'S AN ACCIDENT" EXCUSE ANY-MORE!
L-LET'S...
...TAKE A SHORT BREAK FOR THESE MES-SAGES...

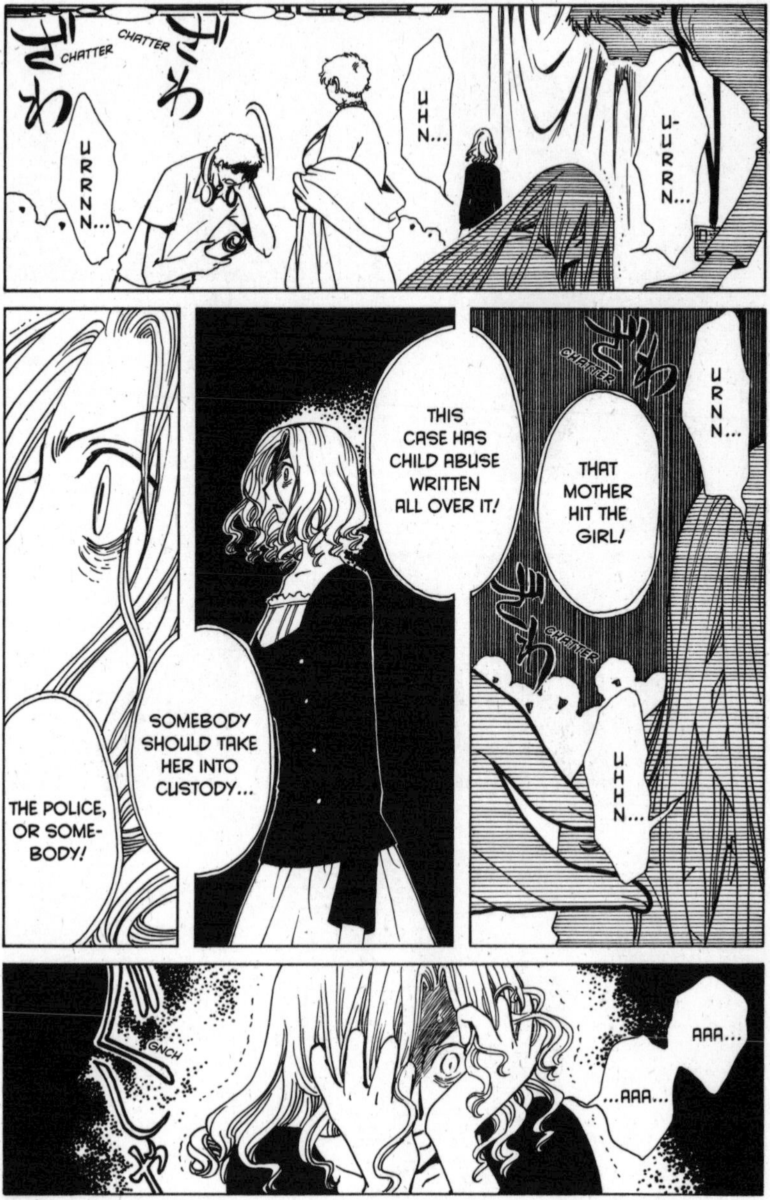

U-URRN...
UHN...
ざわ
CHATTER
CHATTER
ざわ
URRNN...
URNN...
ざわ
CHATTER
THAT MOTHER HIT THE GIRL!
ざわ
CHATTER
UHHN...
THIS CASE HAS CHILD ABUSE WRITTEN ALL OVER IT!
SOMEBODY SHOULD TAKE HER INTO CUSTODY...
THE POLICE, OR SOME-BODY!
AAA...
...AAA...
GNCH

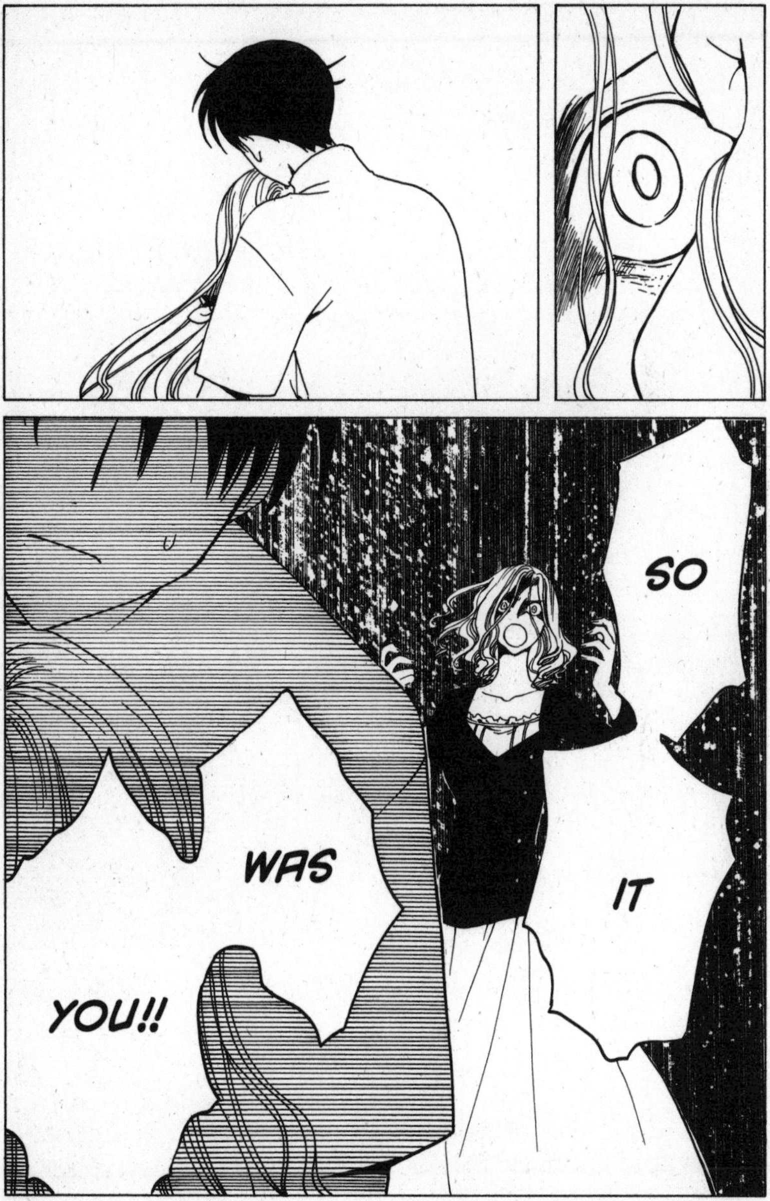
SO IT WAS YOU!!

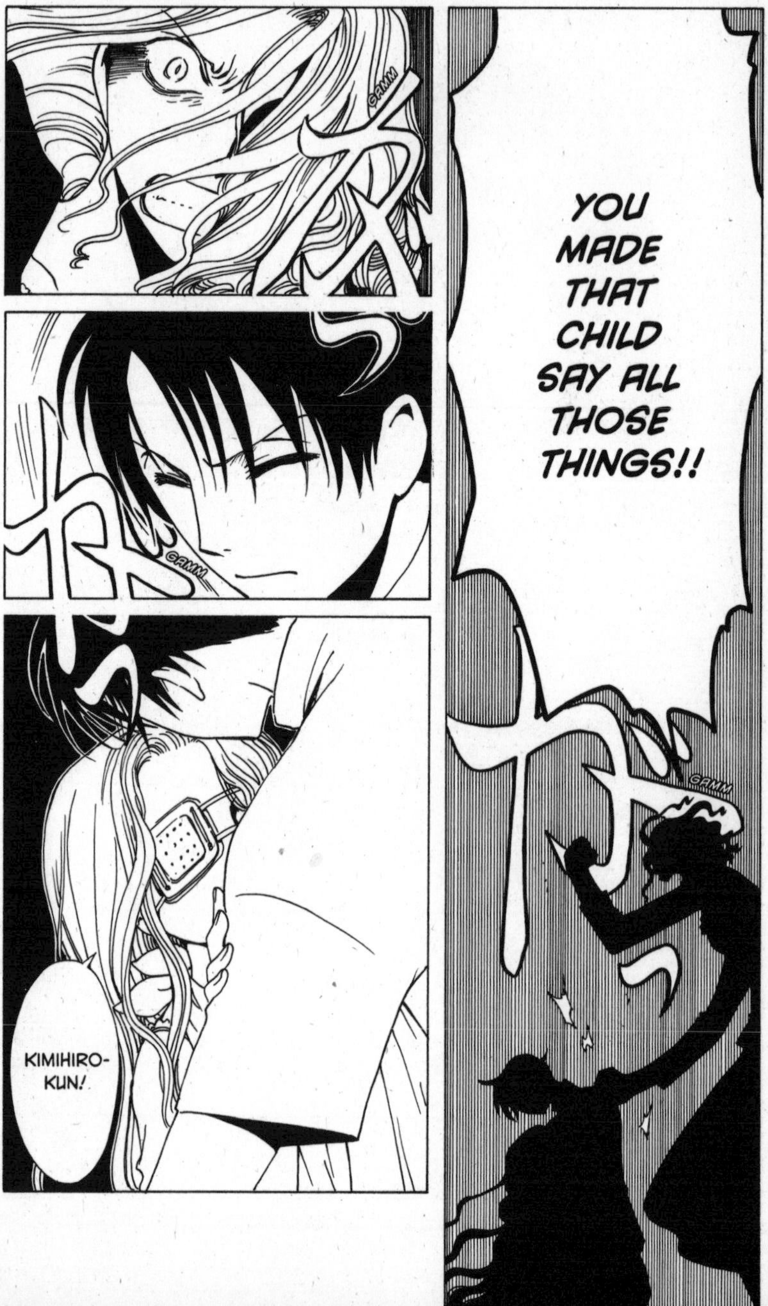
YOU MADE THAT CHILD SAY ALL THOSE THINGS!!
GAMM
GAMM
GAMM
KIMIHIRO-KUN!

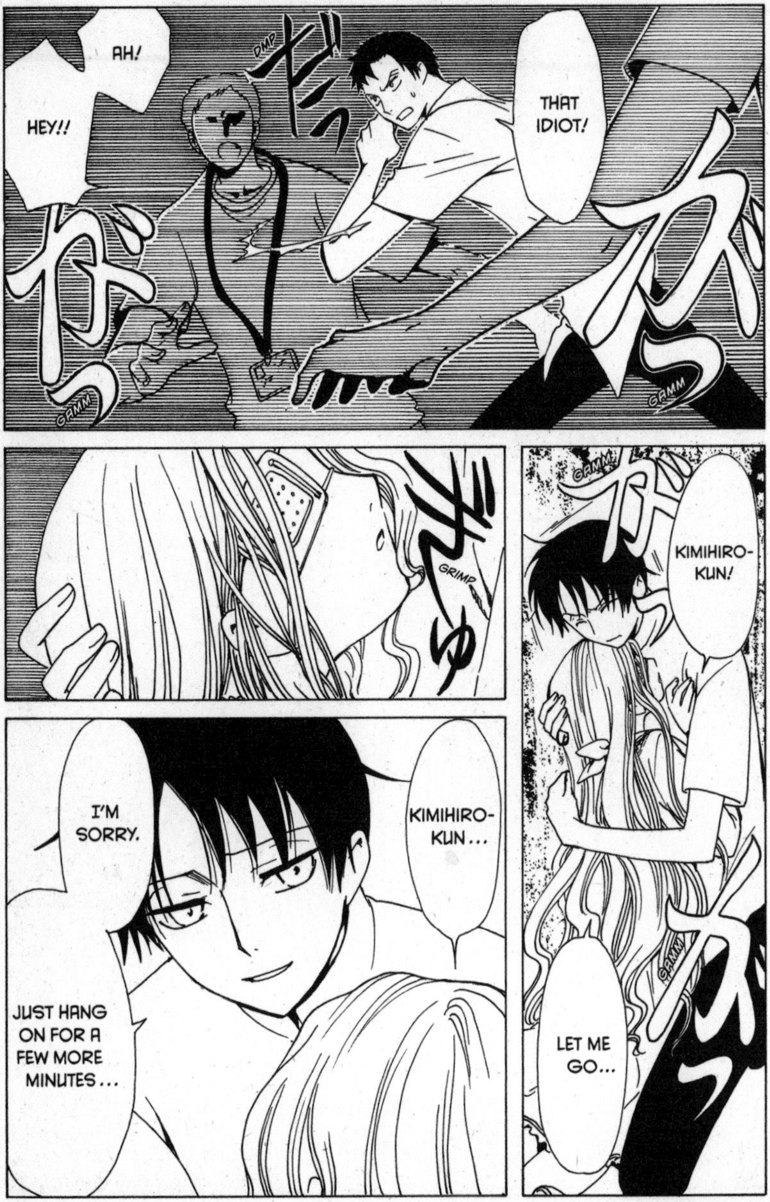
THAT IDIOT!
GAMM
DMP
AH!
HEY!!
GAMM
GAMM
KIMIHIRO-KUN!
GAMM
LET ME GO...
GRIMP
KIMIHIRO-KUN...
I'M SORRY.
JUST HANG ON FOR A FEW MORE MINUTES...

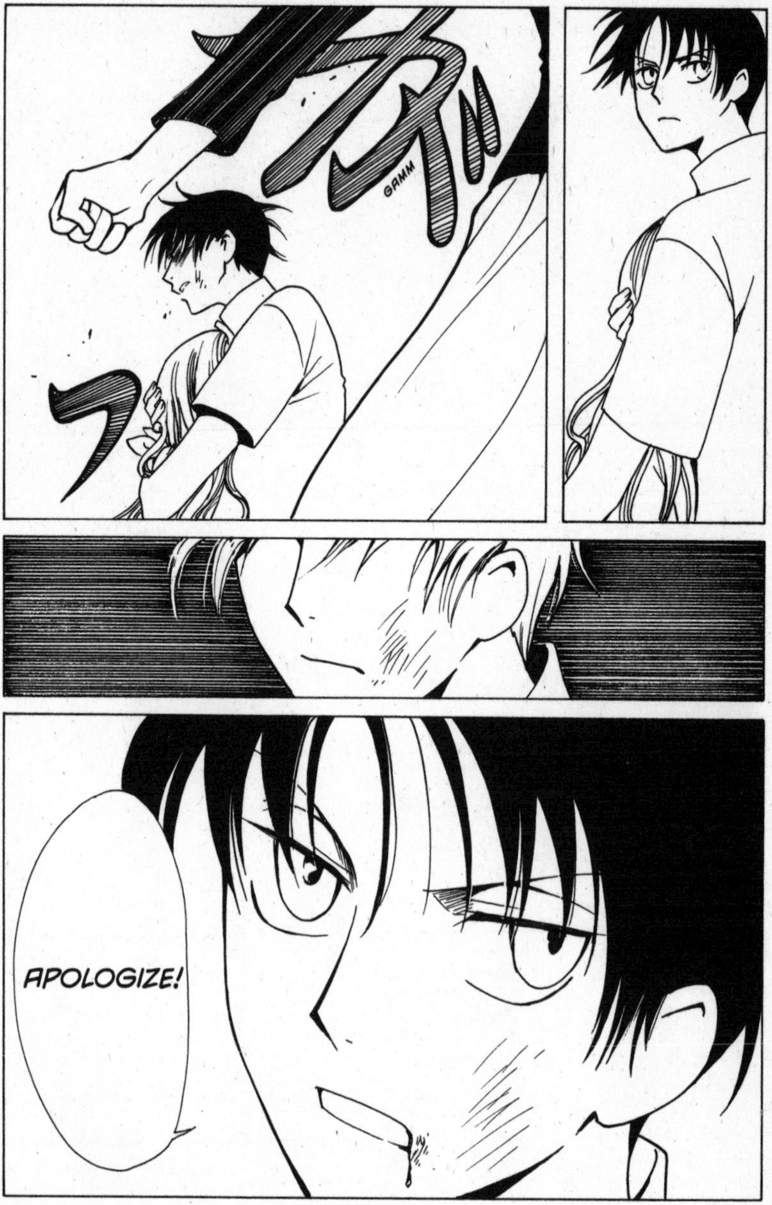
GAMM
APOLOGIZE!

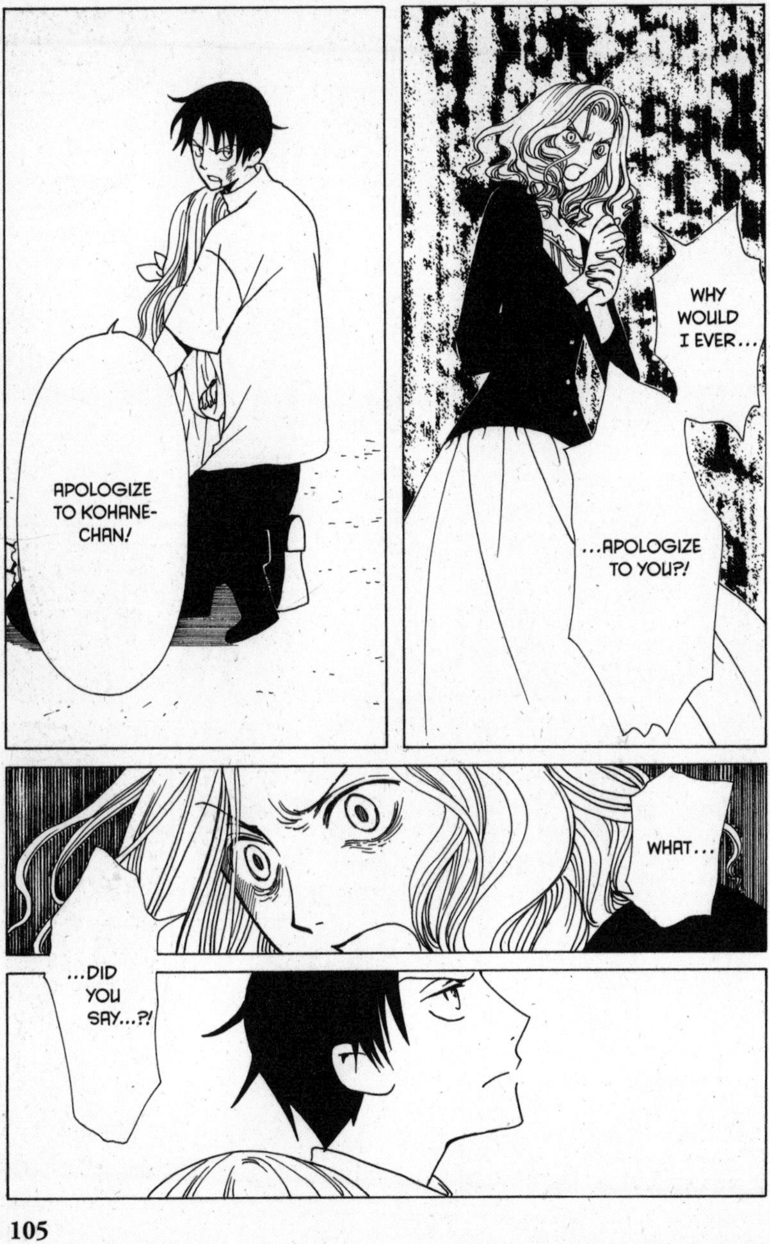
WHY WOULD I EVER...
...APOLOGIZE TO YOU?!
APOLOGIZE TO KOHANE-CHAN!
WHAT...
...DID YOU SAY...?!

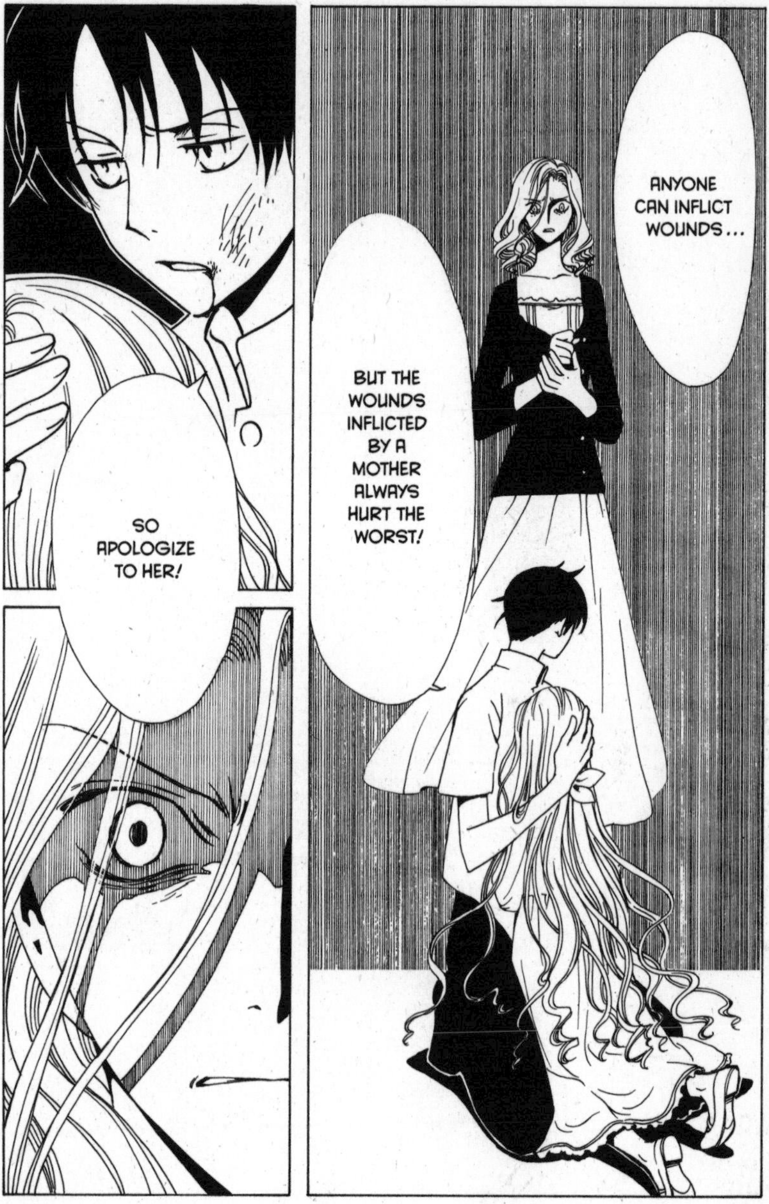
ANYONE CAN INFLICT WOUNDS...
BUT THE WOUNDS INFLICTED BY A MOTHER ALWAYS HURT THE WORST!
SO APOLOGIZE TO HER!

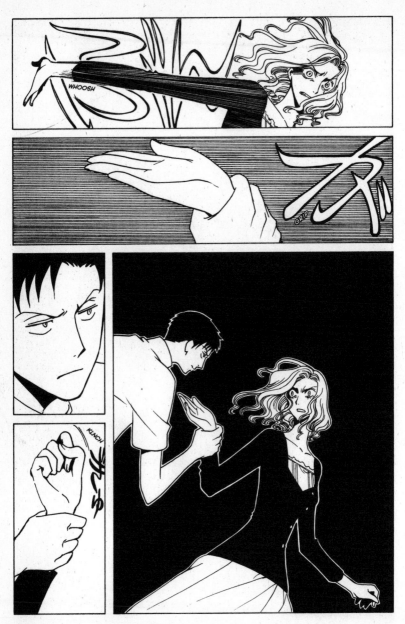

WHOOSH

GRIP

KLNCH

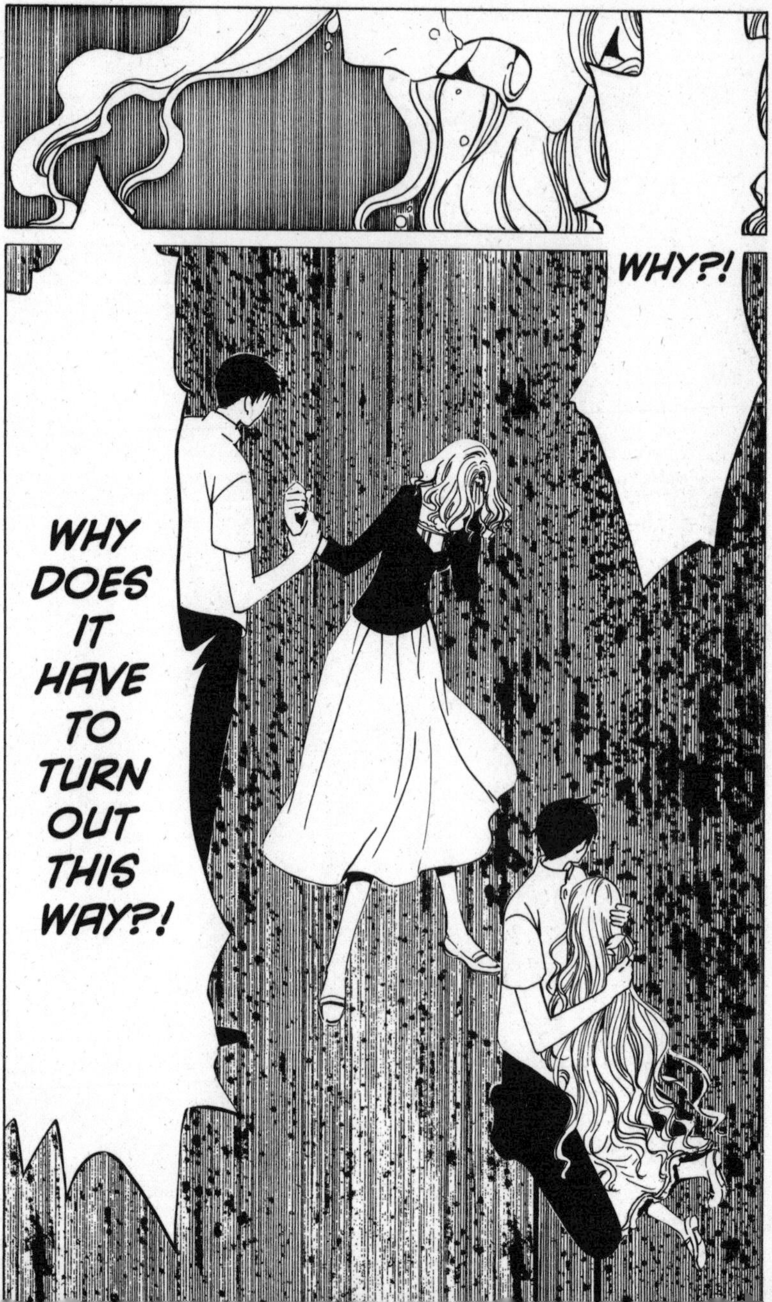
WHY?!
WHY DOES IT HAVE TO TURN OUT THIS WAY?!

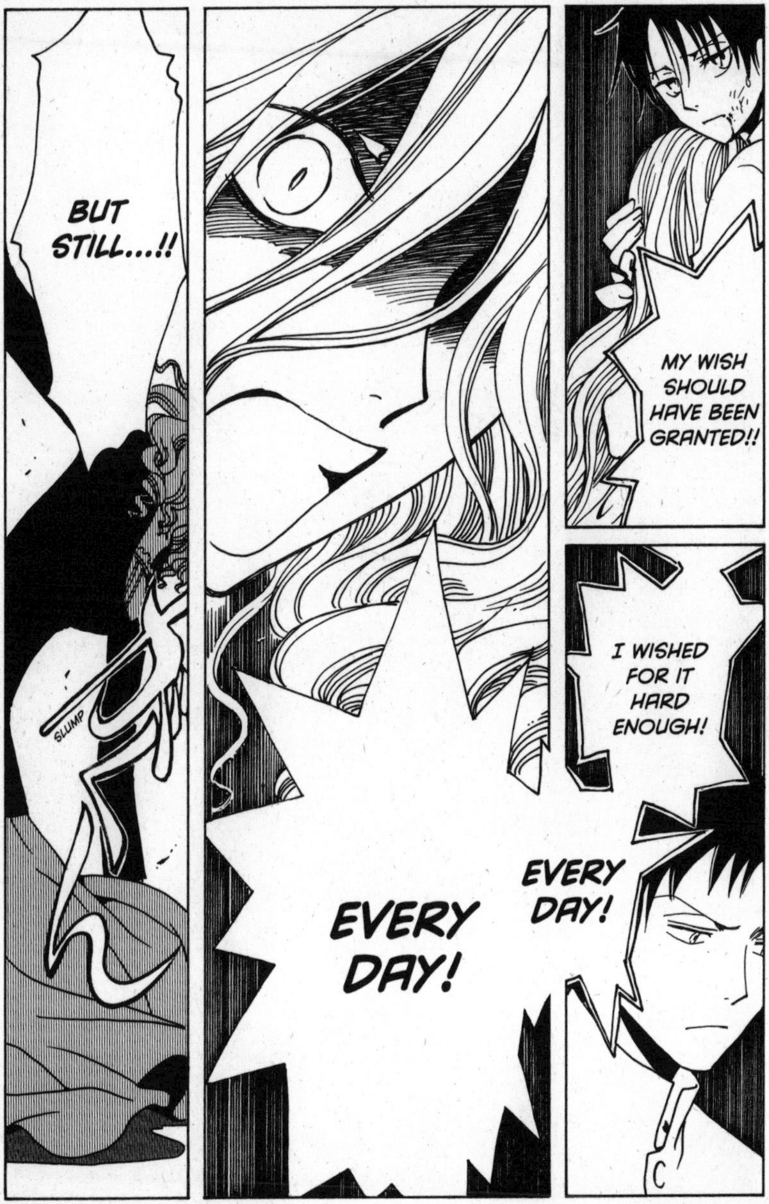
MY WISH SHOULD HAVE BEEN GRANTED!!
I WISHED FOR IT HARD ENOUGH!
EVERY DAY!
EVERY DAY!
BUT STILL...!!
SLUMP

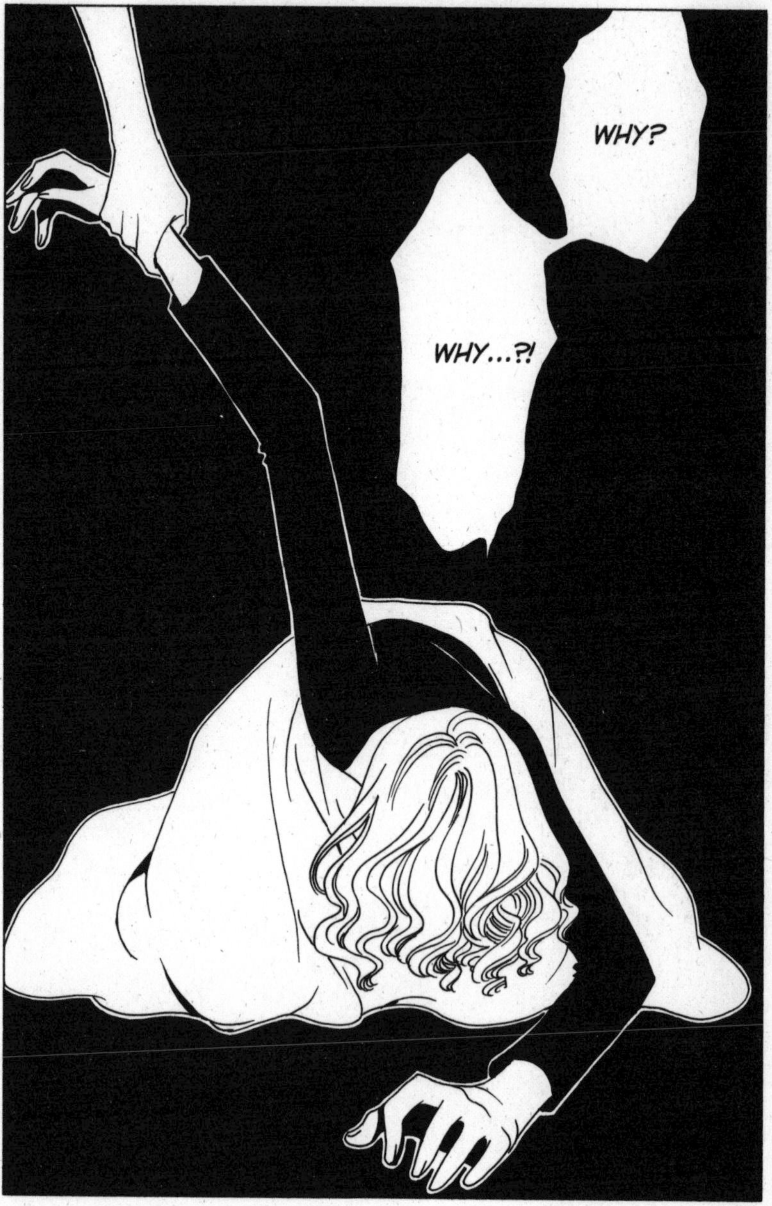
WHY?
WHY...?!

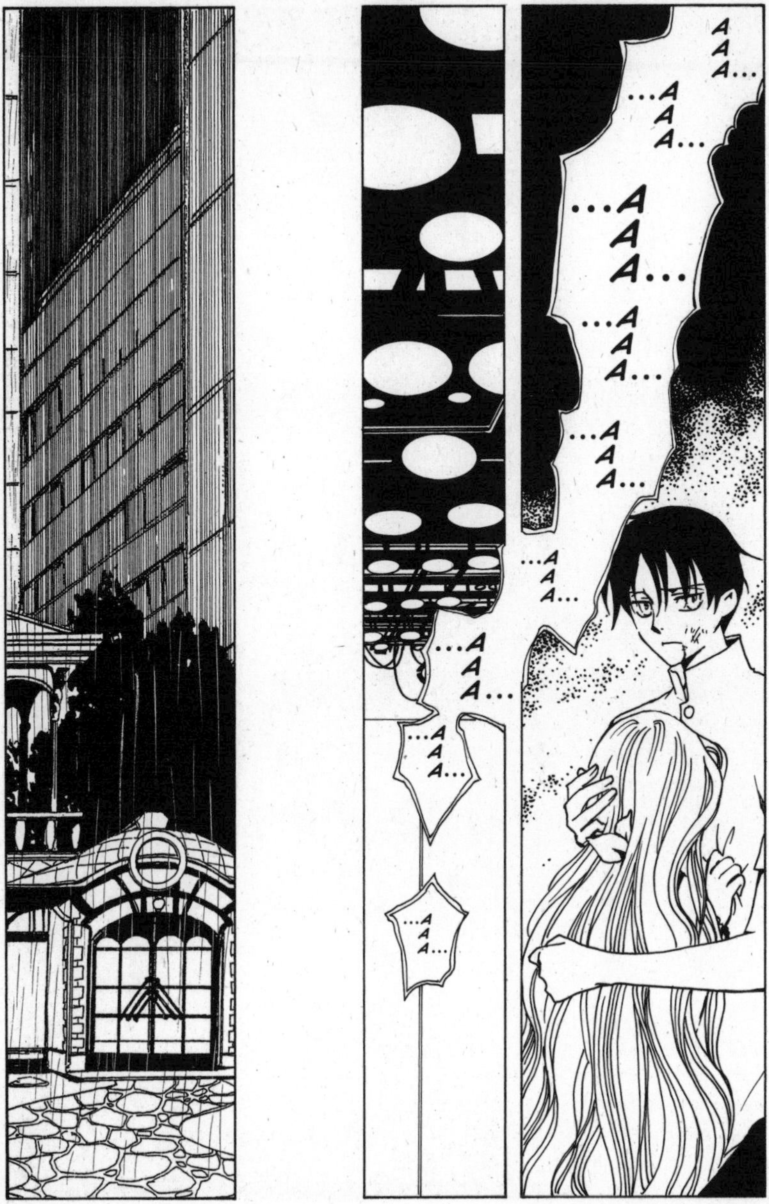
AAA...
...AAA...
...AAA...
...AAA...
...AAA...
...AAA...
...AAA...
...AAA...
...AAA...

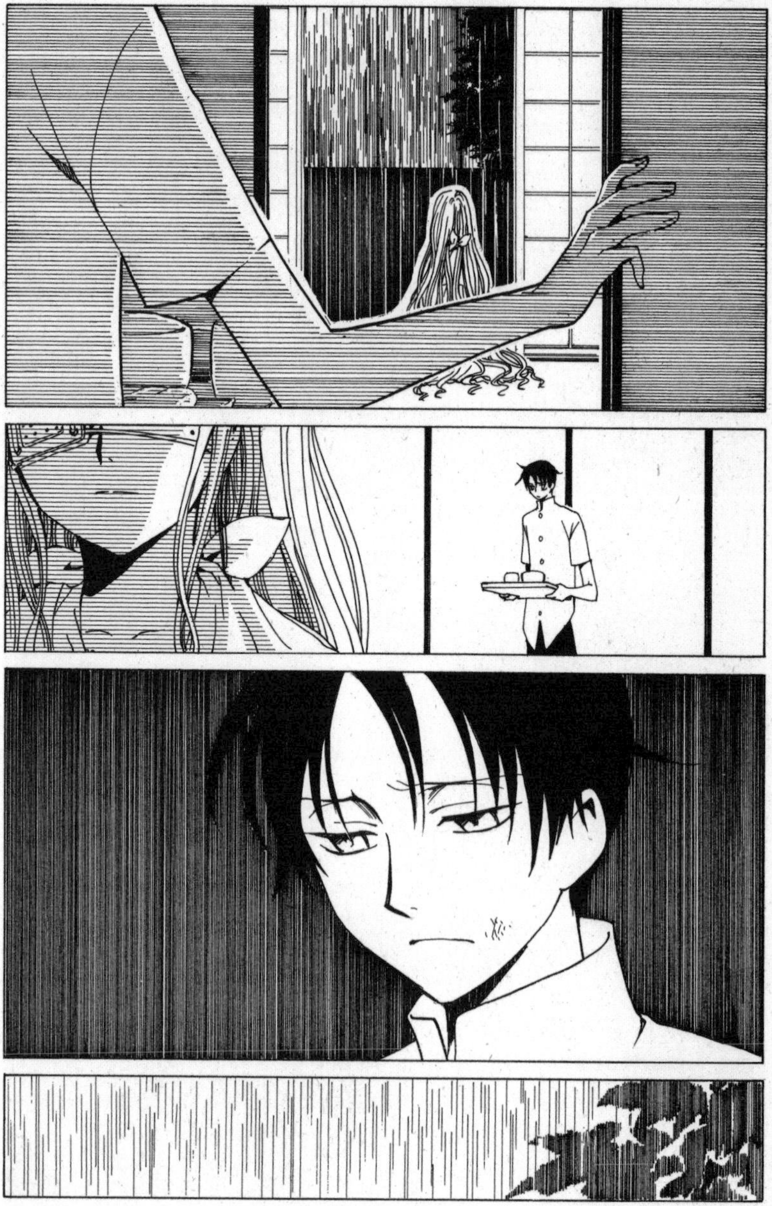

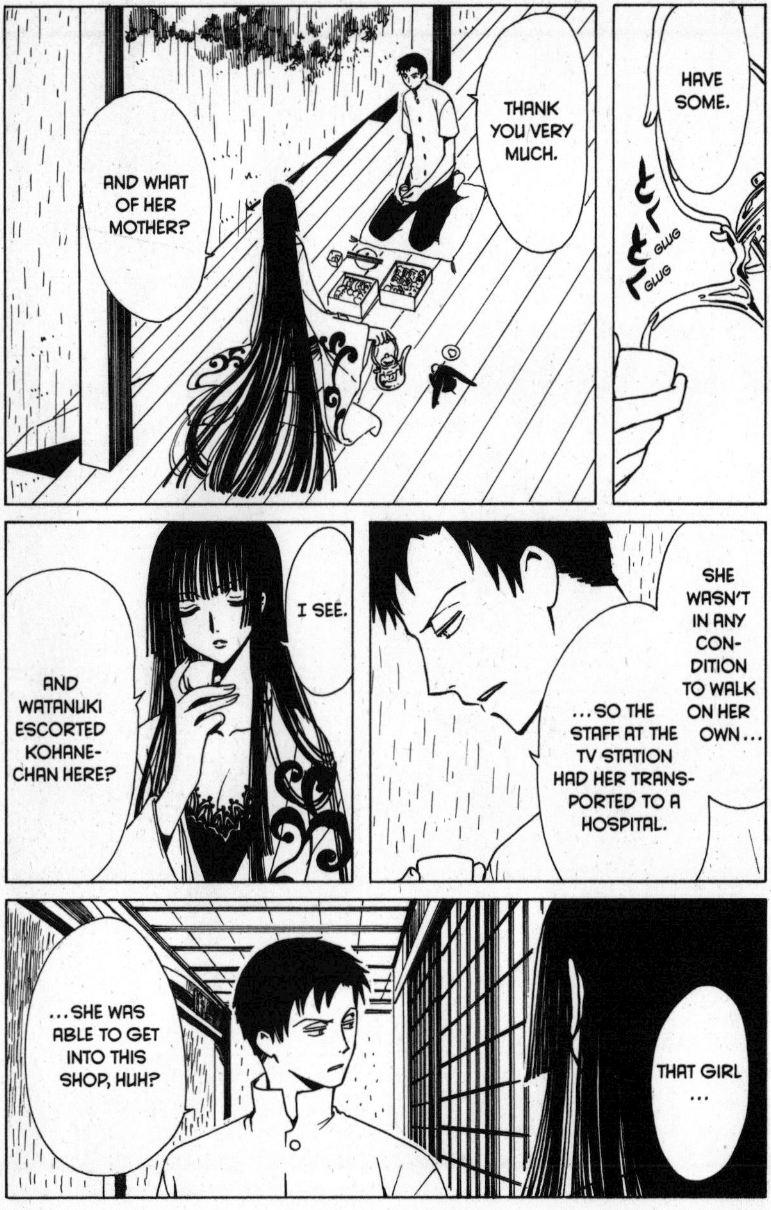
HAVE SOME.
GLUG
GLUG
THANK YOU VERY MUCH.
AND WHAT OF HER MOTHER?
SHE WASN'T IN ANY CON-DITION TO WALK ON HER OWN...
...SO THE STAFF AT THE TV STATION HAD HER TRANS-PORTED TO A HOSPITAL.
I SEE.
AND WATANUKI ESCORTED KOHANE-CHAN HERE?
THAT GIRL ...
...SHE WAS ABLE TO GET INTO THIS SHOP, HUH?

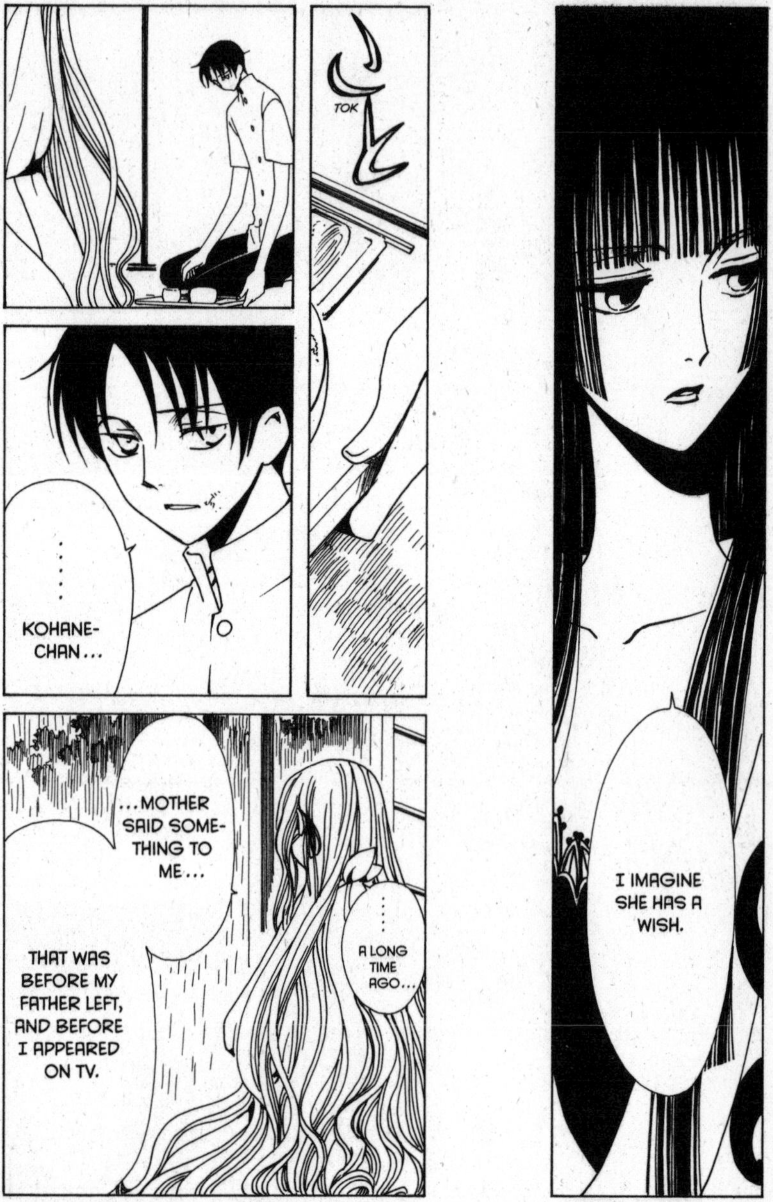
I IMAGINE SHE HAS A WISH.
TOK
.....
KOHANE-CHAN...
.....
A LONG TIME AGO...
...MOTHER SAID SOMETHING TO ME...
THAT WAS BEFORE MY FATHER LEFT, AND BEFORE I APPEARED ON TV.

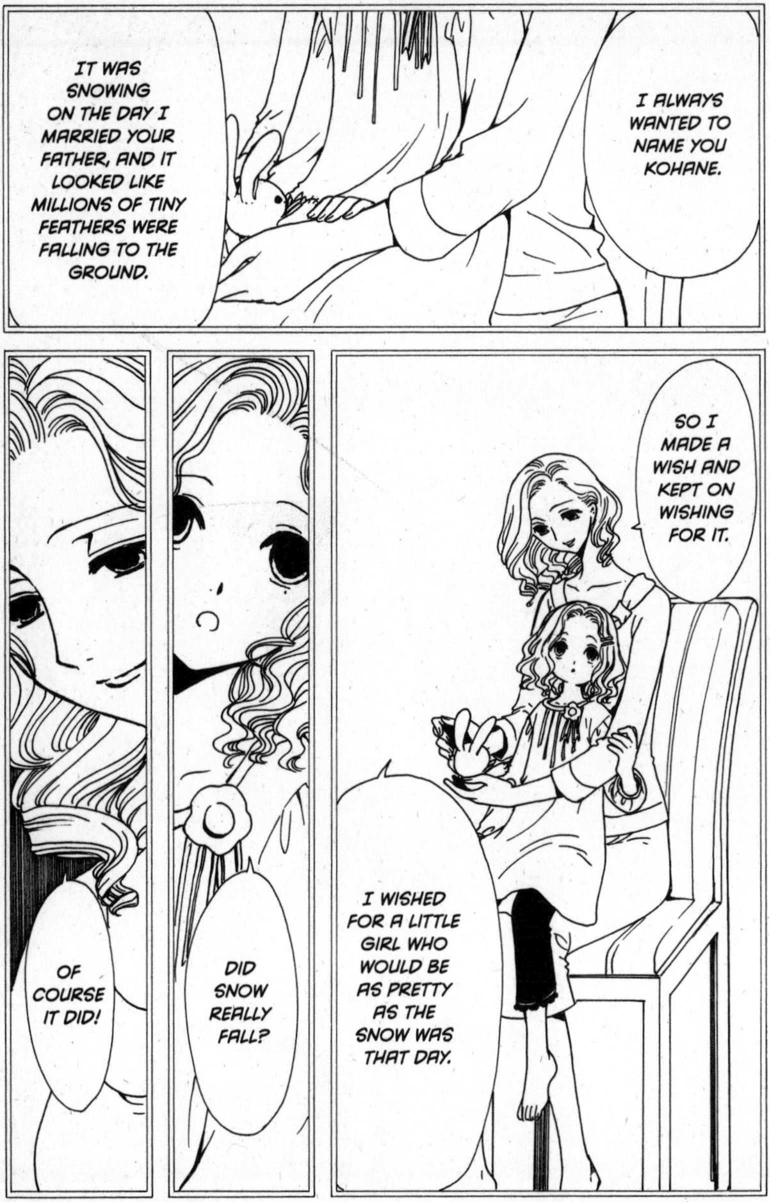
I ALWAYS WANTED TO NAME YOU KOHANE.
IT WAS SNOWING ON THE DAY I MARRIED YOUR FATHER, AND IT LOOKED LIKE MILLIONS OF TINY FEATHERS WERE FALLING TO THE GROUND.
SO I MADE A WISH AND KEPT ON WISHING FOR IT.
I WISHED FOR A LITTLE GIRL WHO WOULD BE AS PRETTY AS THE SNOW WAS THAT DAY.
DID SNOW REALLY FALL?
OF COURSE IT DID!

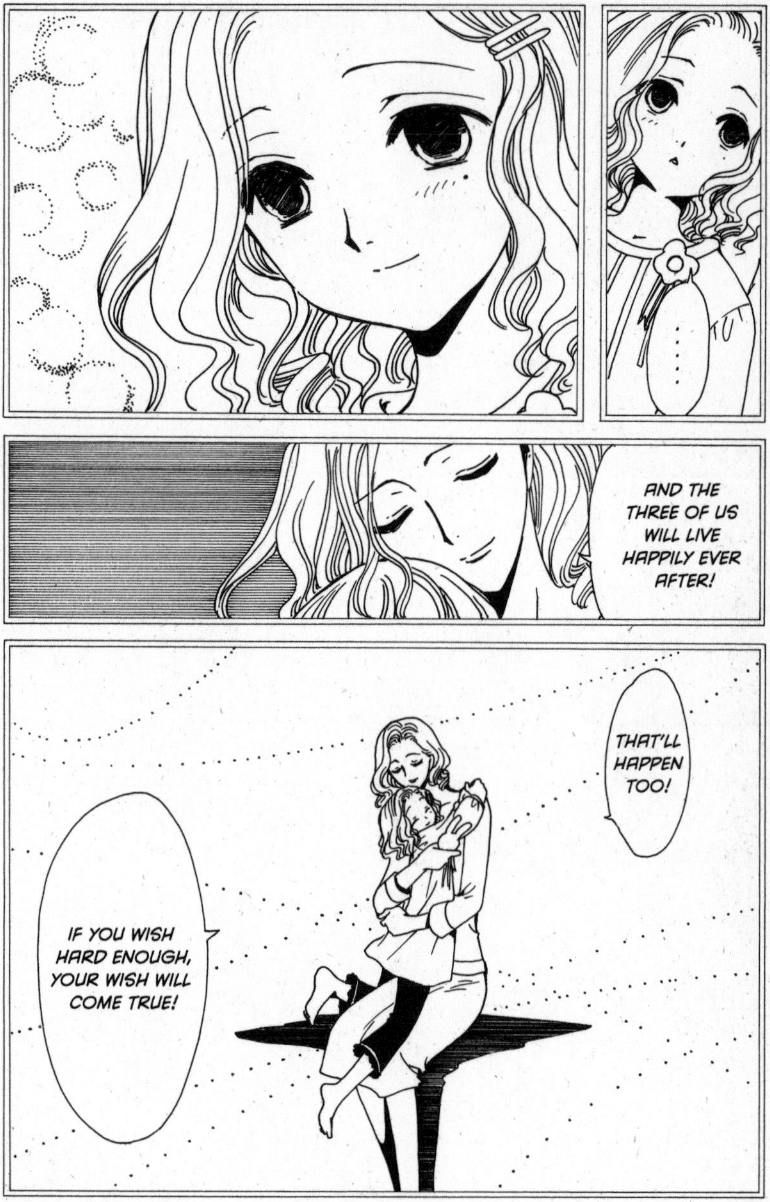
AND THE THREE OF US WILL LIVE HAPPILY EVER AFTER!
THAT'LL HAPPEN TOO!
IF YOU WISH HARD ENOUGH, YOUR WISH WILL COME TRUE!

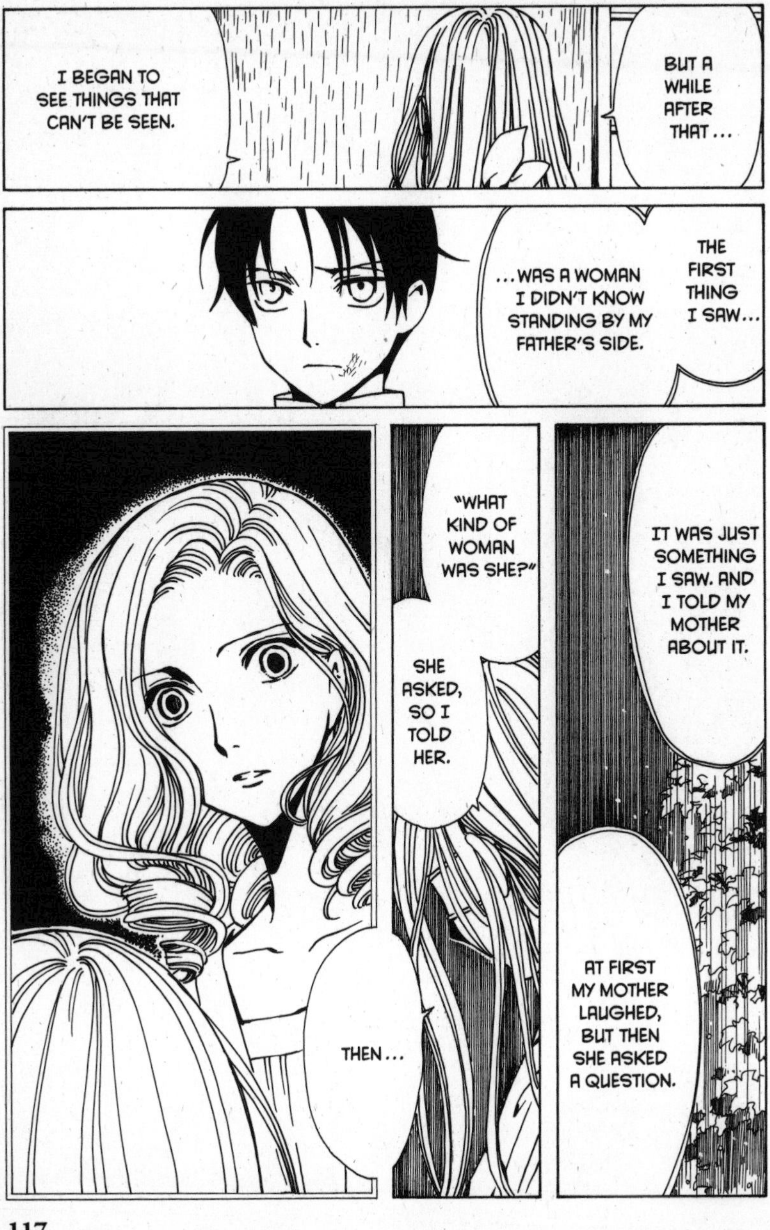
BUT A WHILE AFTER THAT...
I BEGAN TO SEE THINGS THAT CAN'T BE SEEN.
THE FIRST THING I SAW...
...WAS A WOMAN I DIDN'T KNOW STANDING BY MY FATHER'S SIDE.
IT WAS JUST SOMETHING I SAW. AND I TOLD MY MOTHER ABOUT IT.
AT FIRST MY MOTHER LAUGHED, BUT THEN SHE ASKED A QUESTION.
"WHAT KIND OF WOMAN WAS SHE?"
SHE ASKED, SO I TOLD HER.
THEN...

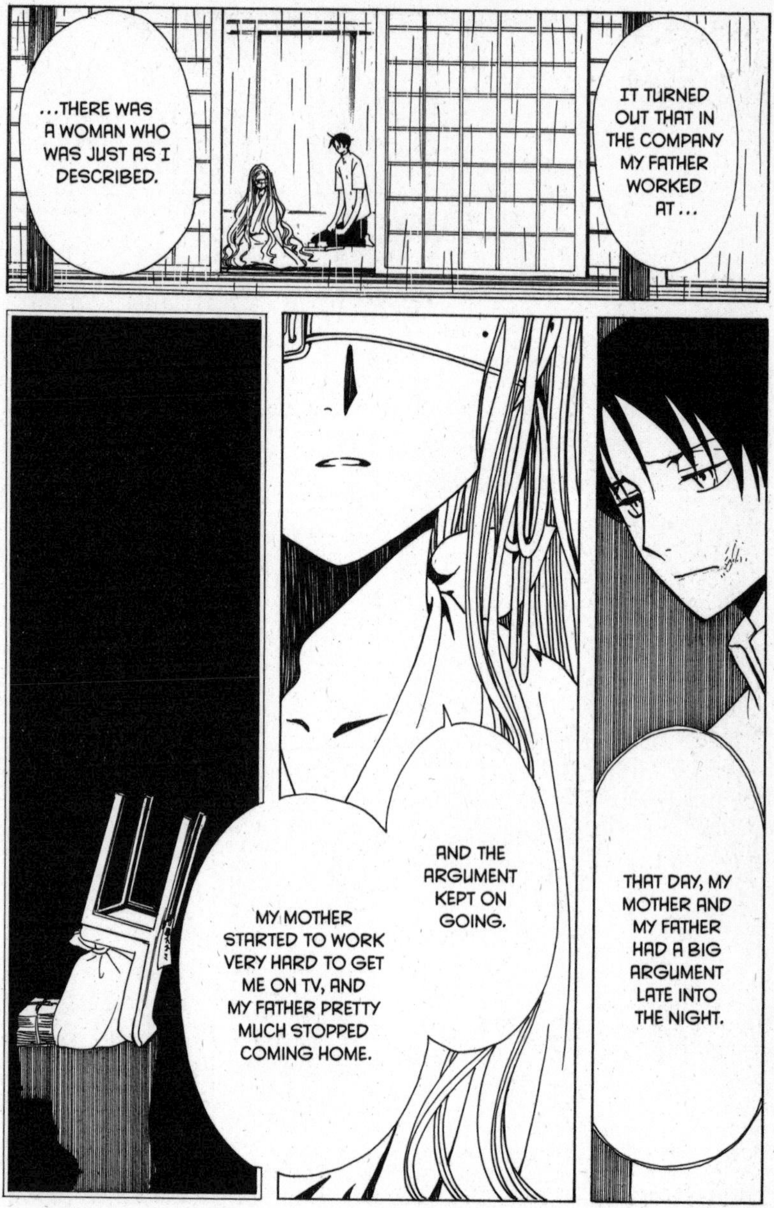
IT TURNED OUT THAT IN THE COMPANY MY FATHER WORKED AT...
...THERE WAS A WOMAN WHO WAS JUST AS I DESCRIBED.
THAT DAY, MY MOTHER AND MY FATHER HAD A BIG ARGUMENT LATE INTO THE NIGHT.
AND THE ARGUMENT KEPT ON GOING.
MY MOTHER STARTED TO WORK VERY HARD TO GET ME ON TV, AND MY FATHER PRETTY MUCH STOPPED COMING HOME.

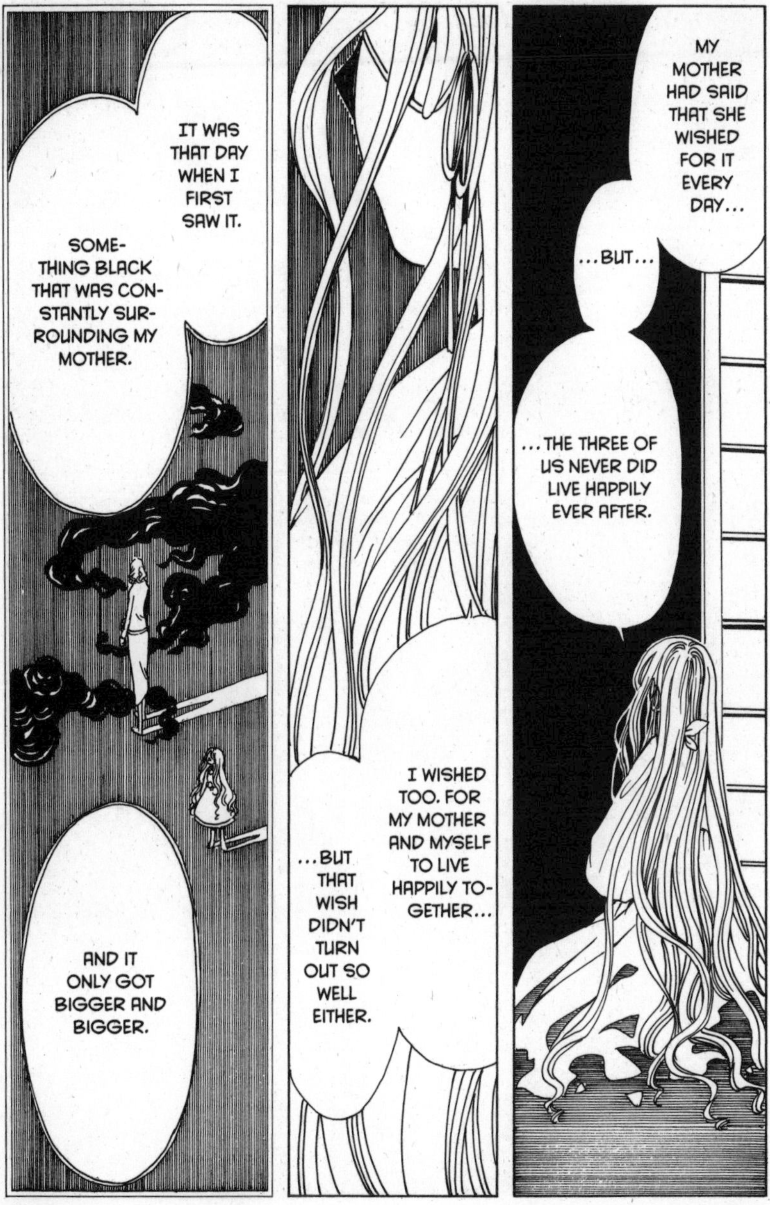
MY MOTHER HAD SAID THAT SHE WISHED FOR IT EVERY DAY...
...BUT...
...THE THREE OF US NEVER DID LIVE HAPPILY EVER AFTER.
I WISHED TOO. FOR MY MOTHER AND MYSELF TO LIVE HAPPILY TOGETHER...
...BUT THAT WISH DIDN'T TURN OUT SO WELL EITHER.
IT WAS THAT DAY WHEN I FIRST SAW IT.
SOMETHING BLACK THAT WAS CONSTANTLY SURROUNDING MY MOTHER.
AND IT ONLY GOT BIGGER AND BIGGER.

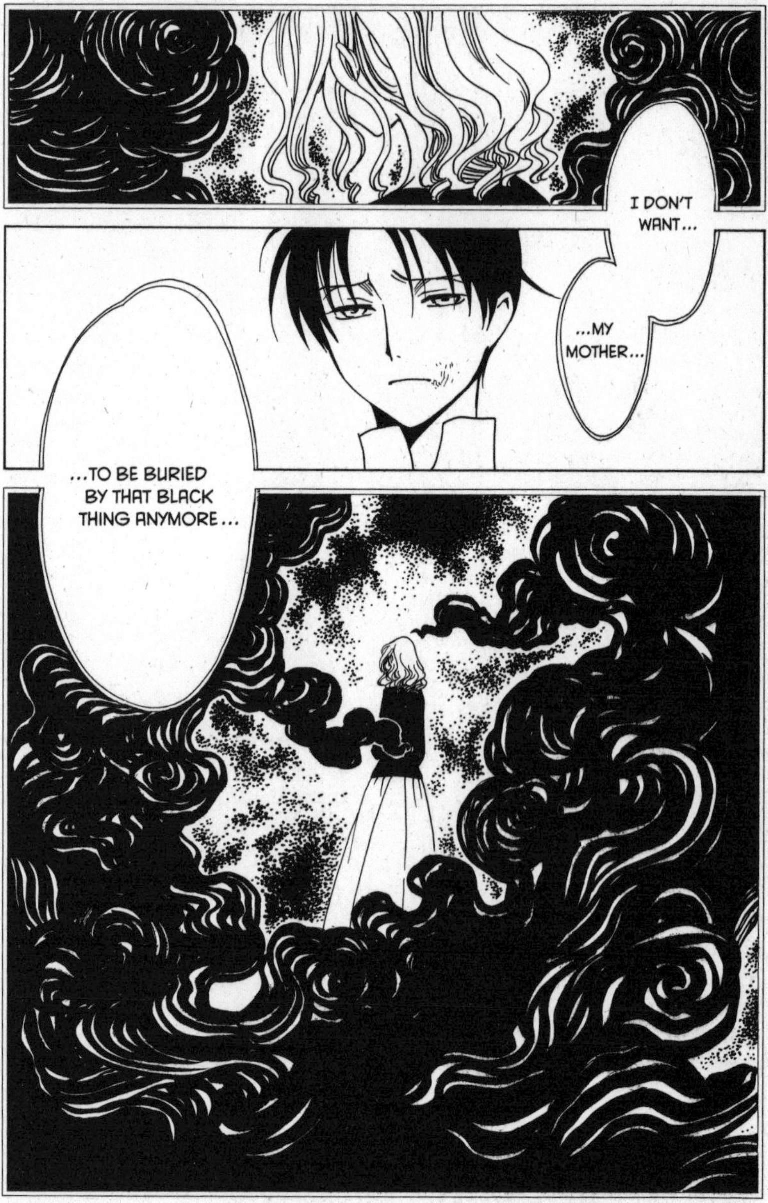
I DON'T WANT...
...MY MOTHER...
...TO BE BURIED BY THAT BLACK THING ANYMORE...

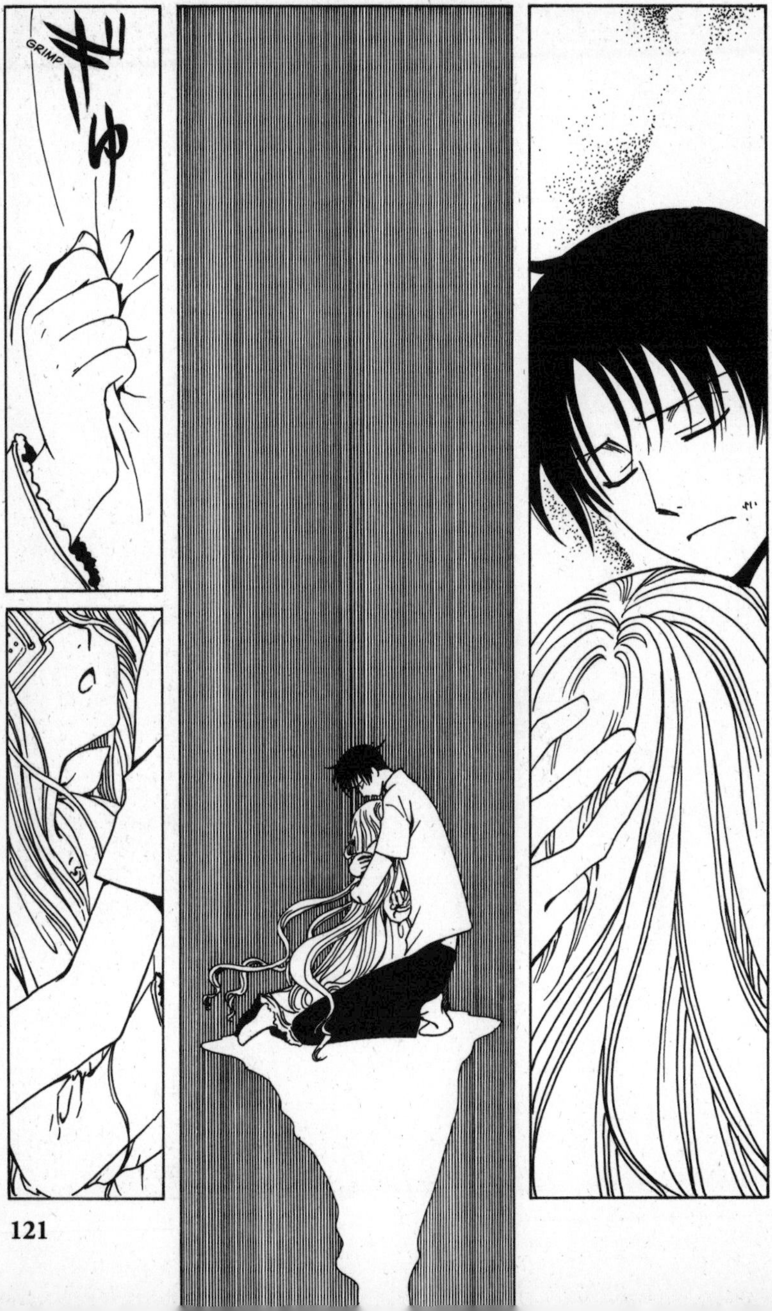
ギュ
GRIMP

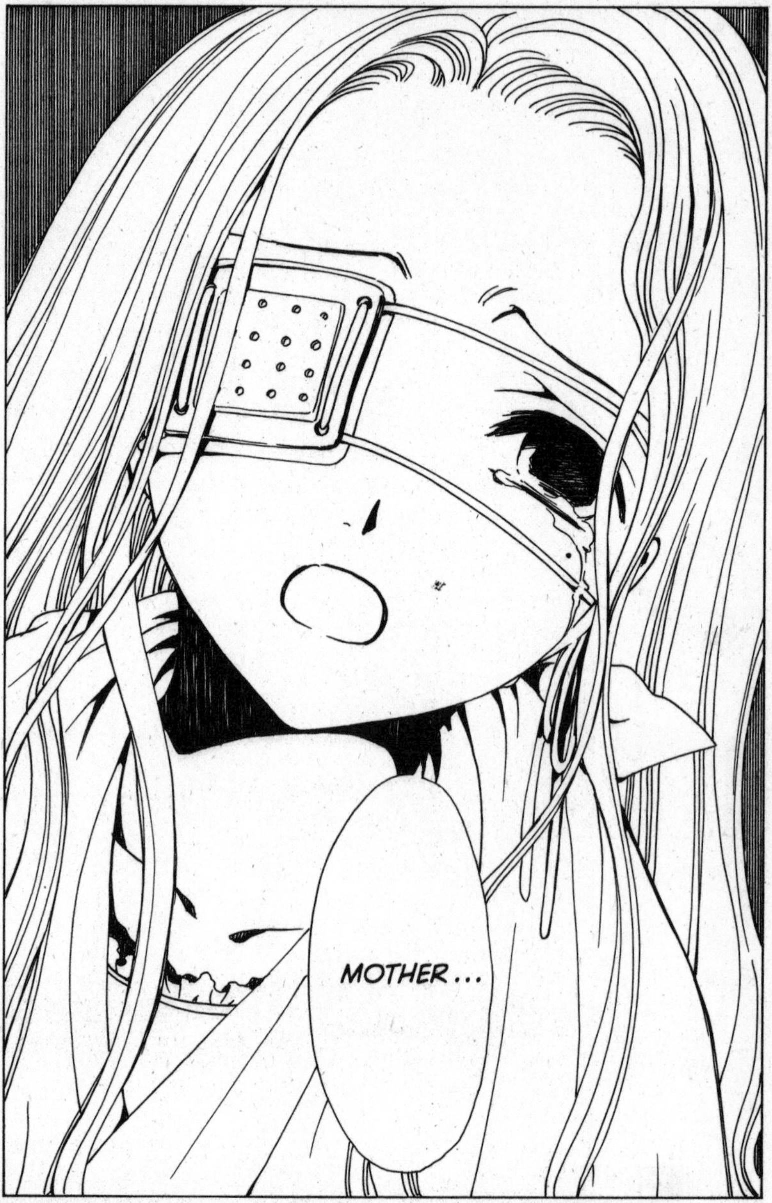
MOTHER...

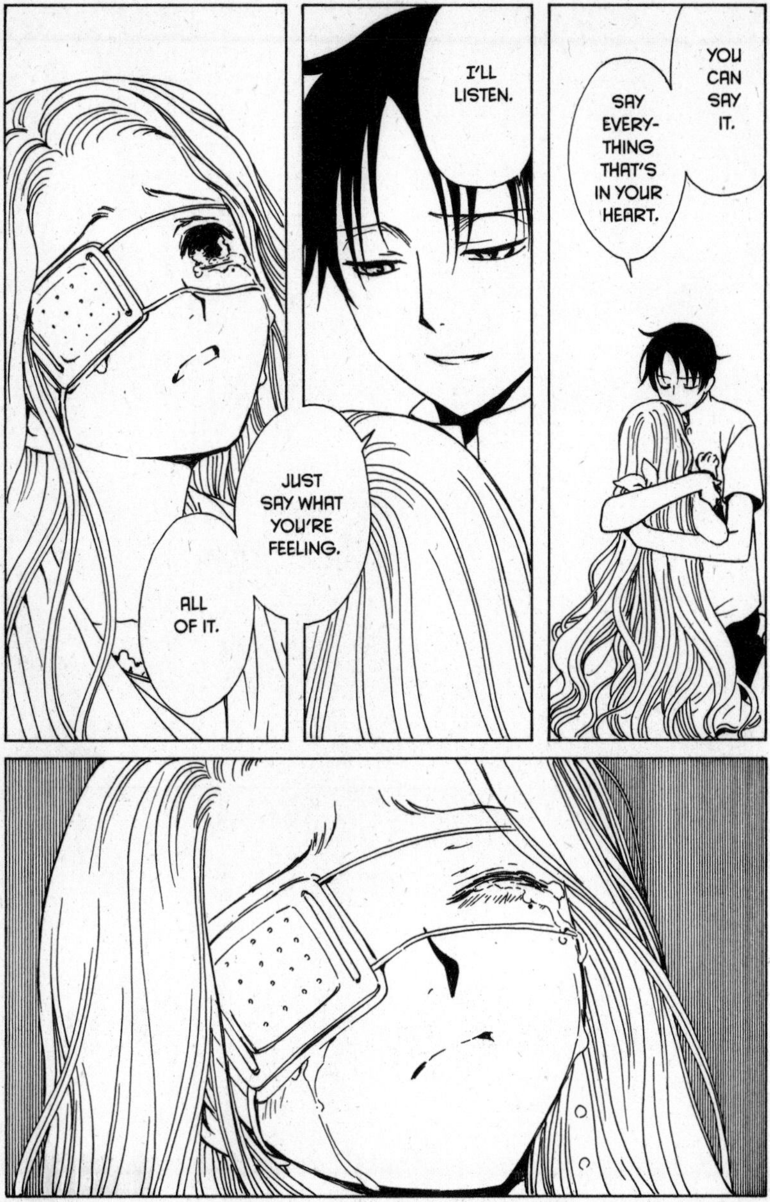
YOU CAN SAY IT.
SAY EVERY-THING THAT'S IN YOUR HEART.
I'LL LISTEN.
JUST SAY WHAT YOU'RE FEELING.
ALL OF IT.

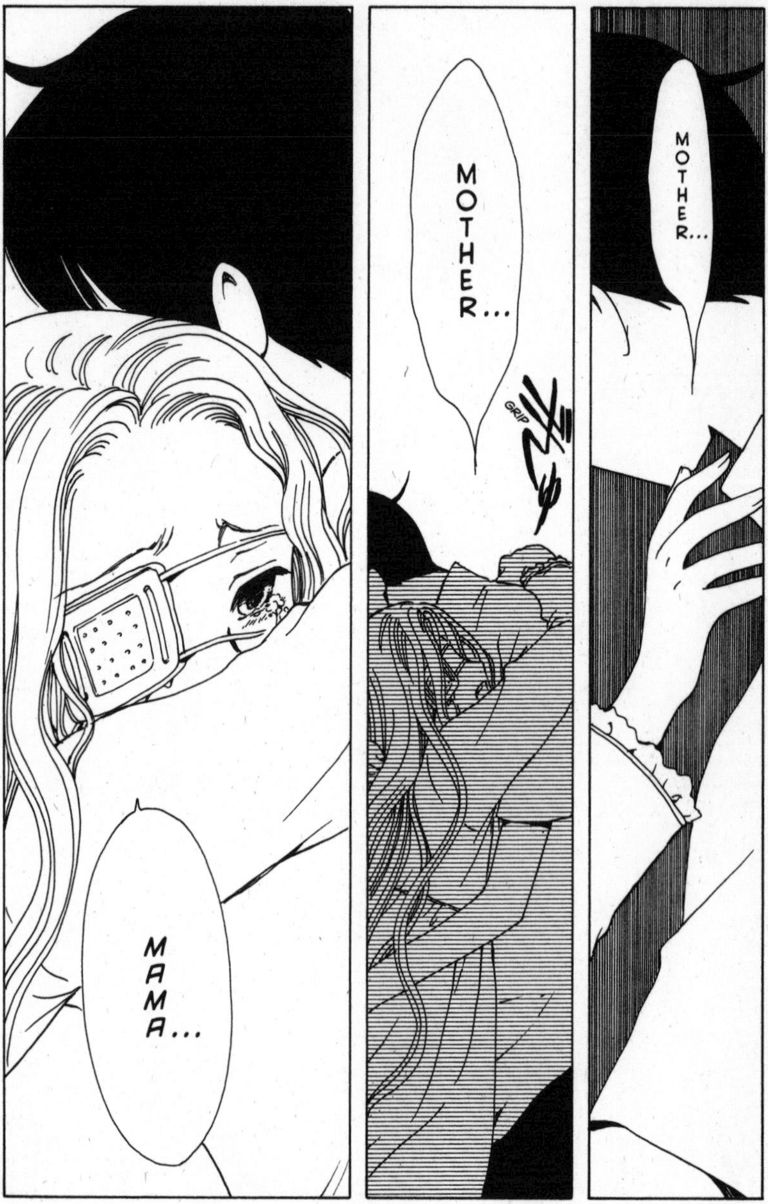
MOTHER...
MOTHER...
GRIP
MAMA...

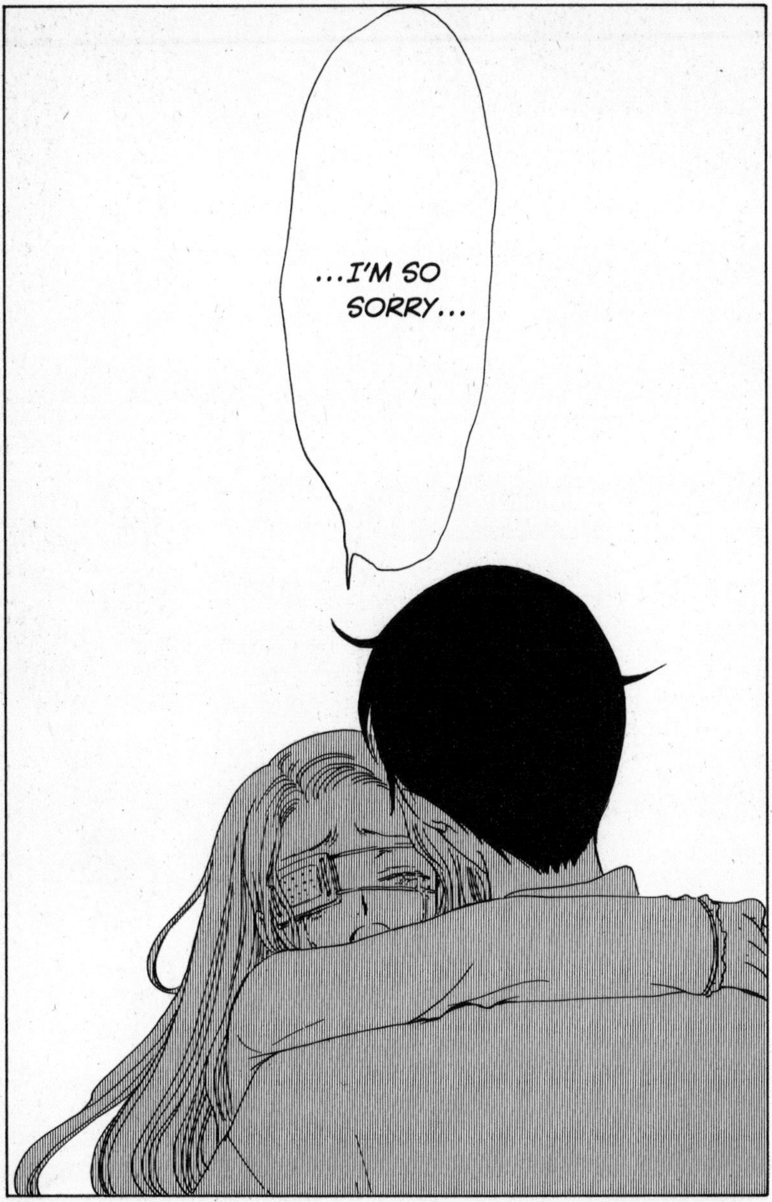
...I'M SO SORRY...

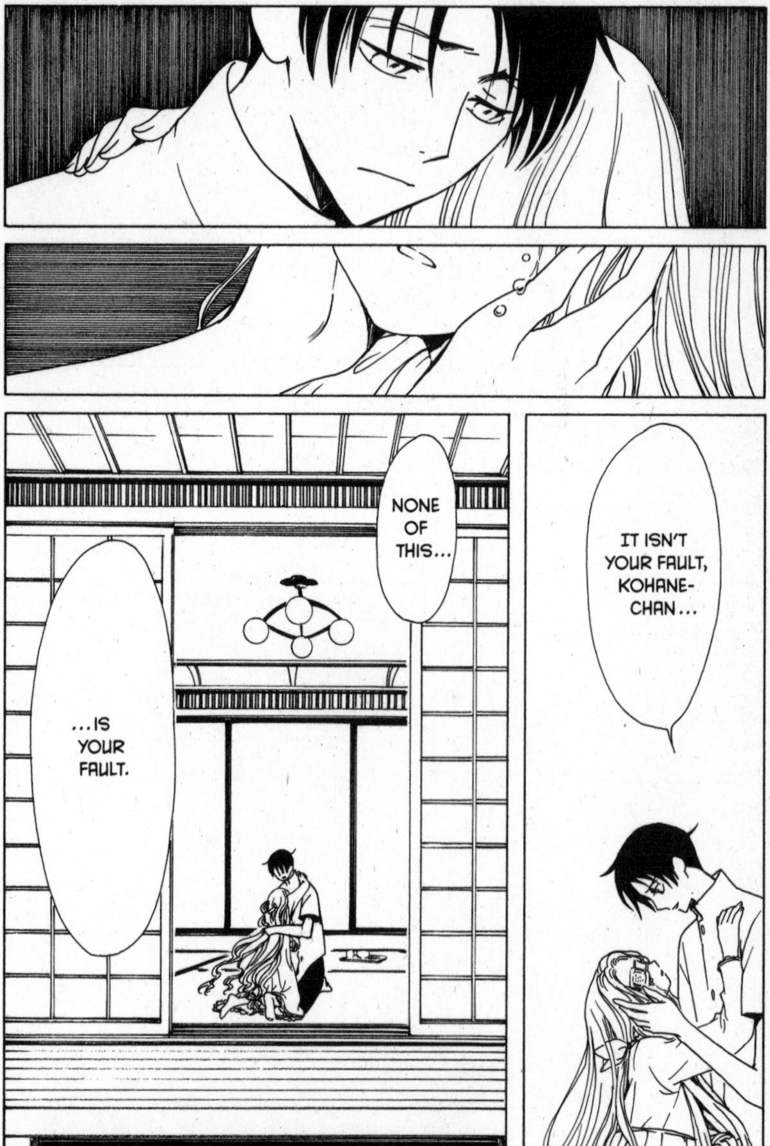
IT ISN'T YOUR FAULT, KOHANE-CHAN...
NONE OF THIS...
...IS YOUR FAULT.

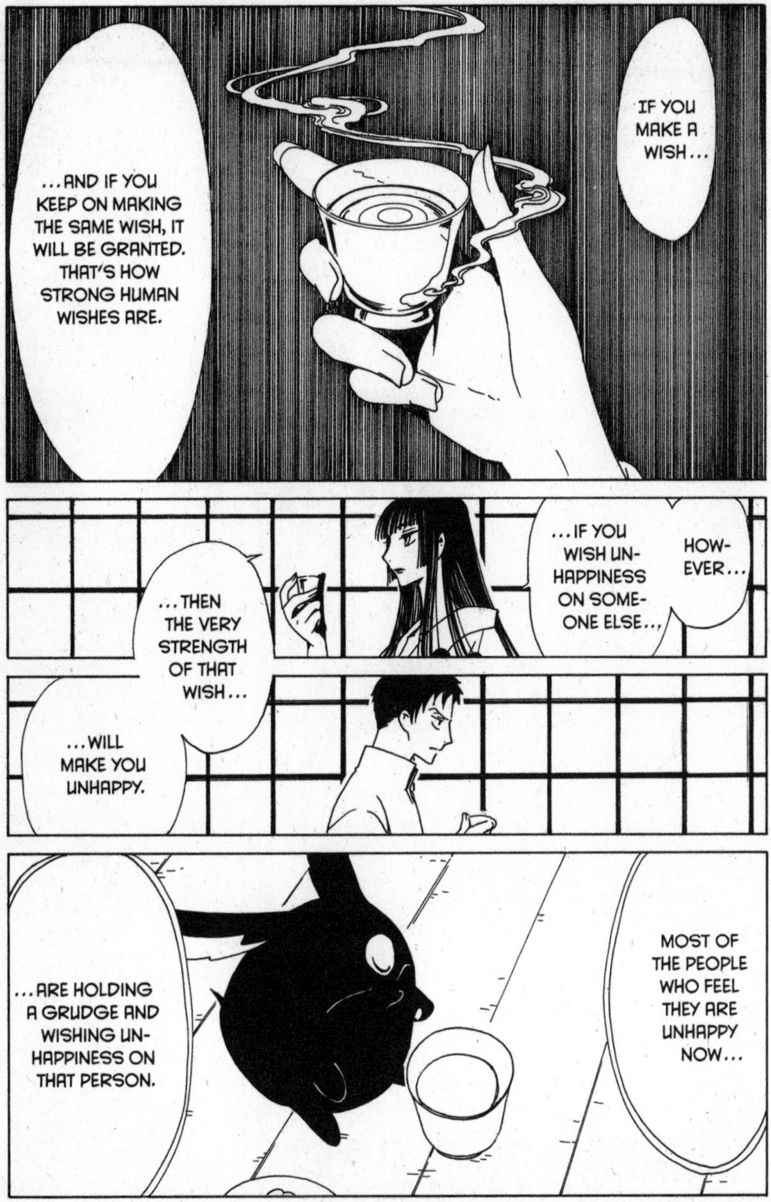
IF YOU MAKE A WISH...
...AND IF YOU KEEP ON MAKING THE SAME WISH, IT WILL BE GRANTED. THAT'S HOW STRONG HUMAN WISHES ARE.
HOW-EVER...
...IF YOU WISH UN-HAPPINESS ON SOME-ONE ELSE...,
...THEN THE VERY STRENGTH OF THAT WISH...
...WILL MAKE YOU UNHAPPY.
MOST OF THE PEOPLE WHO FEEL THEY ARE UNHAPPY NOW...
...ARE HOLDING A GRUDGE AND WISHING UN-HAPPINESS ON THAT PERSON.

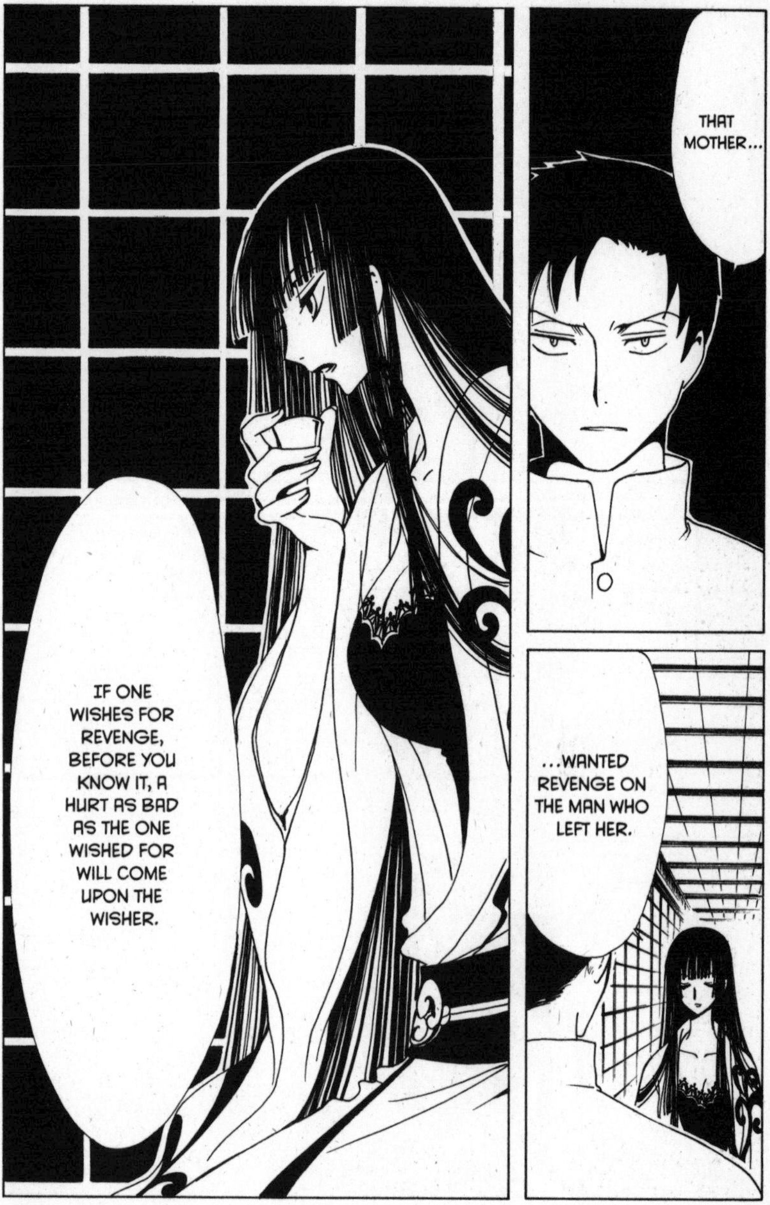
THAT MOTHER...
...WANTED REVENGE ON THE MAN WHO LEFT HER.
IF ONE WISHES FOR REVENGE, BEFORE YOU KNOW IT, A HURT AS BAD AS THE ONE WISHED FOR WILL COME UPON THE WISHER.

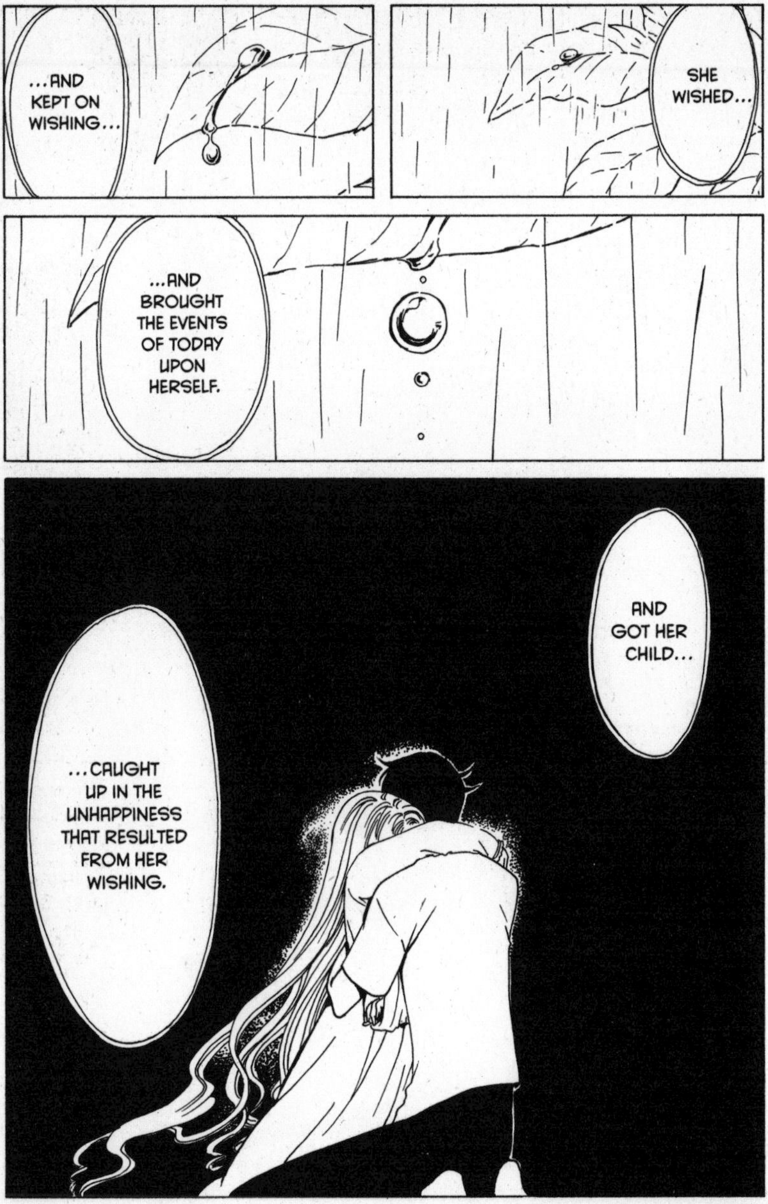
SHE WISHED...
...AND KEPT ON WISHING...
...AND BROUGHT THE EVENTS OF TODAY UPON HERSELF.
AND GOT HER CHILD...
...CAUGHT UP IN THE UNHAPPINESS THAT RESULTED FROM HER WISHING.

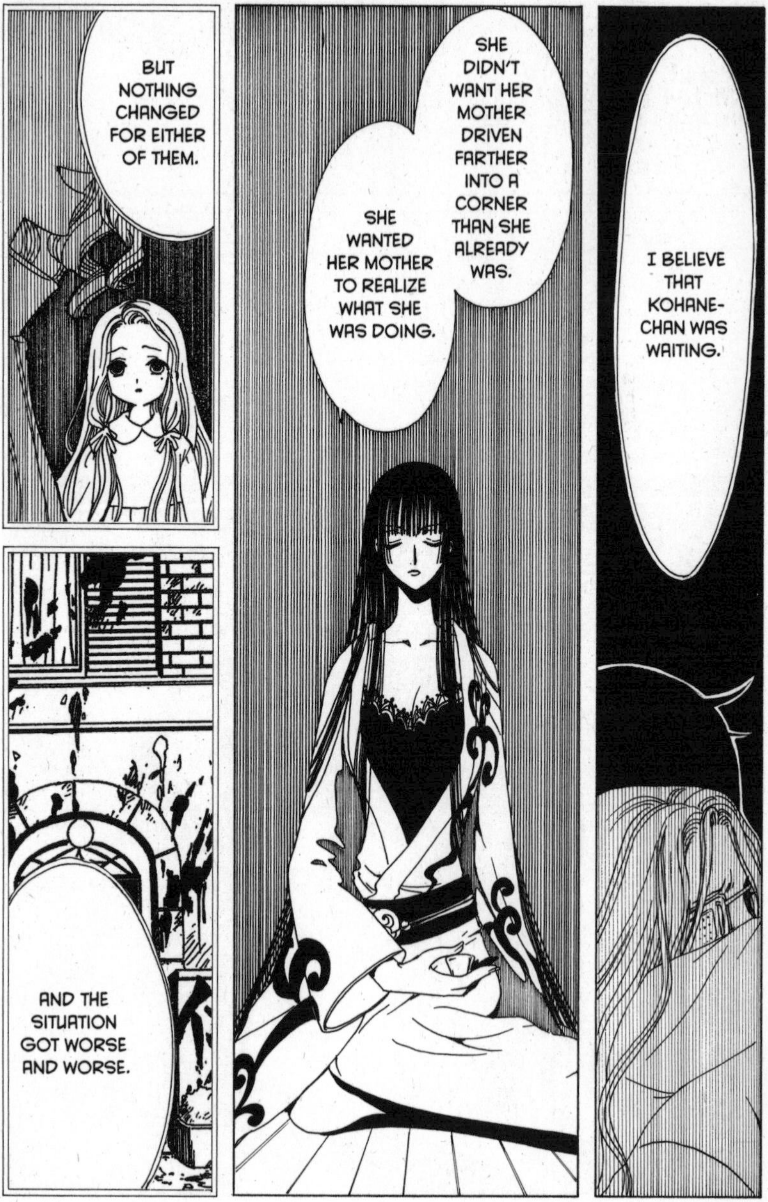
I BELIEVE THAT KOHANE-CHAN WAS WAITING.
SHE DIDN'T WANT HER MOTHER DRIVEN FARTHER INTO A CORNER THAN SHE ALREADY WAS.
SHE WANTED HER MOTHER TO REALIZE WHAT SHE WAS DOING.
BUT NOTHING CHANGED FOR EITHER OF THEM.
AND THE SITUATION GOT WORSE AND WORSE.

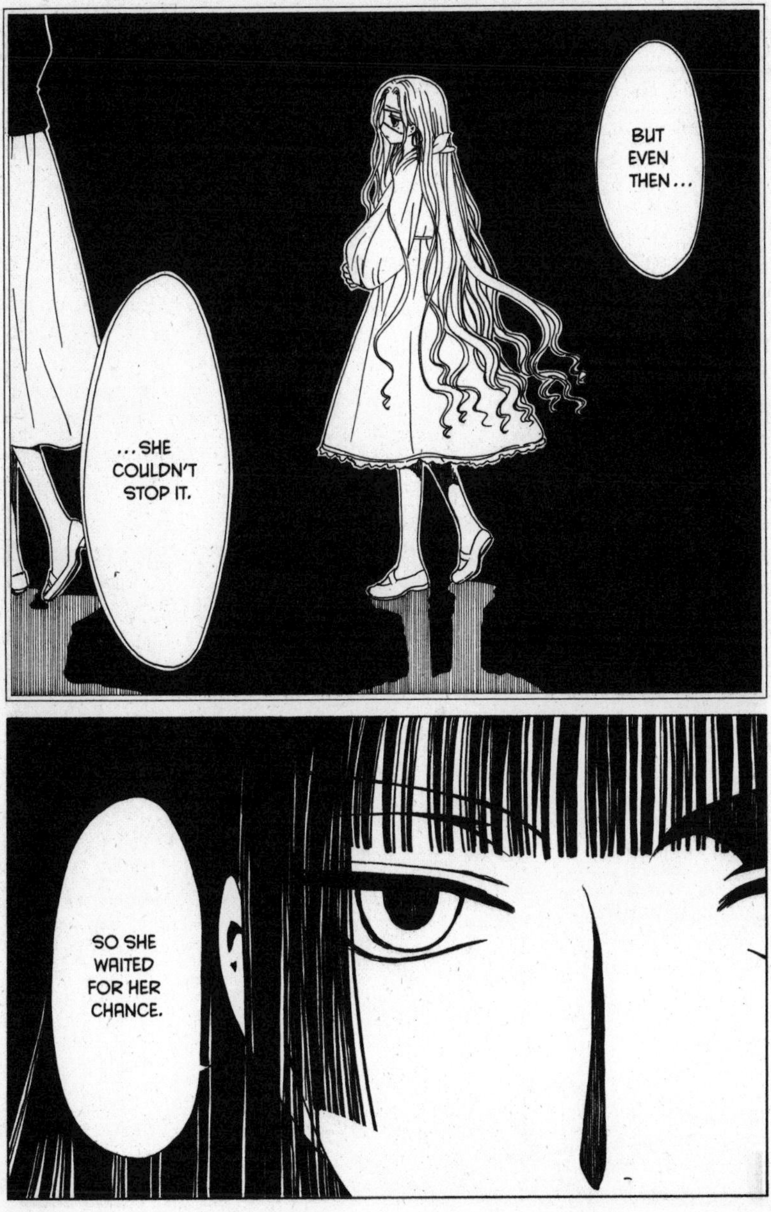
BUT EVEN THEN...
...SHE COULDN'T STOP IT.
SO SHE WAITED FOR HER CHANCE.

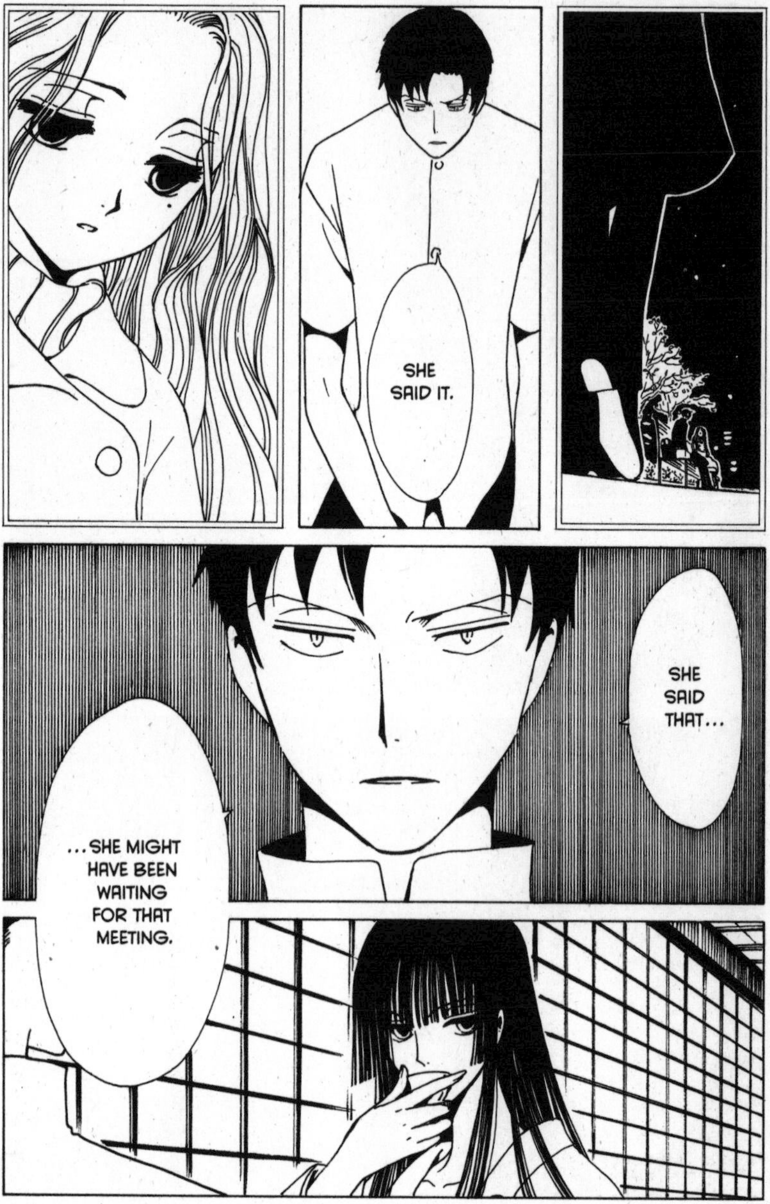
SHE SAID IT.
SHE SAID THAT...
...SHE MIGHT HAVE BEEN WAITING FOR THAT MEETING.

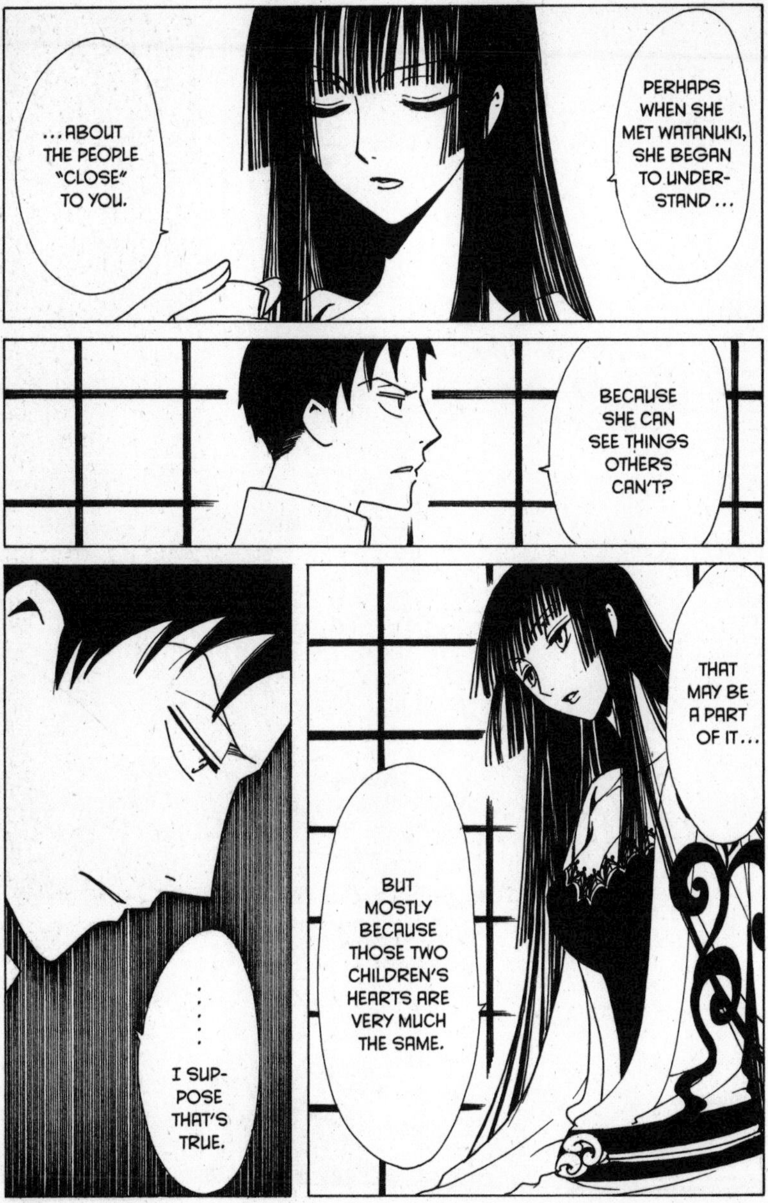
PERHAPS WHEN SHE MET WATANUKI, SHE BEGAN TO UNDERSTAND ...
... ABOUT THE PEOPLE "CLOSE" TO YOU.
BECAUSE SHE CAN SEE THINGS OTHERS CAN'T?
THAT MAY BE A PART OF IT...
BUT MOSTLY BECAUSE THOSE TWO CHILDREN'S HEARTS ARE VERY MUCH THE SAME.
.....
I SUPPOSE THAT'S TRUE.

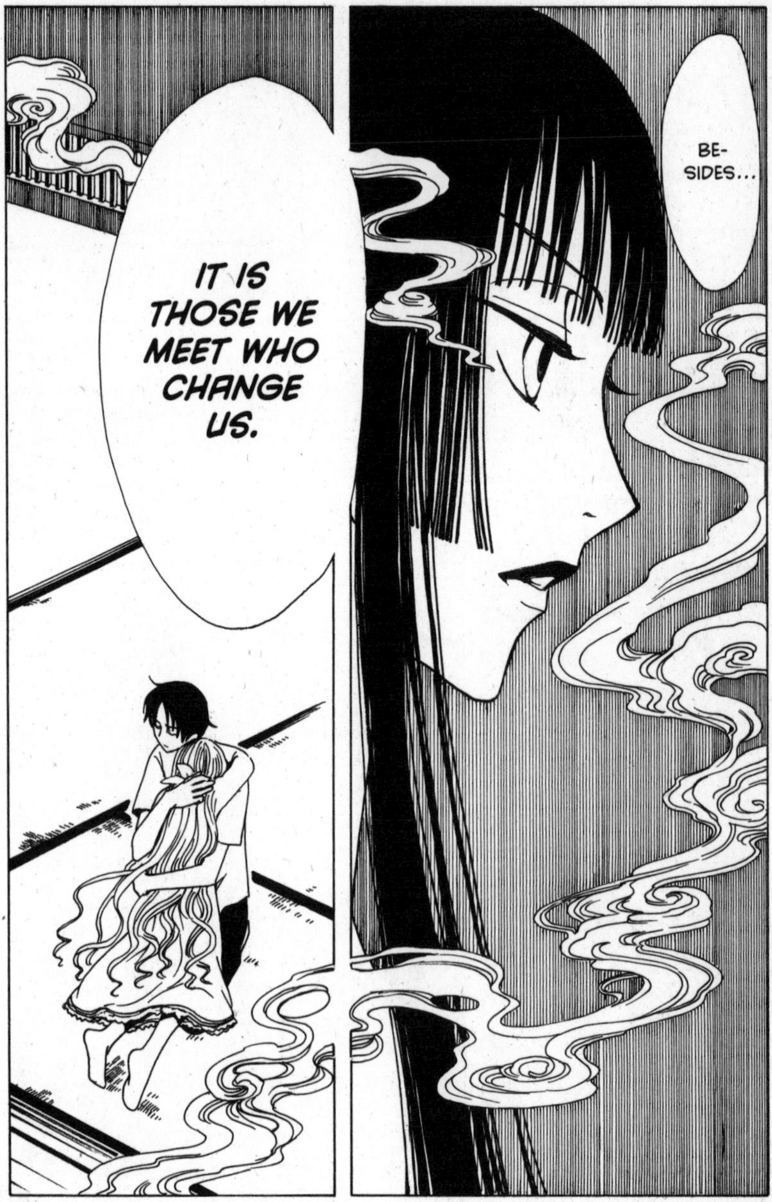
BE-SIDES...
IT IS THOSE WE MEET WHO CHANGE US.

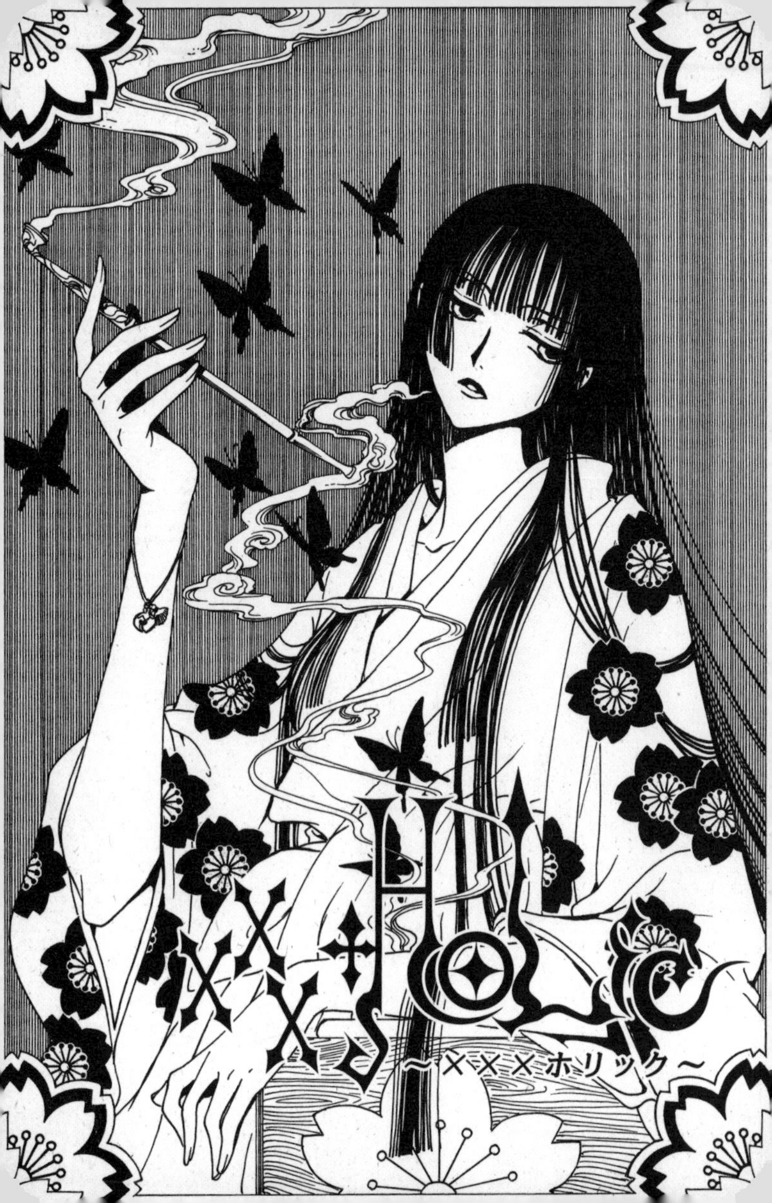
xxxHOLiC
~×××ホリック~

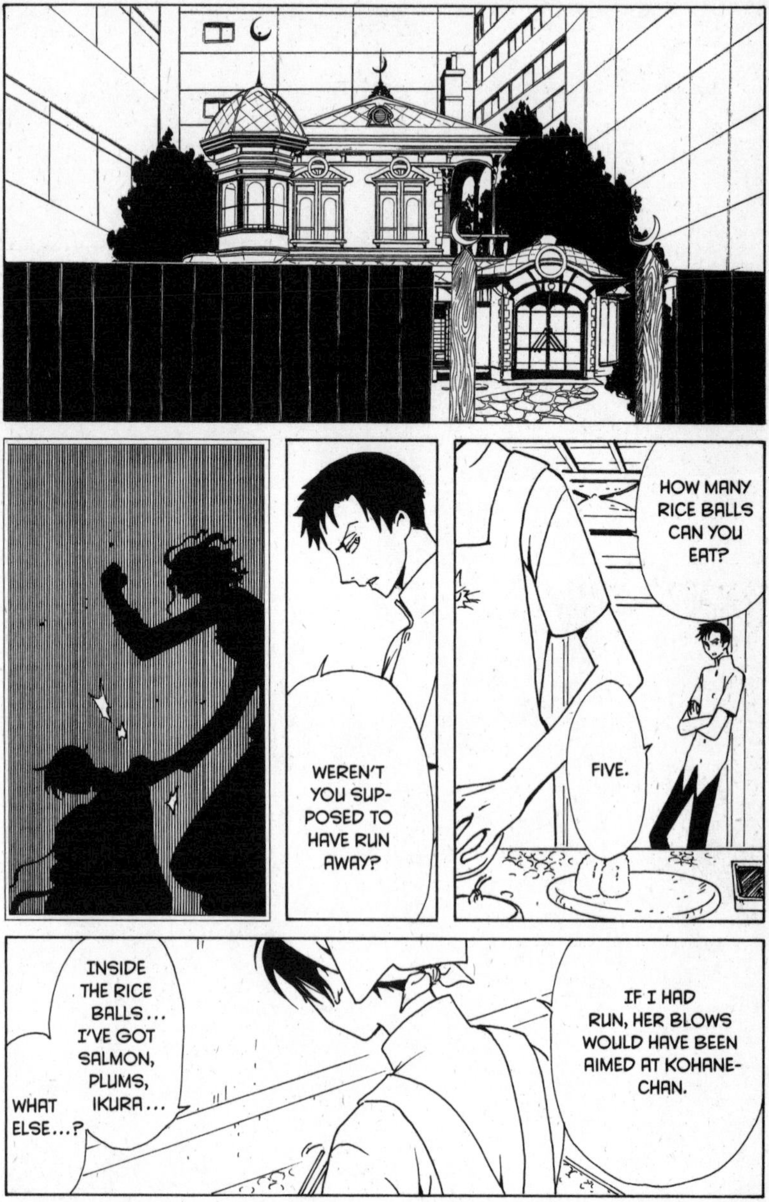
HOW MANY RICE BALLS CAN YOU EAT?
FIVE.
WEREN'T YOU SUPPOSED TO HAVE RUN AWAY?
IF I HAD RUN, HER BLOWS WOULD HAVE BEEN AIMED AT KOHANE-CHAN.
INSIDE THE RICE BALLS... I'VE GOT SALMON, PLUMS, IKURA...
WHAT ELSE...?

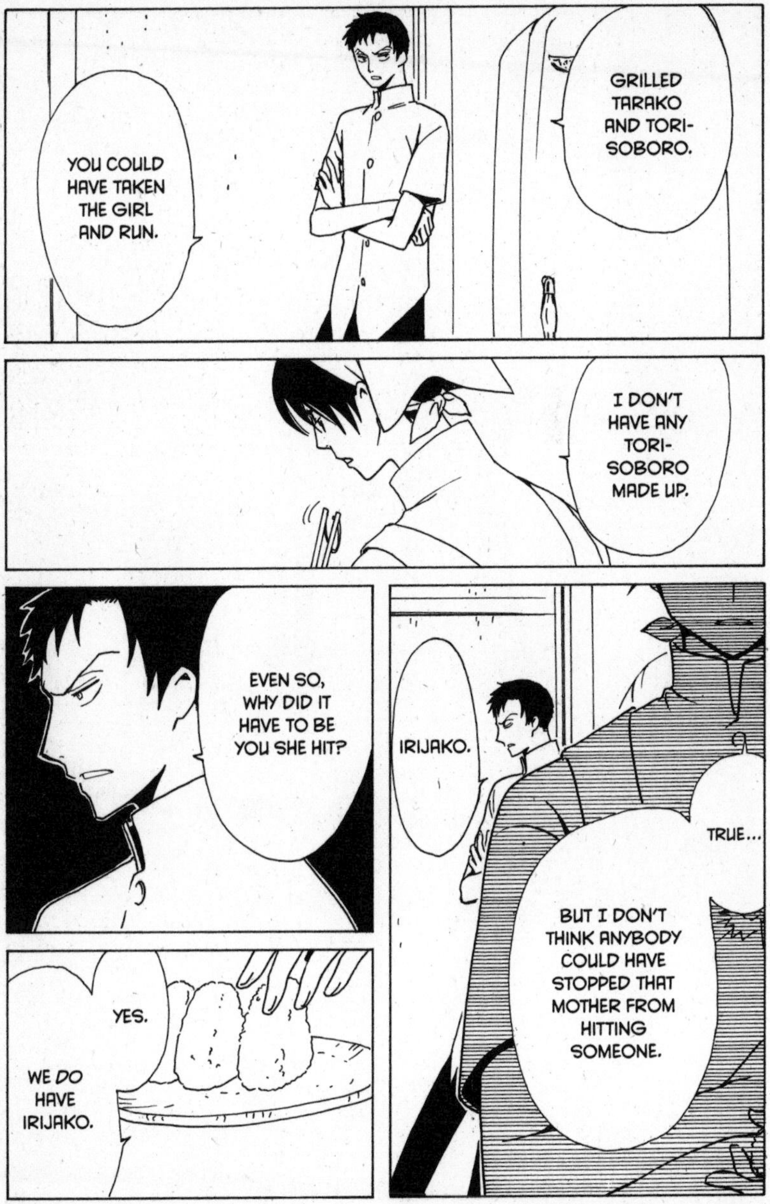
GRILLED TARAKO AND TORI-SOBORO.
YOU COULD HAVE TAKEN THE GIRL AND RUN.
I DON'T HAVE ANY TORI-SOBORO MADE UP.
IRIJAKO.
TRUE...
BUT I DON'T THINK ANYBODY COULD HAVE STOPPED THAT MOTHER FROM HITTING SOMEONE.
EVEN SO, WHY DID IT HAVE TO BE YOU SHE HIT?
YES.
WE *DO* HAVE IRIJAKO.

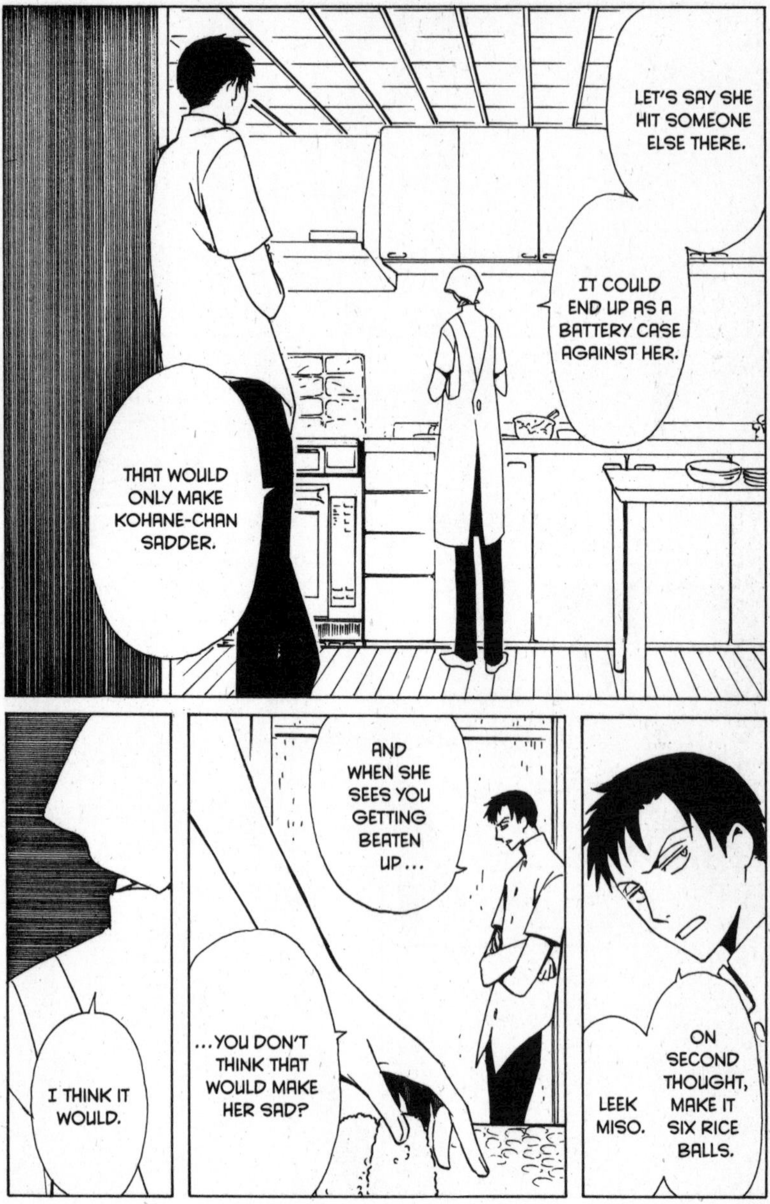
LET'S SAY SHE HIT SOMEONE ELSE THERE.
IT COULD END UP AS A BATTERY CASE AGAINST HER.
THAT WOULD ONLY MAKE KOHANE-CHAN SADDER.
ON SECOND THOUGHT, MAKE IT SIX RICE BALLS.
LEEK MISO.
AND WHEN SHE SEES YOU GETTING BEATEN UP...
...YOU DON'T THINK THAT WOULD MAKE HER SAD?
I THINK IT WOULD.

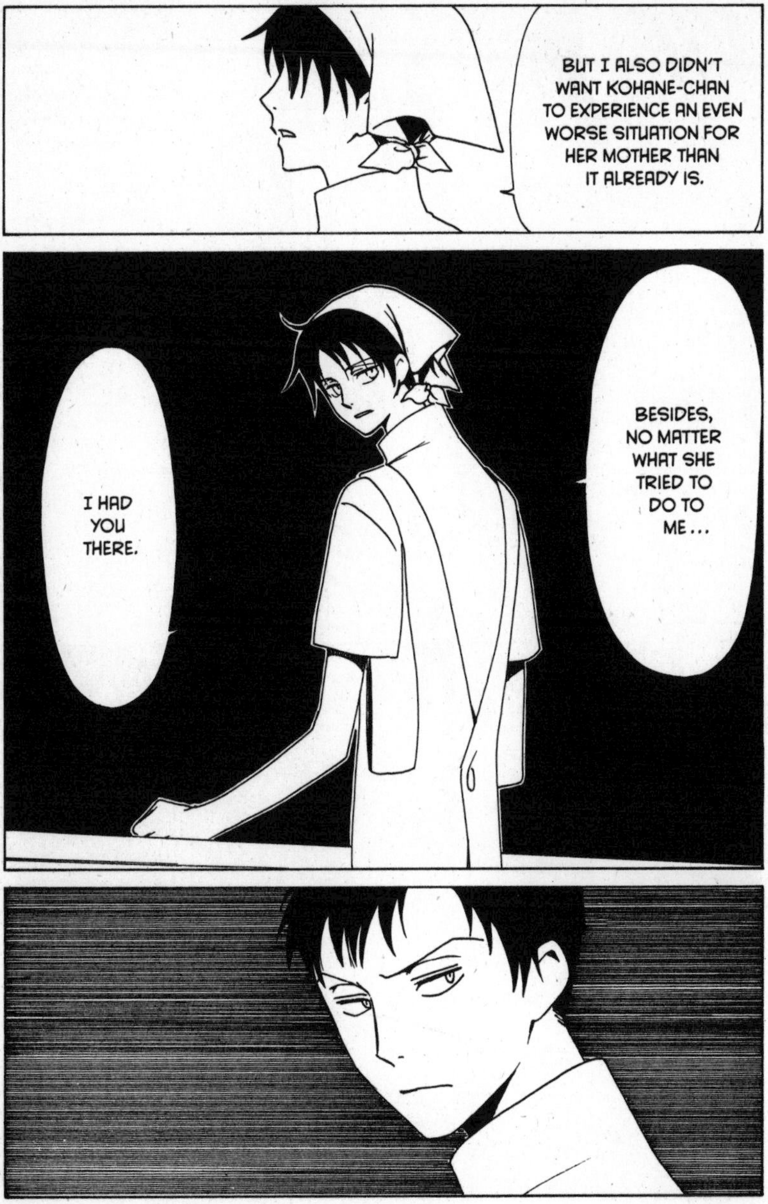
BUT I ALSO DIDN'T WANT KOHANE-CHAN TO EXPERIENCE AN EVEN WORSE SITUATION FOR HER MOTHER THAN IT ALREADY IS.
BESIDES, NO MATTER WHAT SHE TRIED TO DO TO ME...
I HAD YOU THERE.

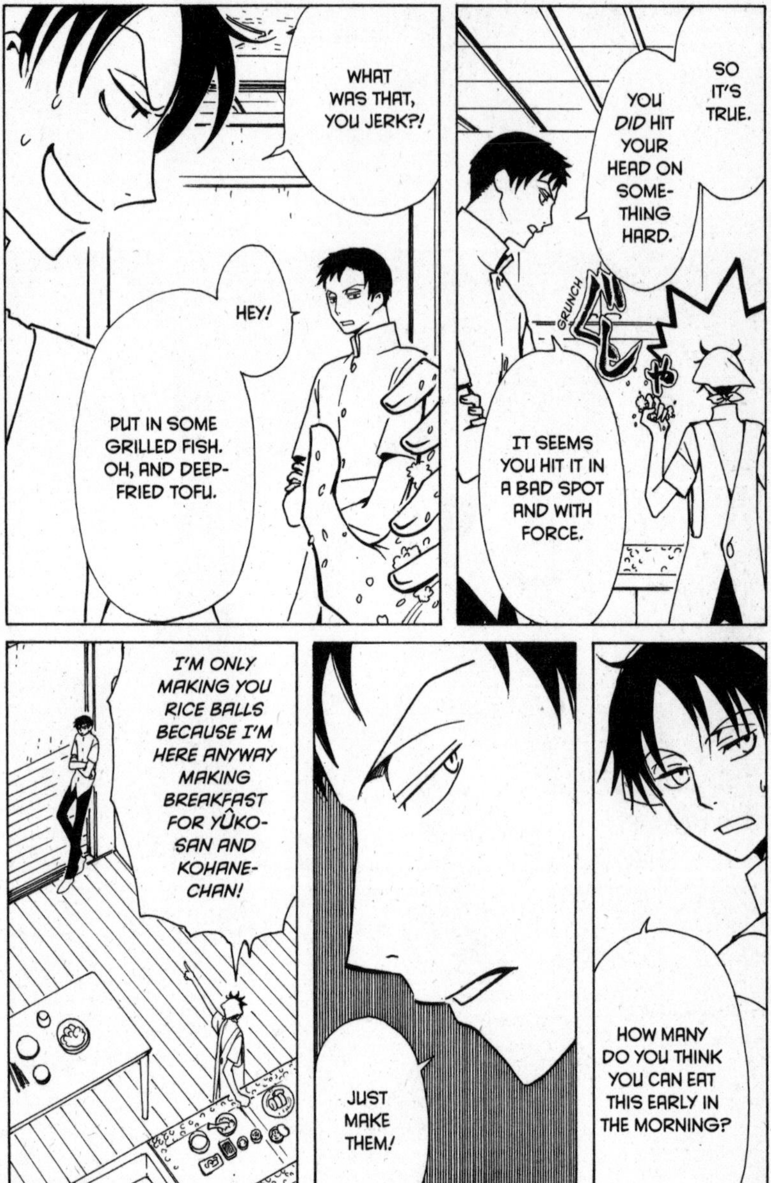
SO IT'S TRUE.
YOU *DID* HIT YOUR HEAD ON SOMETHING HARD.
GRUNCH
IT SEEMS YOU HIT IT IN A BAD SPOT AND WITH FORCE.
WHAT WAS THAT, YOU JERK?!
HEY!
PUT IN SOME GRILLED FISH. OH, AND DEEP-FRIED TOFU.
HOW MANY DO YOU THINK YOU CAN EAT THIS EARLY IN THE MORNING?
JUST MAKE THEM!
*I'M ONLY MAKING YOU RICE BALLS BECAUSE I'M HERE ANYWAY MAKING BREAKFAST FOR YÛKO-SAN AND KOHANE-CHAN!*

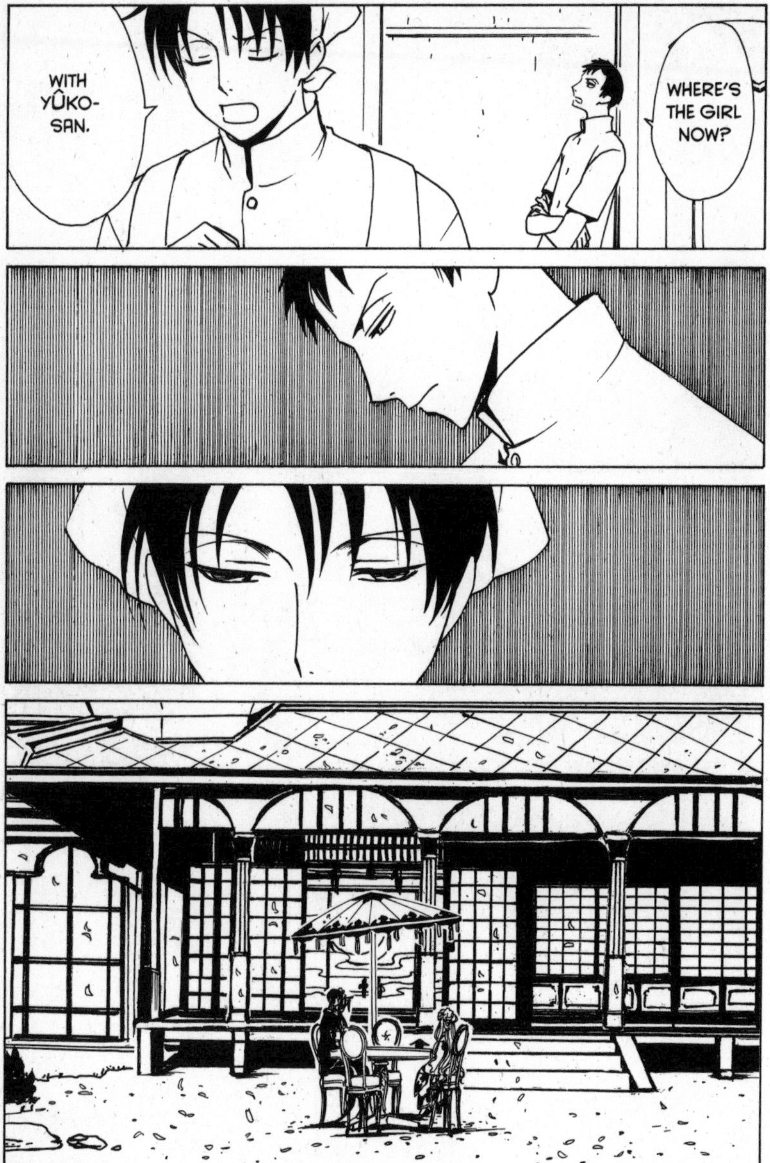
WHERE'S THE GIRL NOW?
WITH YÛKO-SAN.

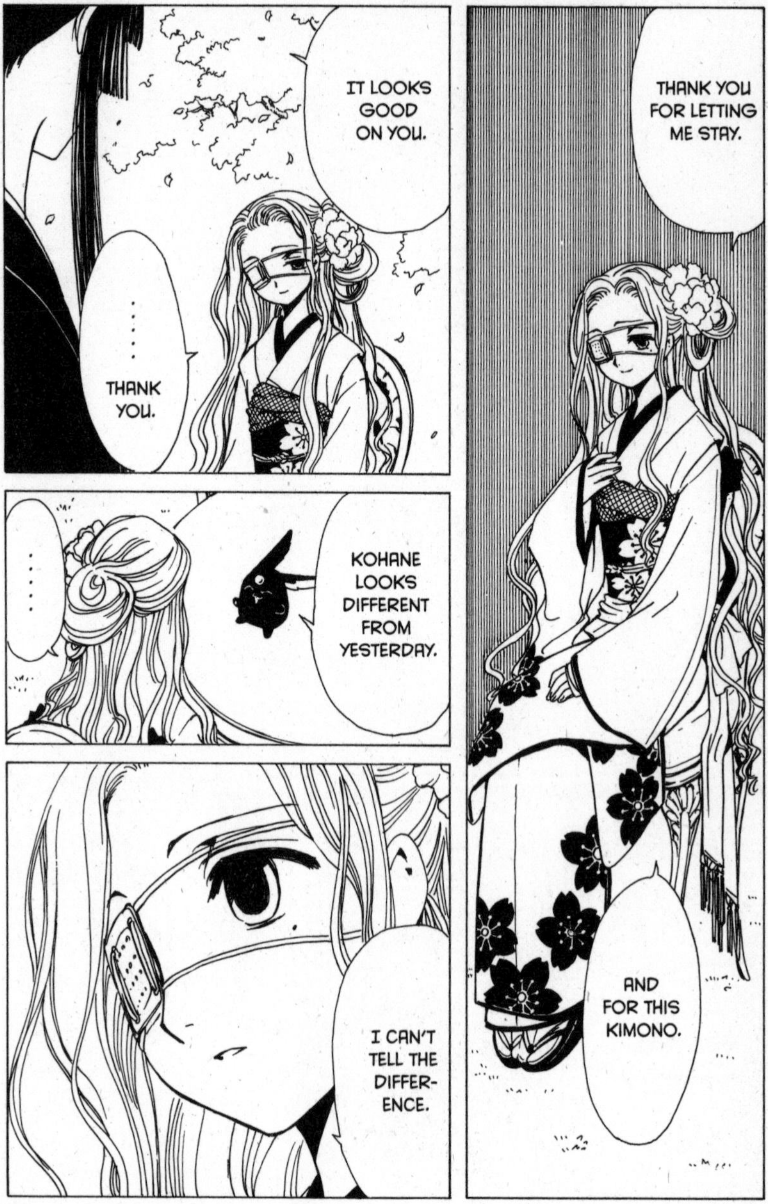
THANK YOU FOR LETTING ME STAY.
AND FOR THIS KIMONO.
IT LOOKS GOOD ON YOU.
......
THANK YOU.
KOHANE LOOKS DIFFERENT FROM YESTERDAY.
......
I CAN'T TELL THE DIFFER-ENCE.

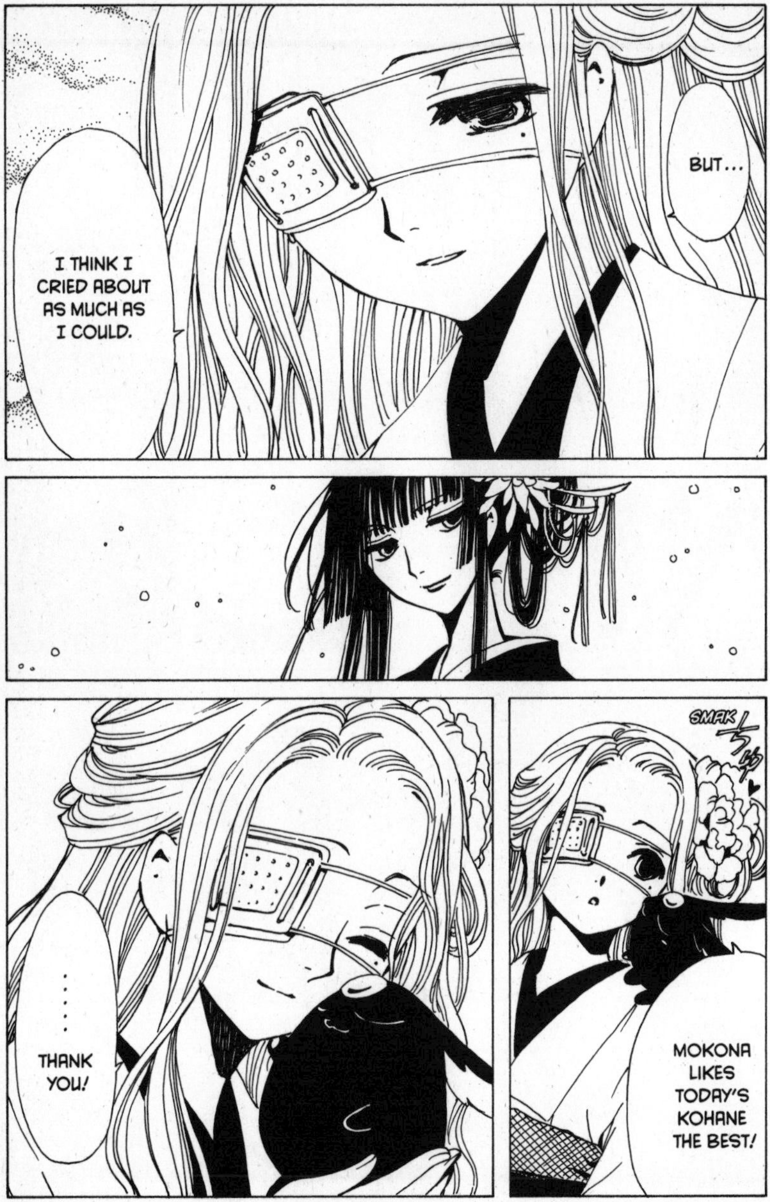
BUT...
I THINK I CRIED ABOUT AS MUCH AS I COULD.
SMAK
MOKONA LIKES TODAY'S KOHANE THE BEST!
......
THANK YOU!

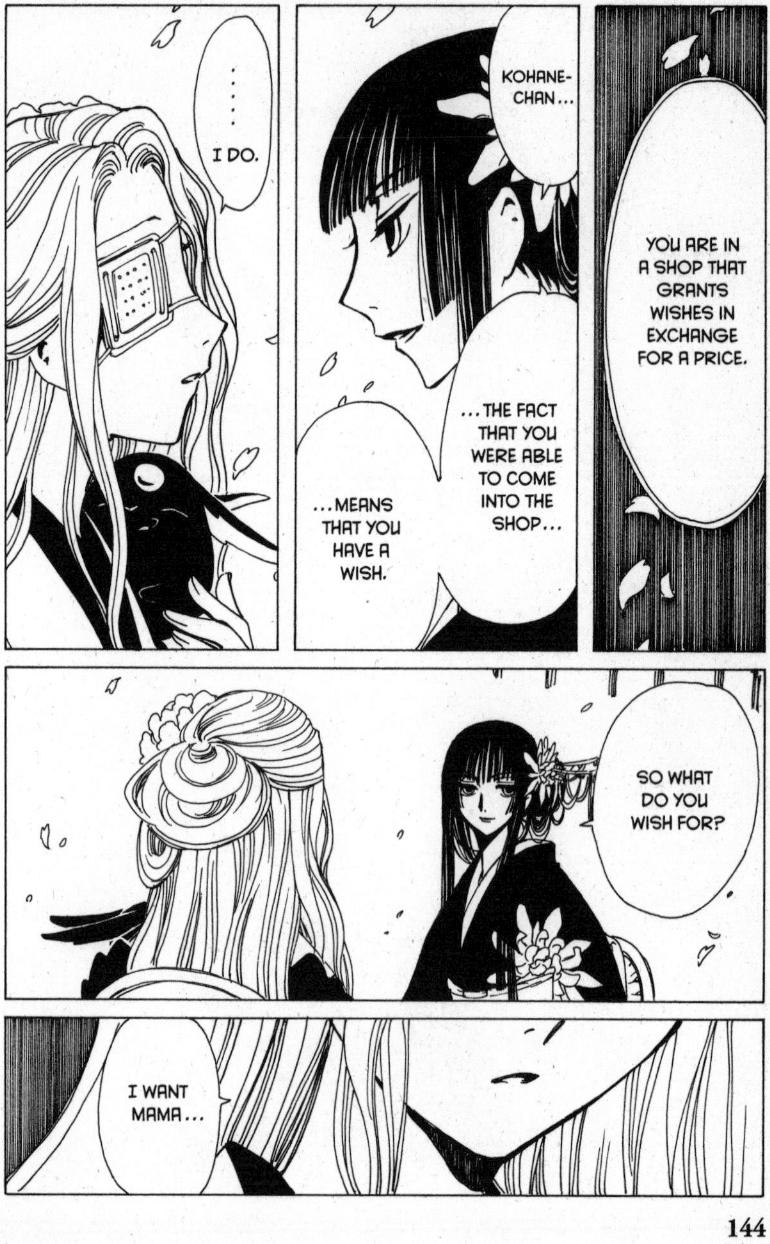
YOU ARE IN A SHOP THAT GRANTS WISHES IN EXCHANGE FOR A PRICE.
KOHANE-CHAN...
...THE FACT THAT YOU WERE ABLE TO COME INTO THE SHOP...
...MEANS THAT YOU HAVE A WISH.
..... I DO.
SO WHAT DO YOU WISH FOR?
I WANT MAMA...

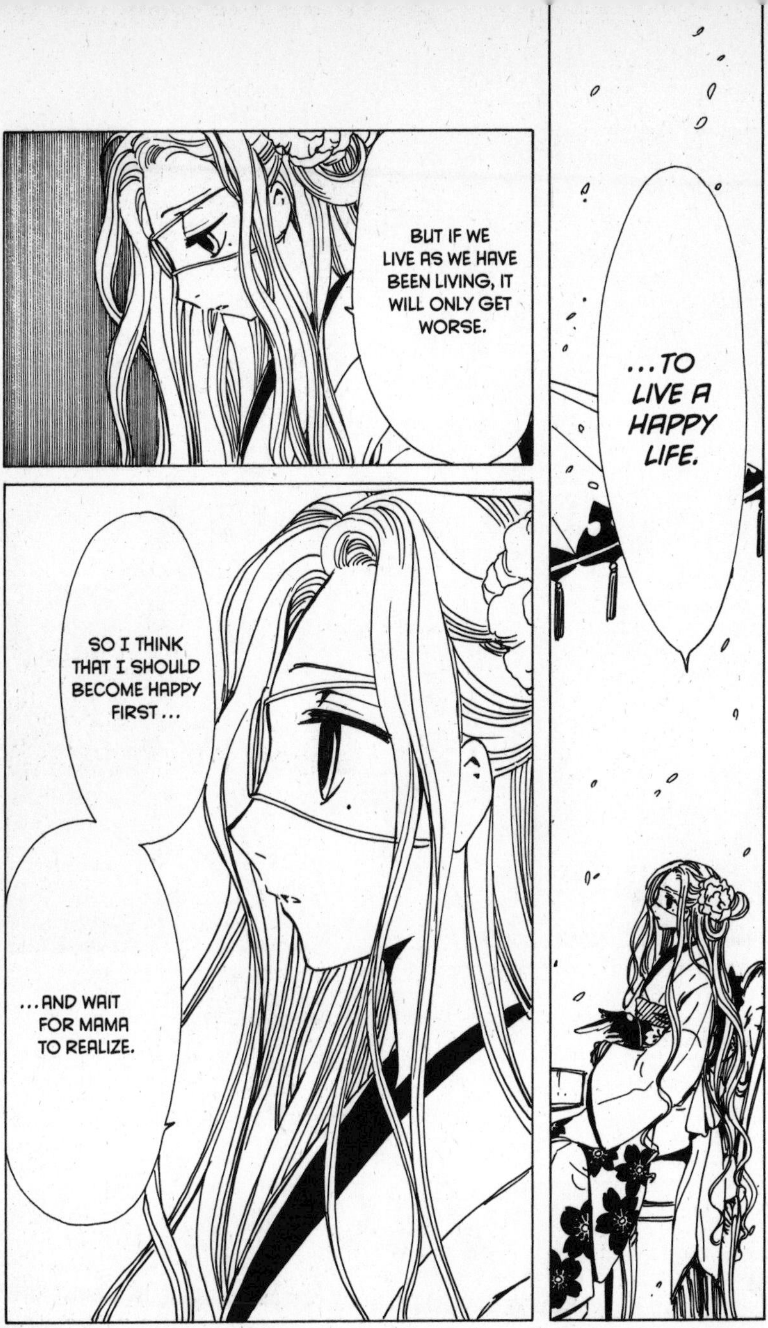
...TO LIVE A HAPPY LIFE.
BUT IF WE LIVE AS WE HAVE BEEN LIVING, IT WILL ONLY GET WORSE.
SO I THINK THAT I SHOULD BECOME HAPPY FIRST...
...AND WAIT FOR MAMA TO REALIZE.

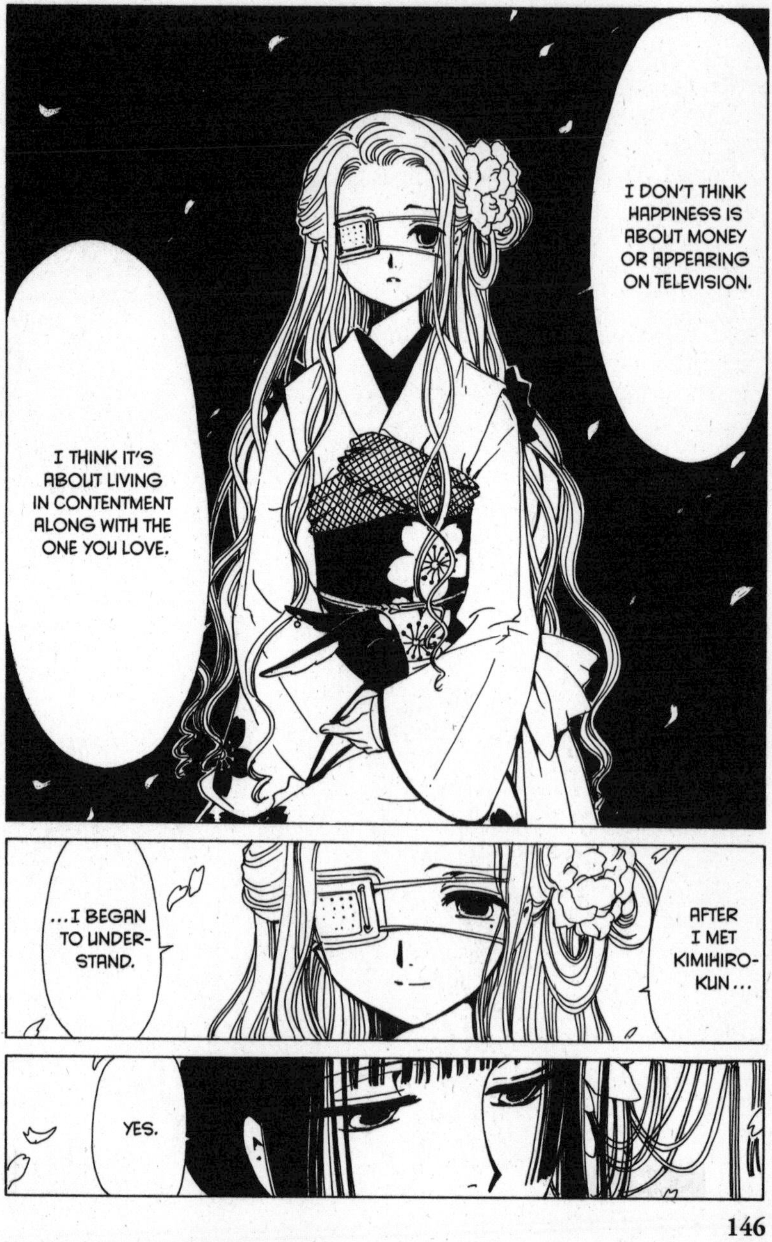
I DON'T THINK HAPPINESS IS ABOUT MONEY OR APPEARING ON TELEVISION.
I THINK IT'S ABOUT LIVING IN CONTENTMENT ALONG WITH THE ONE YOU LOVE.
AFTER I MET KIMIHIRO-KUN...
...I BEGAN TO UNDER-STAND.
YES.

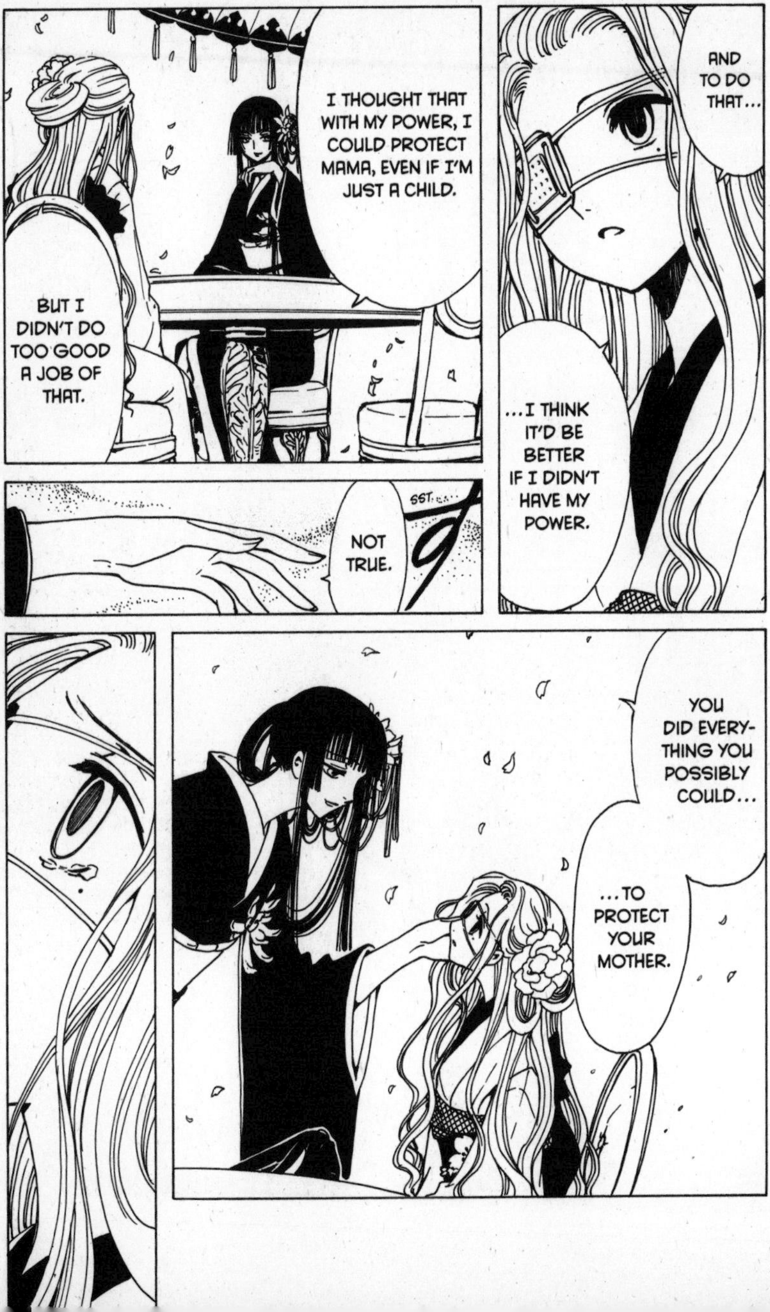
AND TO DO THAT...
...I THINK IT'D BE BETTER IF I DIDN'T HAVE MY POWER.
I THOUGHT THAT WITH MY POWER, I COULD PROTECT MAMA, EVEN IF I'M JUST A CHILD.
BUT I DIDN'T DO TOO GOOD A JOB OF THAT.
SST...
NOT TRUE.
YOU DID EVERY-THING YOU POSSIBLY COULD...
...TO PROTECT YOUR MOTHER.

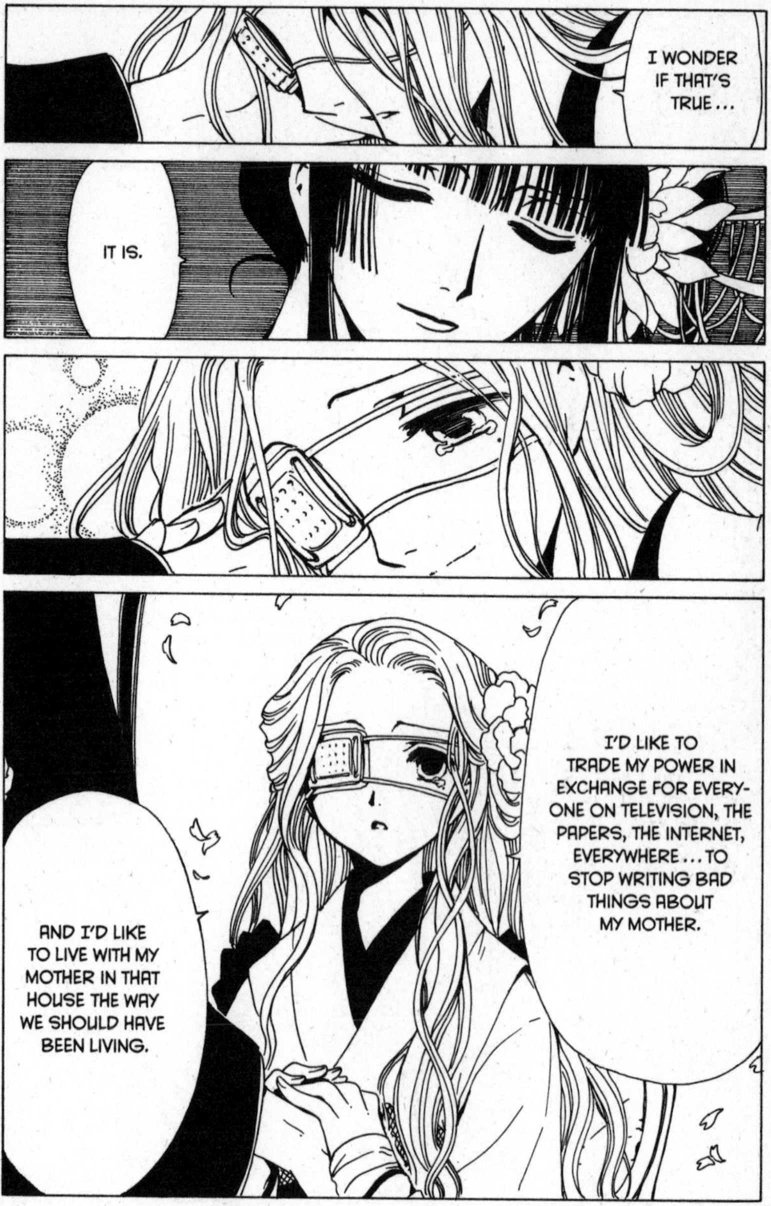
I WONDER IF THAT'S TRUE...
IT IS.
I'D LIKE TO TRADE MY POWER IN EXCHANGE FOR EVERYONE ON TELEVISION, THE PAPERS, THE INTERNET, EVERYWHERE... TO STOP WRITING BAD THINGS ABOUT MY MOTHER.
AND I'D LIKE TO LIVE WITH MY MOTHER IN THAT HOUSE THE WAY WE SHOULD HAVE BEEN LIVING.

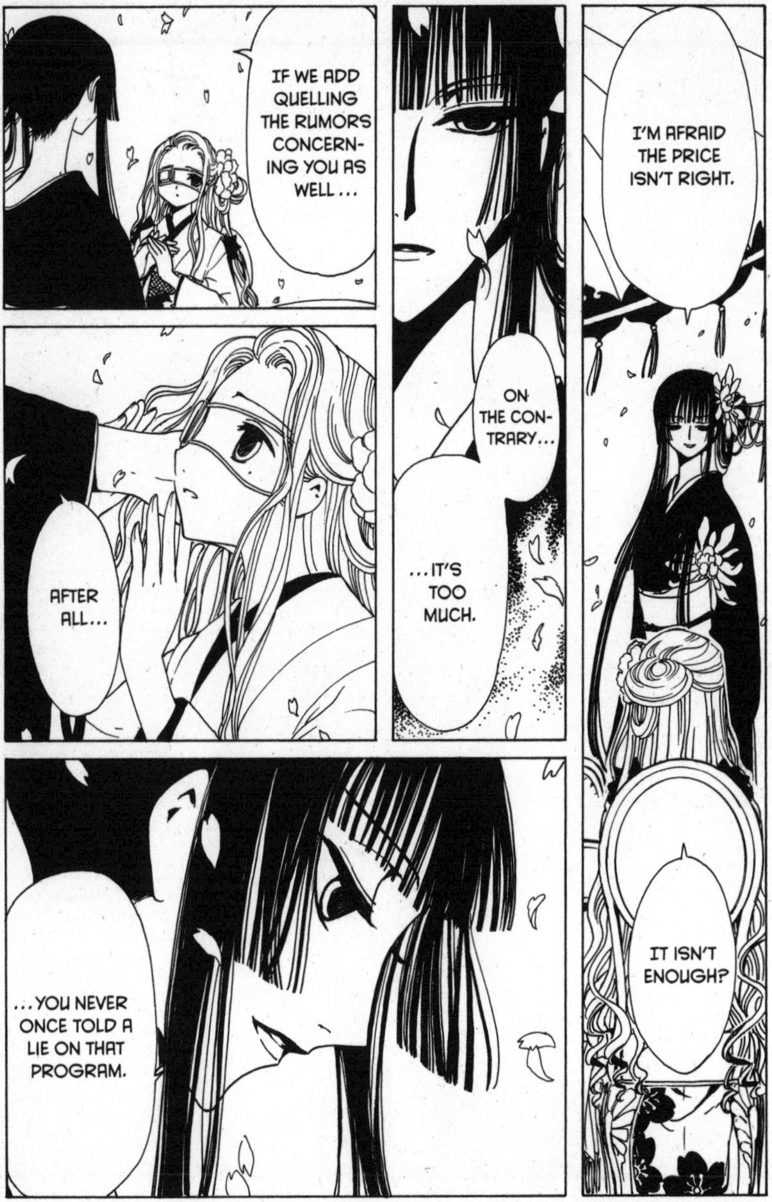
I'M AFRAID THE PRICE ISN'T RIGHT.
IT ISN'T ENOUGH?
ON THE CONTRARY...
...IT'S TOO MUCH.
IF WE ADD QUELLING THE RUMORS CONCERNING YOU AS WELL...
AFTER ALL...
...YOU NEVER ONCE TOLD A LIE ON THAT PROGRAM.

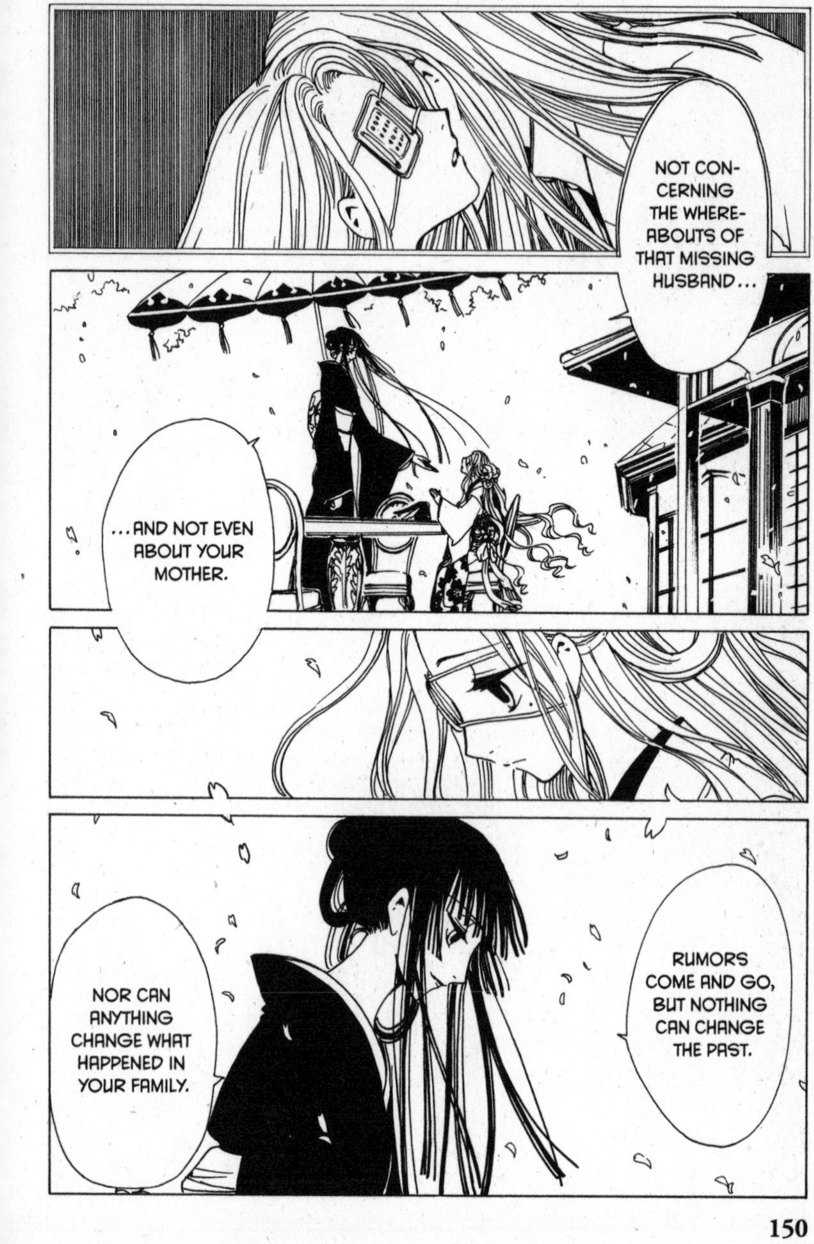
NOT CON-CERNING THE WHERE-ABOUTS OF THAT MISSING HUSBAND...
...AND NOT EVEN ABOUT YOUR MOTHER.
RUMORS COME AND GO, BUT NOTHING CAN CHANGE THE PAST.
NOR CAN ANYTHING CHANGE WHAT HAPPENED IN YOUR FAMILY.

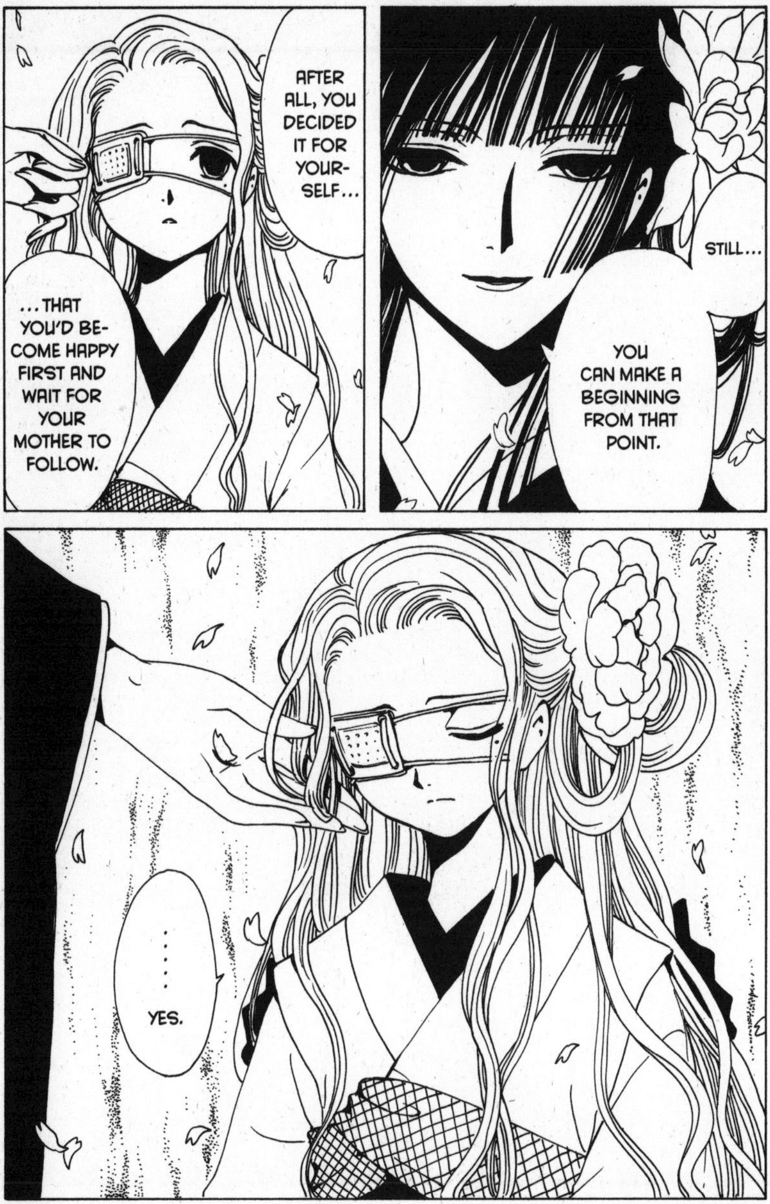
STILL...
YOU CAN MAKE A BEGINNING FROM THAT POINT.
AFTER ALL, YOU DECIDED IT FOR YOURSELF...
...THAT YOU'D BECOME HAPPY FIRST AND WAIT FOR YOUR MOTHER TO FOLLOW.
...... YES.

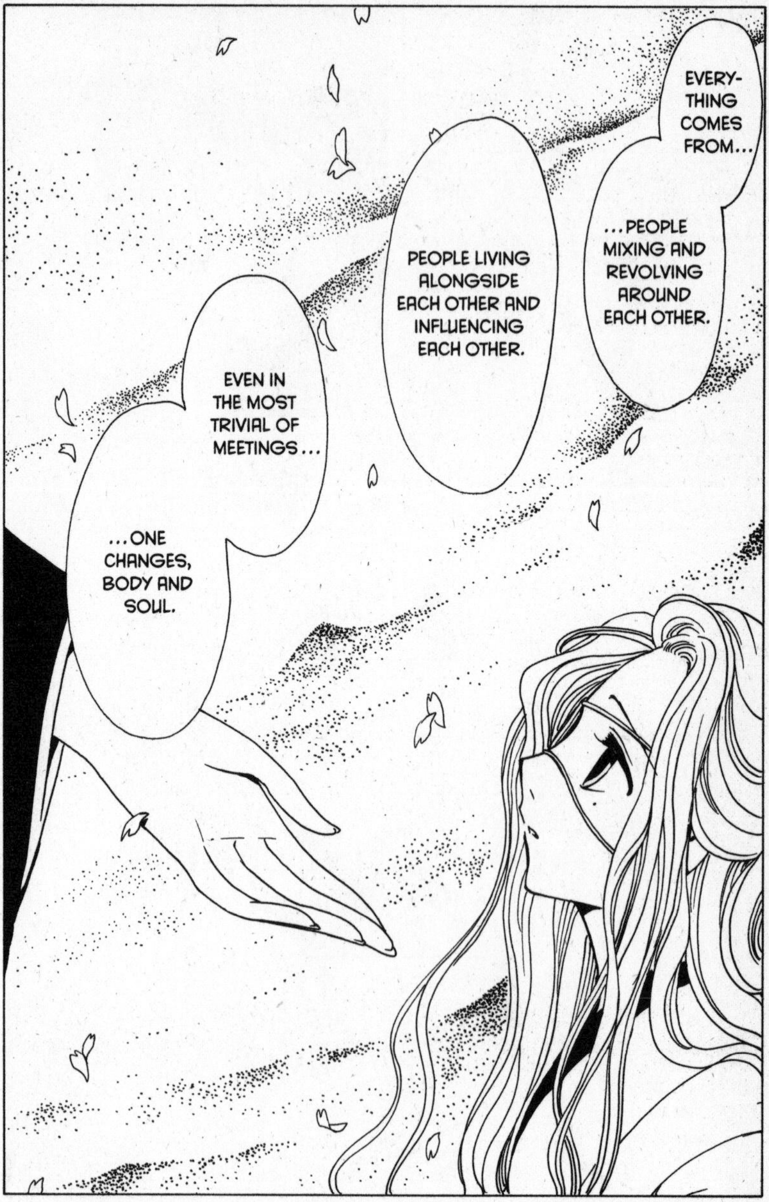
EVERY-THING COMES FROM...
...PEOPLE MIXING AND REVOLVING AROUND EACH OTHER.
PEOPLE LIVING ALONGSIDE EACH OTHER AND INFLUENCING EACH OTHER.
EVEN IN THE MOST TRIVIAL OF MEETINGS...
...ONE CHANGES, BODY AND SOUL.

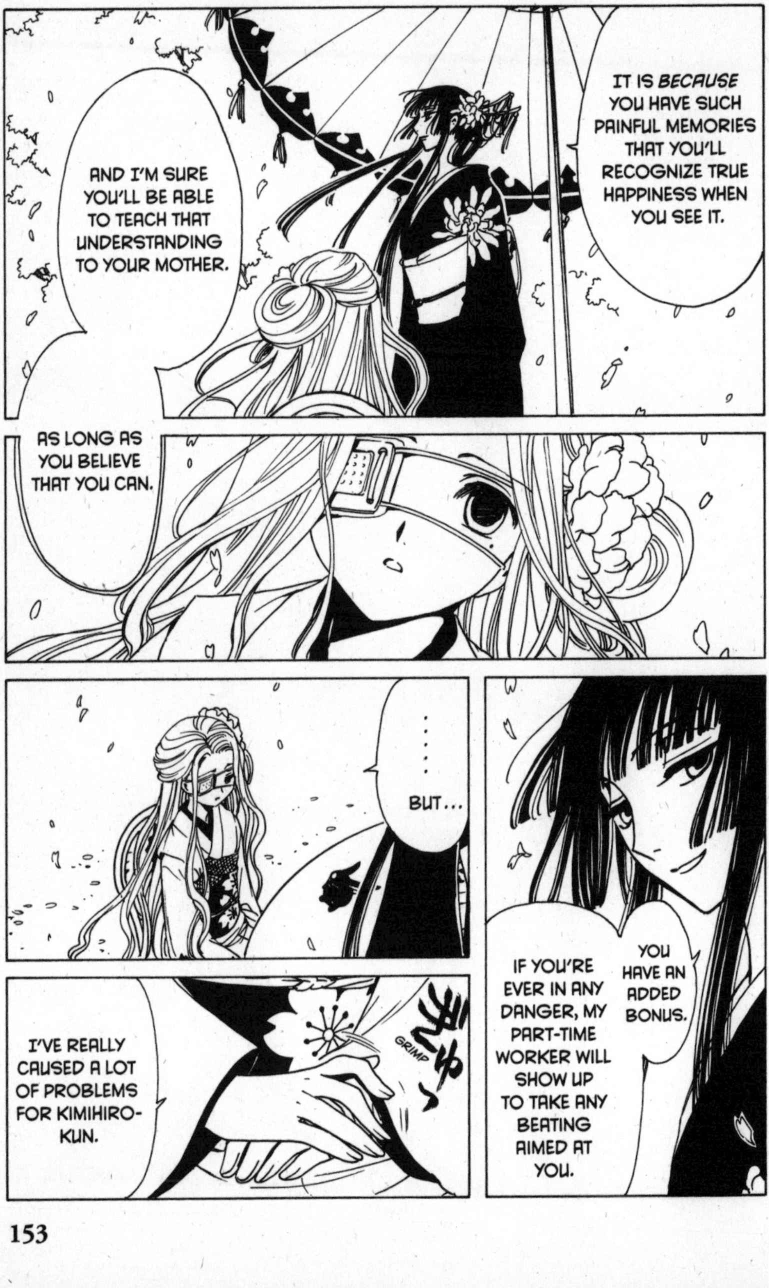
IT IS *BECAUSE* YOU HAVE SUCH PAINFUL MEMORIES THAT YOU'LL RECOGNIZE TRUE HAPPINESS WHEN YOU SEE IT.
AND I'M SURE YOU'LL BE ABLE TO TEACH THAT UNDERSTANDING TO YOUR MOTHER.
AS LONG AS YOU BELIEVE THAT YOU CAN.
YOU HAVE AN ADDED BONUS.
IF YOU'RE EVER IN ANY DANGER, MY PART-TIME WORKER WILL SHOW UP TO TAKE ANY BEATING AIMED AT YOU.
.....
BUT...
GRIMP
I'VE REALLY CAUSED A LOT OF PROBLEMS FOR KIMIHIRO-KUN.

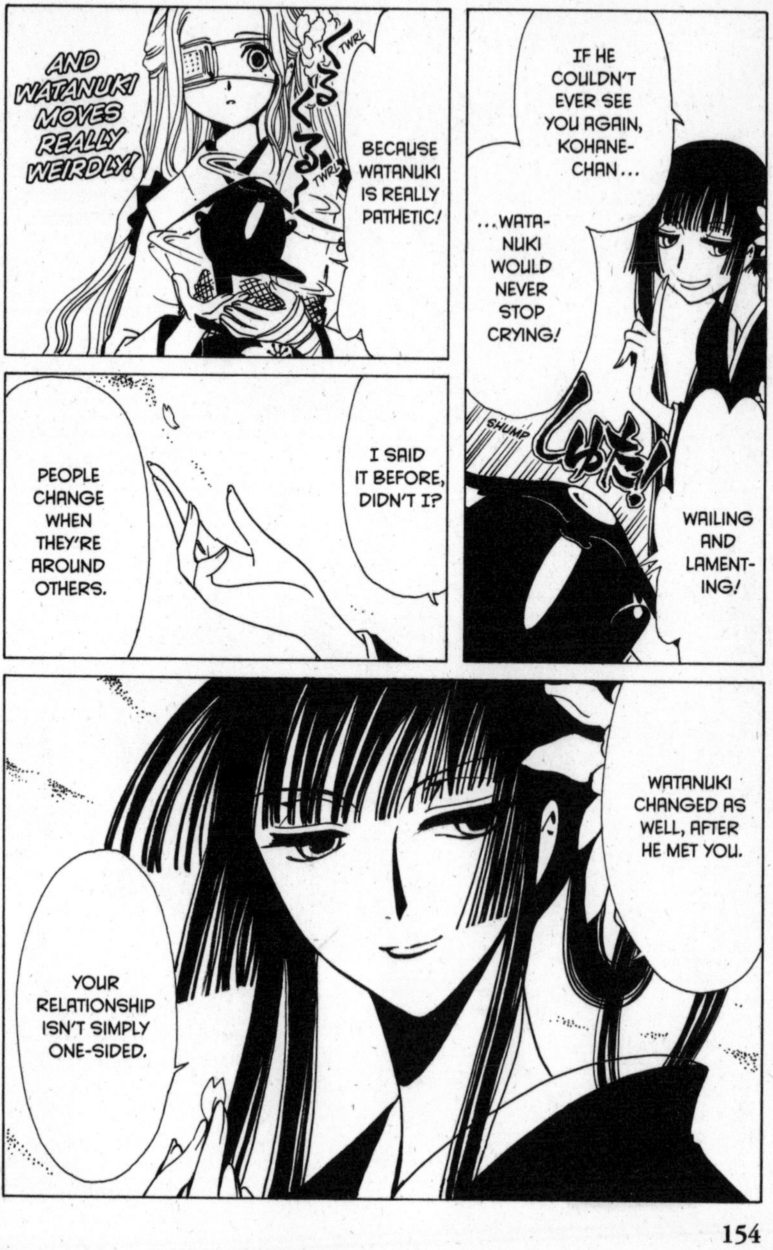
IF HE COULDN'T EVER SEE YOU AGAIN, KOHANE-CHAN...
...WATA-NUKI WOULD NEVER STOP CRYING!
SHUMP
WAILING AND LAMENT-ING!
BECAUSE WATANUKI IS REALLY PATHETIC!
TWRL
TWRL
AND WATANUKI MOVES REALLY WEIRDLY!
I SAID IT BEFORE, DIDN'T I?
PEOPLE CHANGE WHEN THEY'RE AROUND OTHERS.
WATANUKI CHANGED AS WELL, AFTER HE MET YOU.
YOUR RELATIONSHIP ISN'T SIMPLY ONE-SIDED.

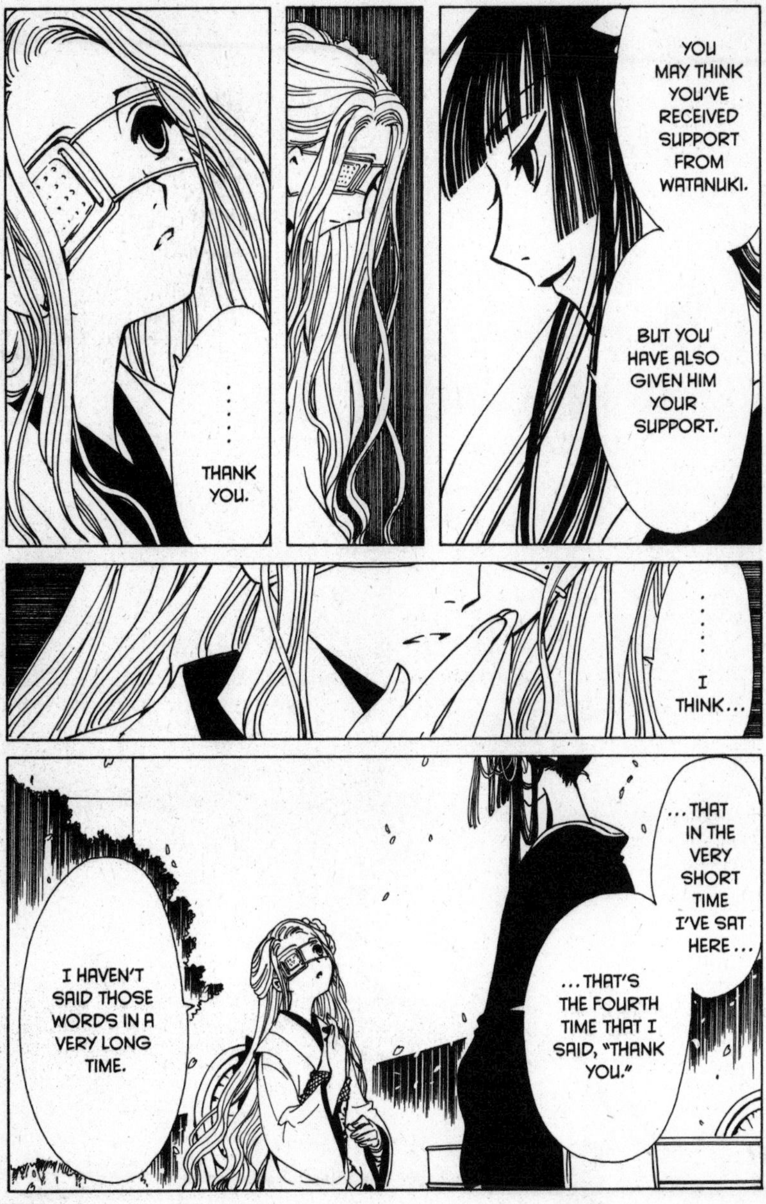
YOU MAY THINK YOU'VE RECEIVED SUPPORT FROM WATANUKI.
BUT YOU HAVE ALSO GIVEN HIM YOUR SUPPORT.
..... THANK YOU.
..... I THINK...
...THAT IN THE VERY SHORT TIME I'VE SAT HERE...
...THAT'S THE FOURTH TIME THAT I SAID, "THANK YOU."
I HAVEN'T SAID THOSE WORDS IN A VERY LONG TIME.

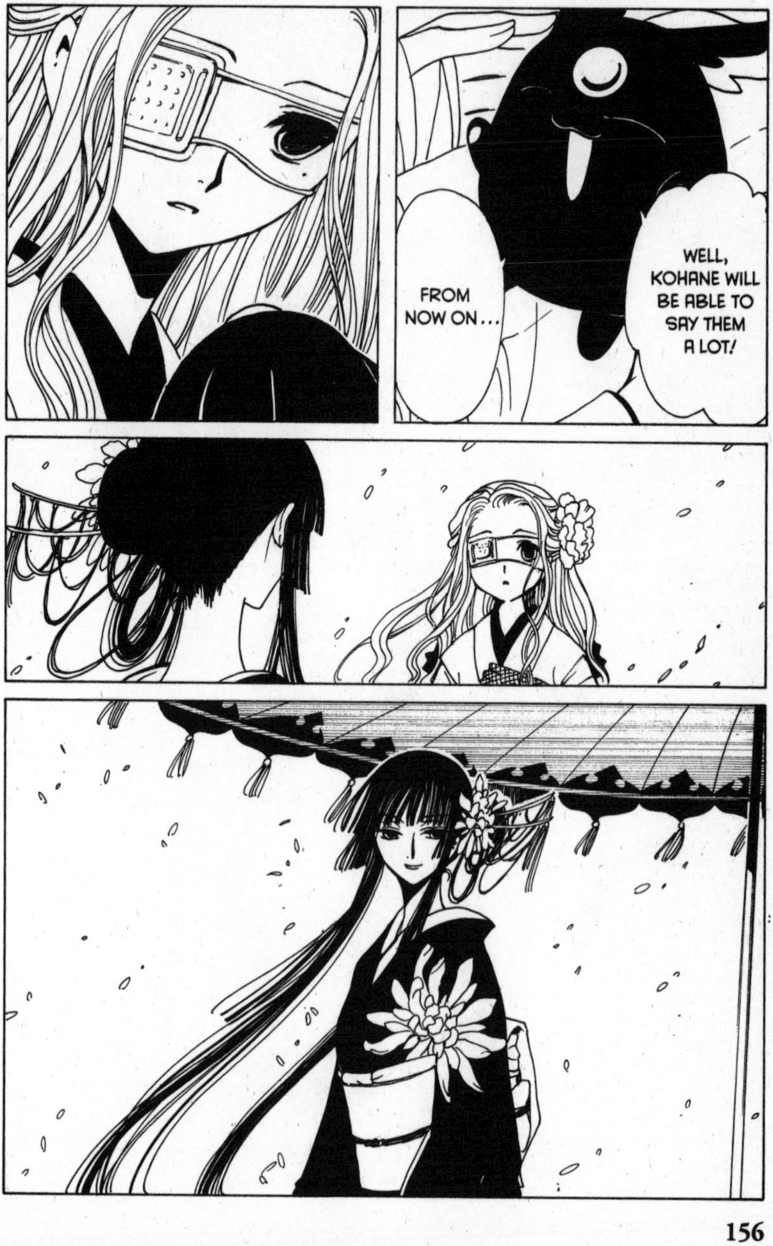
WELL, KOHANE WILL BE ABLE TO SAY THEM A LOT!
FROM NOW ON...

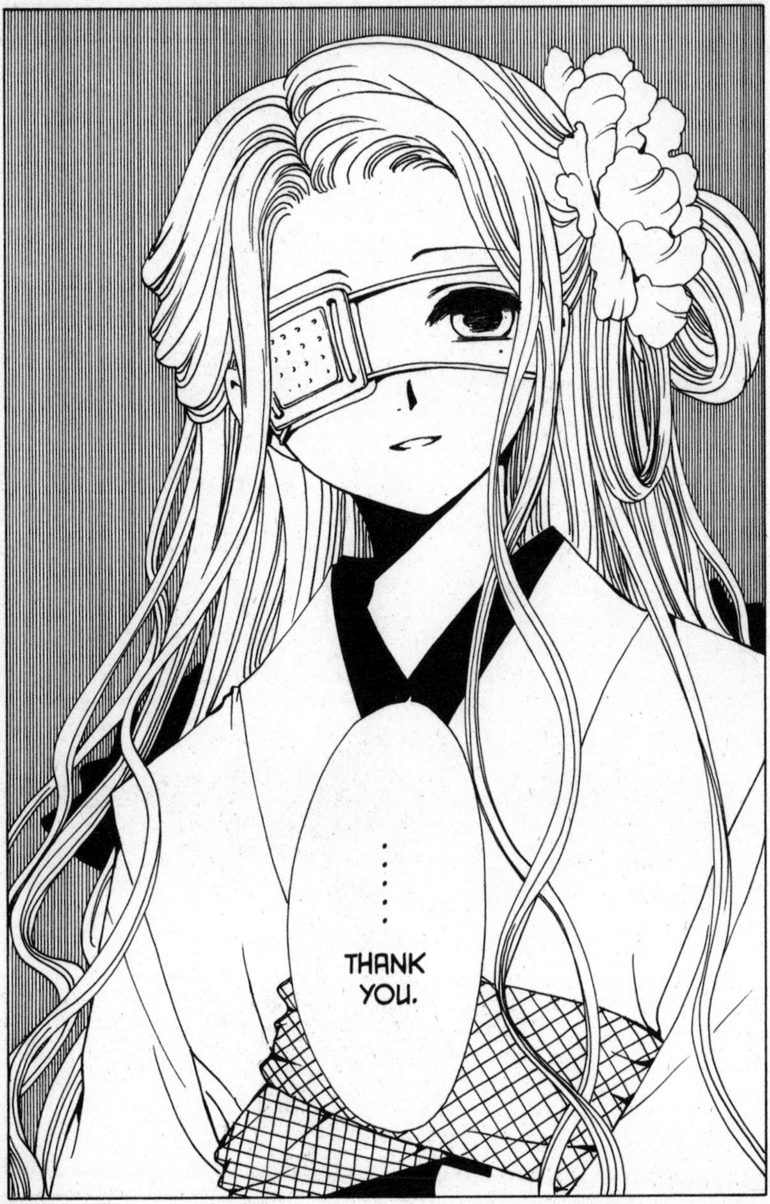
......THANK YOU.

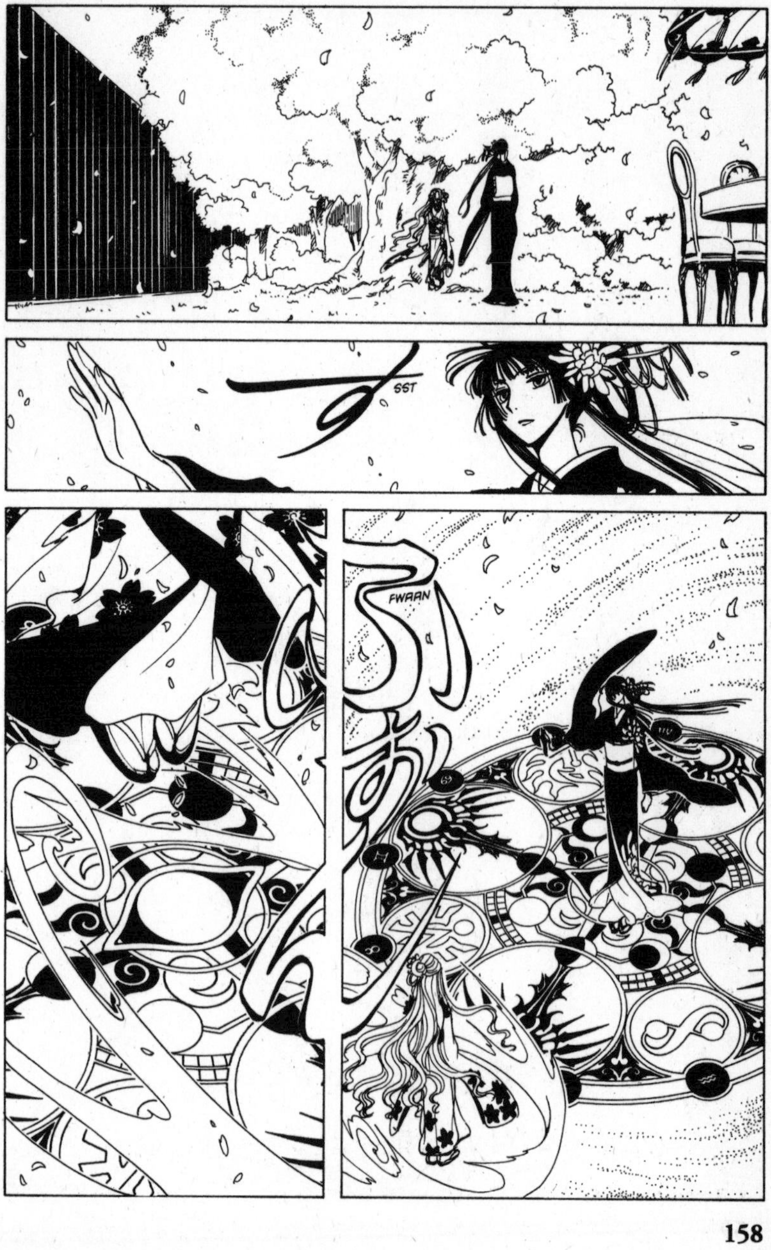
SST
FWAAN

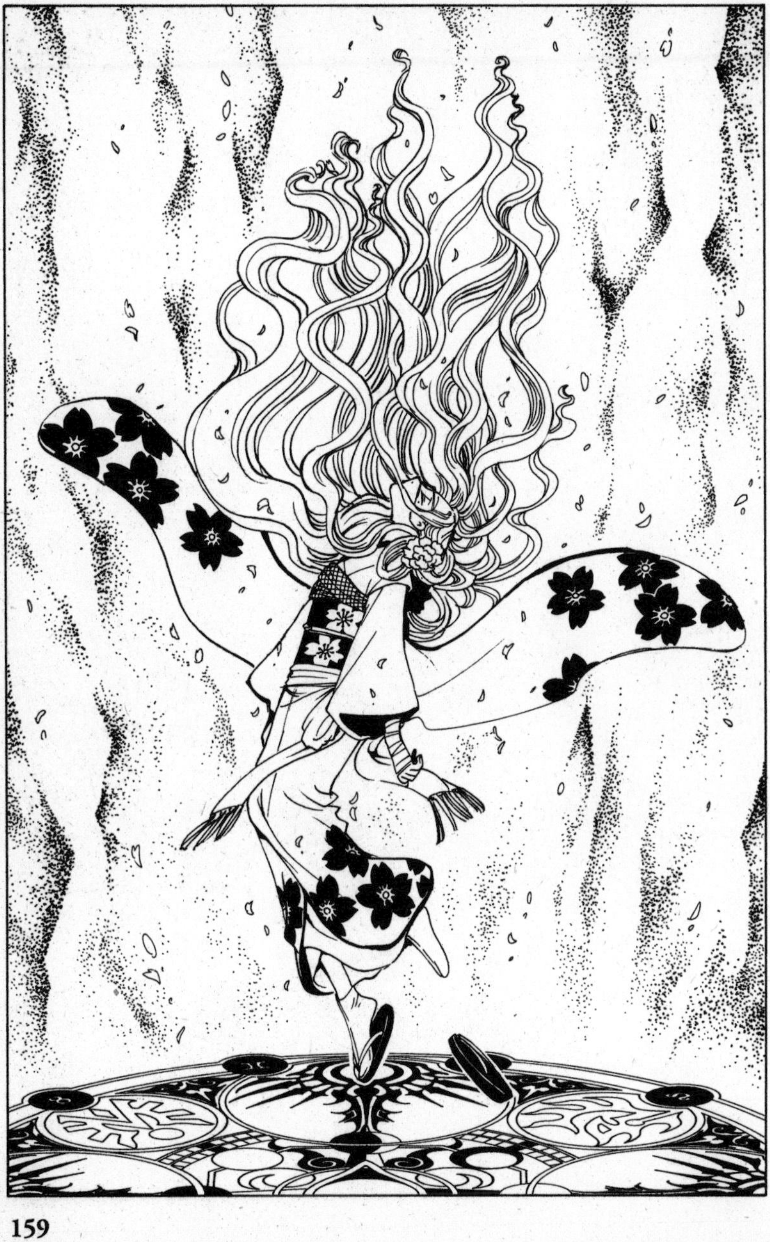

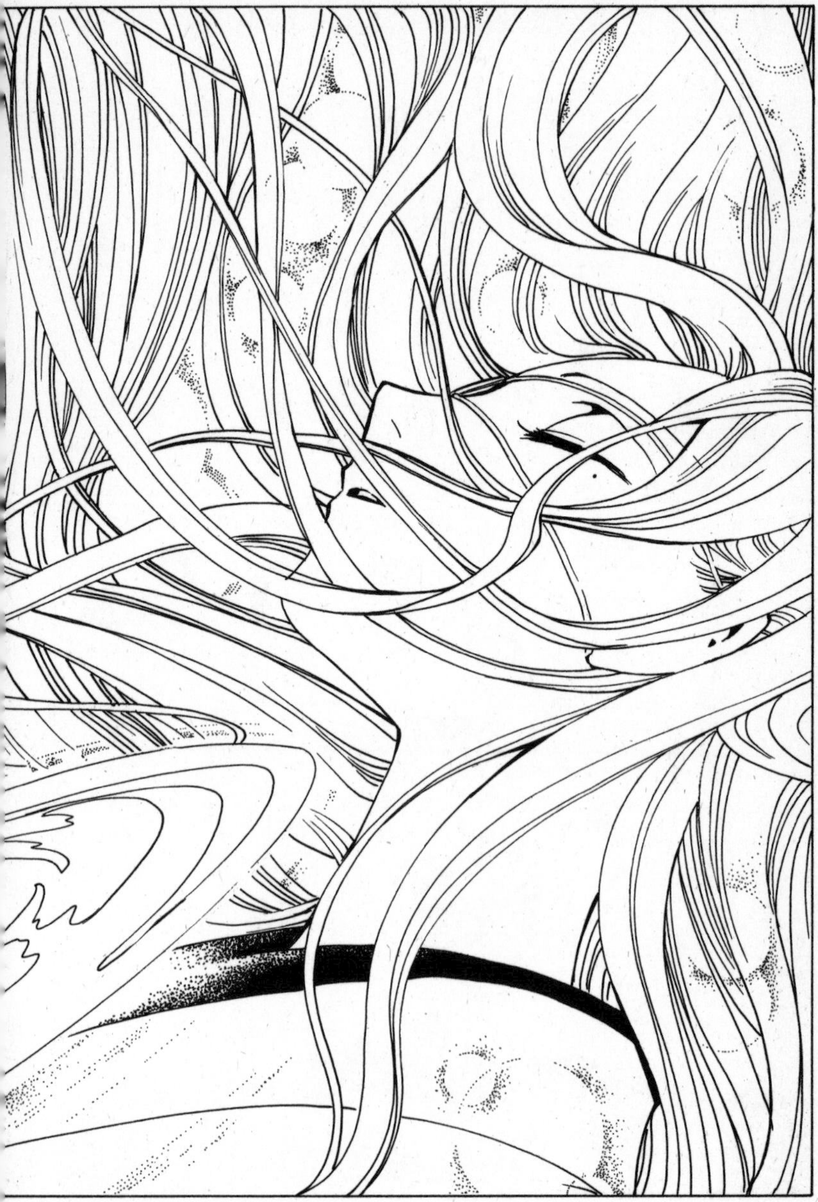

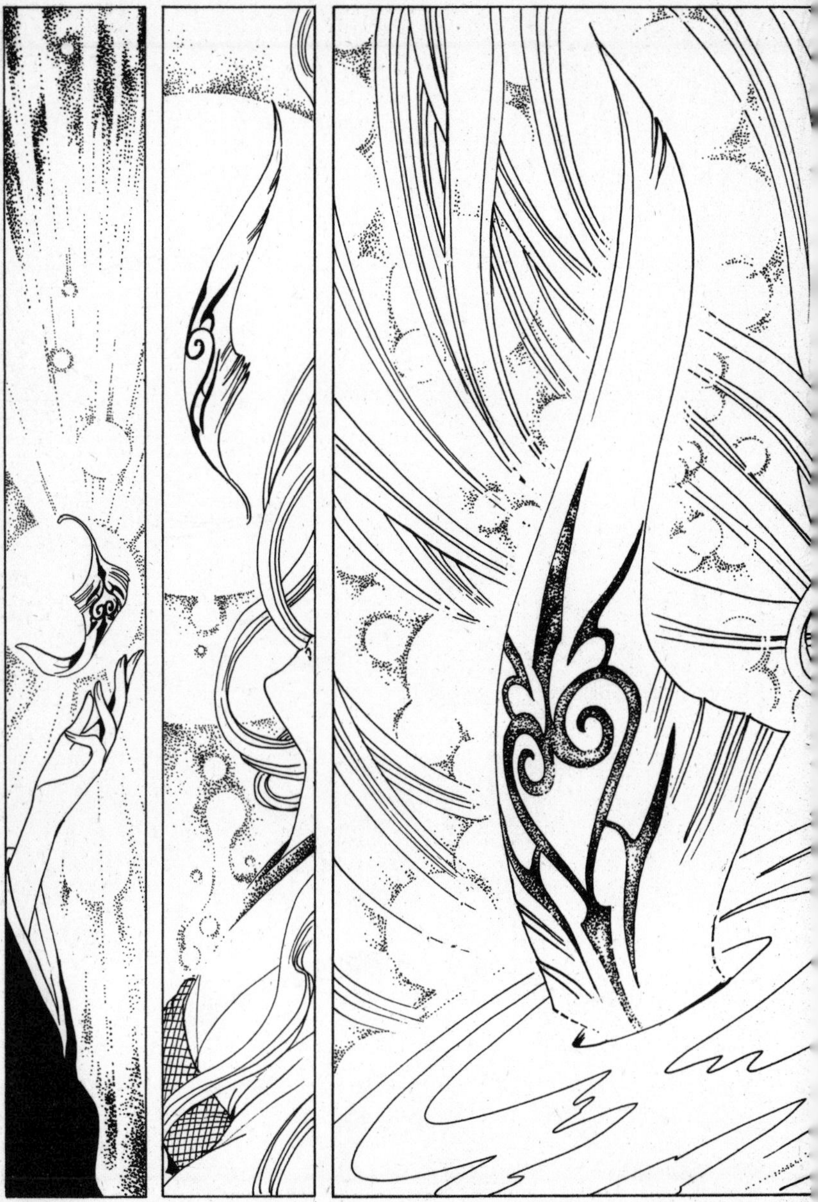

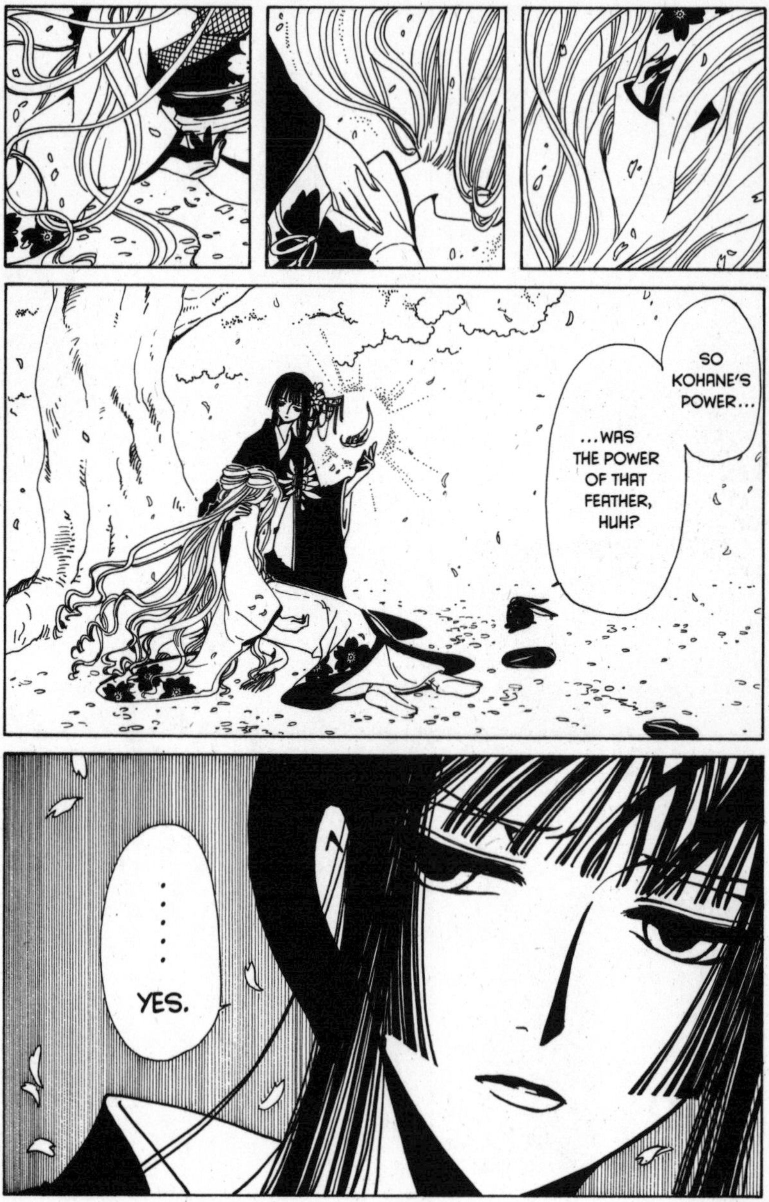
SO KOHANE'S POWER...
...WAS THE POWER OF THAT FEATHER, HUH?
......
YES.

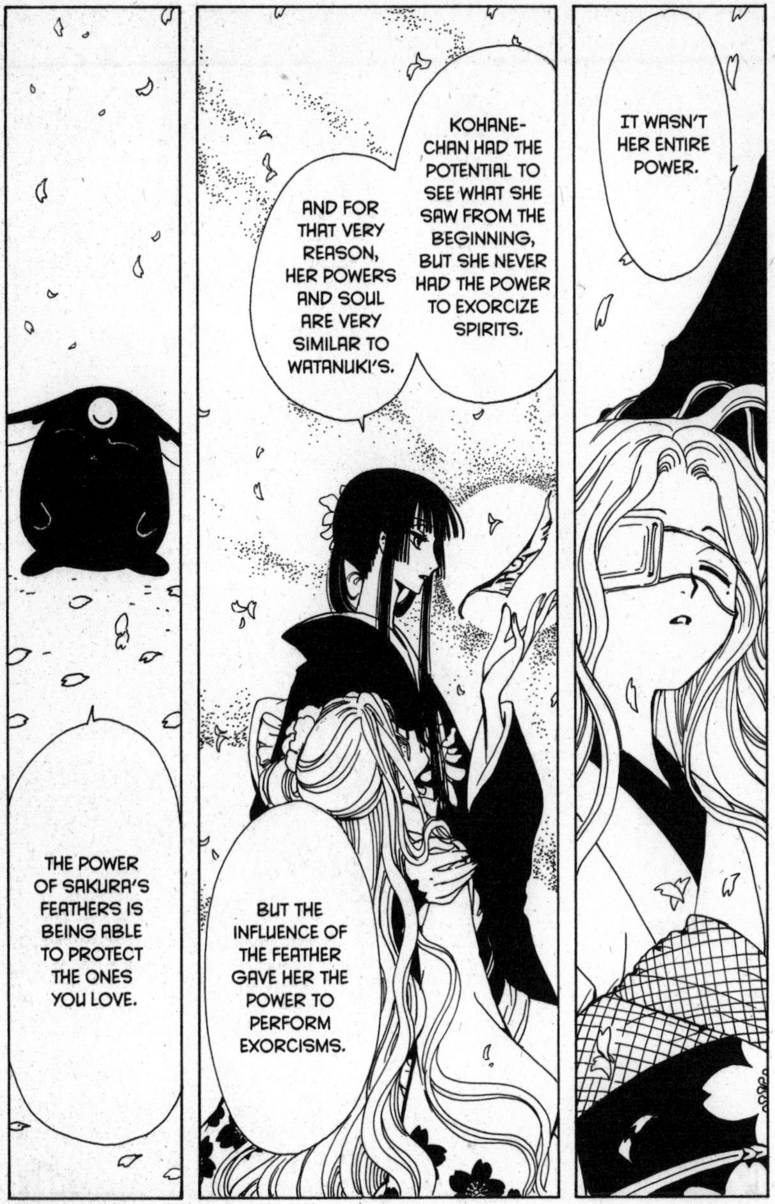
IT WASN'T HER ENTIRE POWER.
KOHANE-CHAN HAD THE POTENTIAL TO SEE WHAT SHE SAW FROM THE BEGINNING, BUT SHE NEVER HAD THE POWER TO EXORCIZE SPIRITS.
AND FOR THAT VERY REASON, HER POWERS AND SOUL ARE VERY SIMILAR TO WATANUKI'S.
BUT THE INFLUENCE OF THE FEATHER GAVE HER THE POWER TO PERFORM EXORCISMS.
THE POWER OF SAKURA'S FEATHERS IS BEING ABLE TO PROTECT THE ONES YOU LOVE.

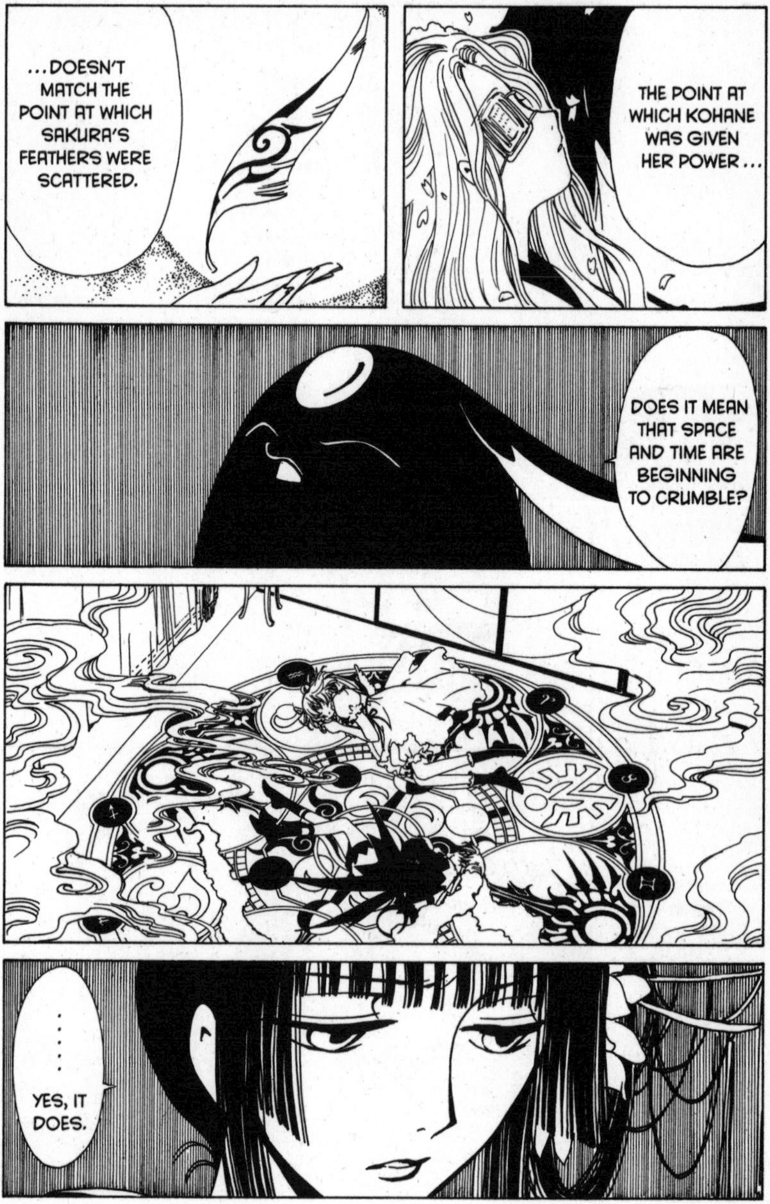
THE POINT AT WHICH KOHANE WAS GIVEN HER POWER...
...DOESN'T MATCH THE POINT AT WHICH SAKURA'S FEATHERS WERE SCATTERED.
DOES IT MEAN THAT SPACE AND TIME ARE BEGINNING TO CRUMBLE?
..... YES, IT DOES.

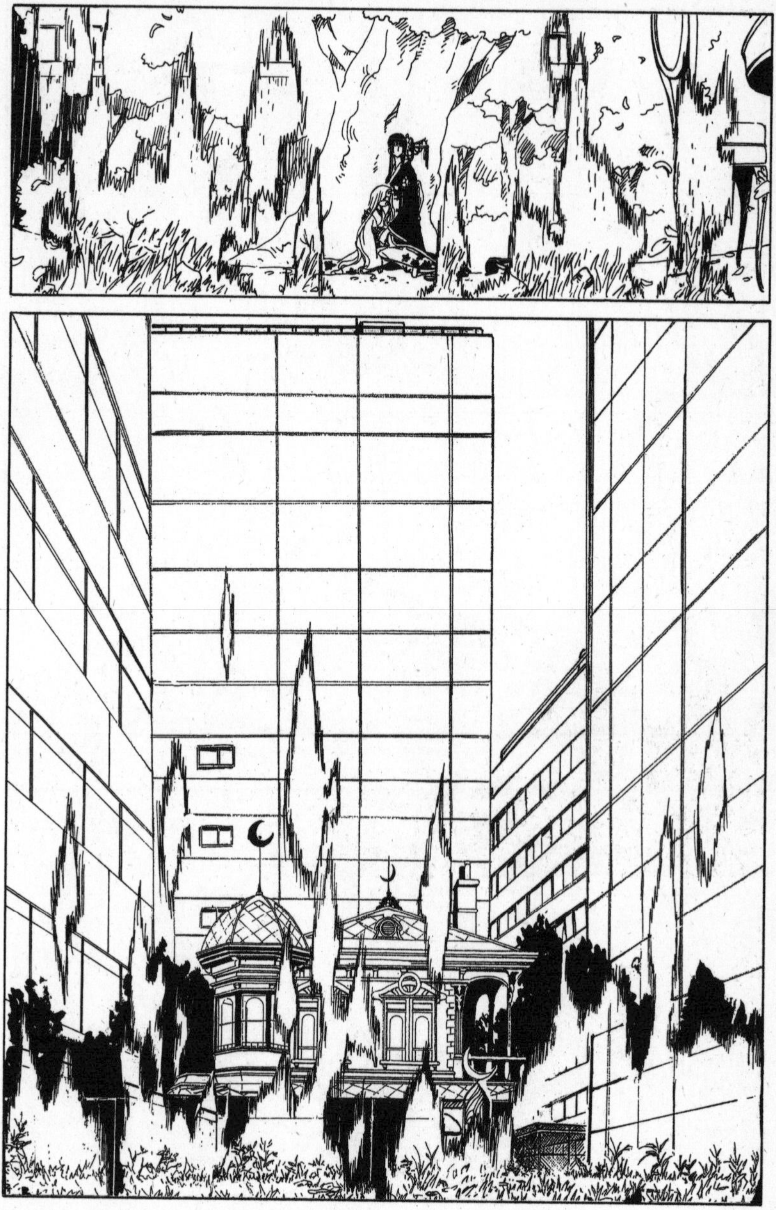

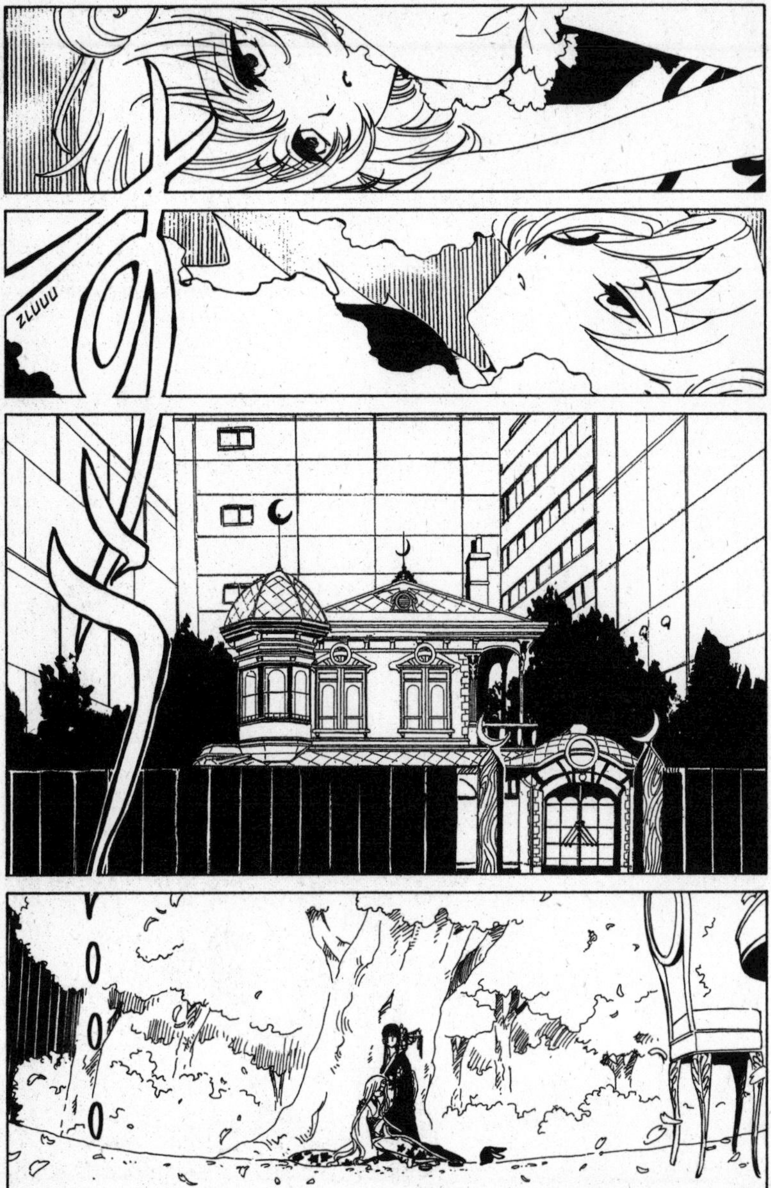
ZLUUU

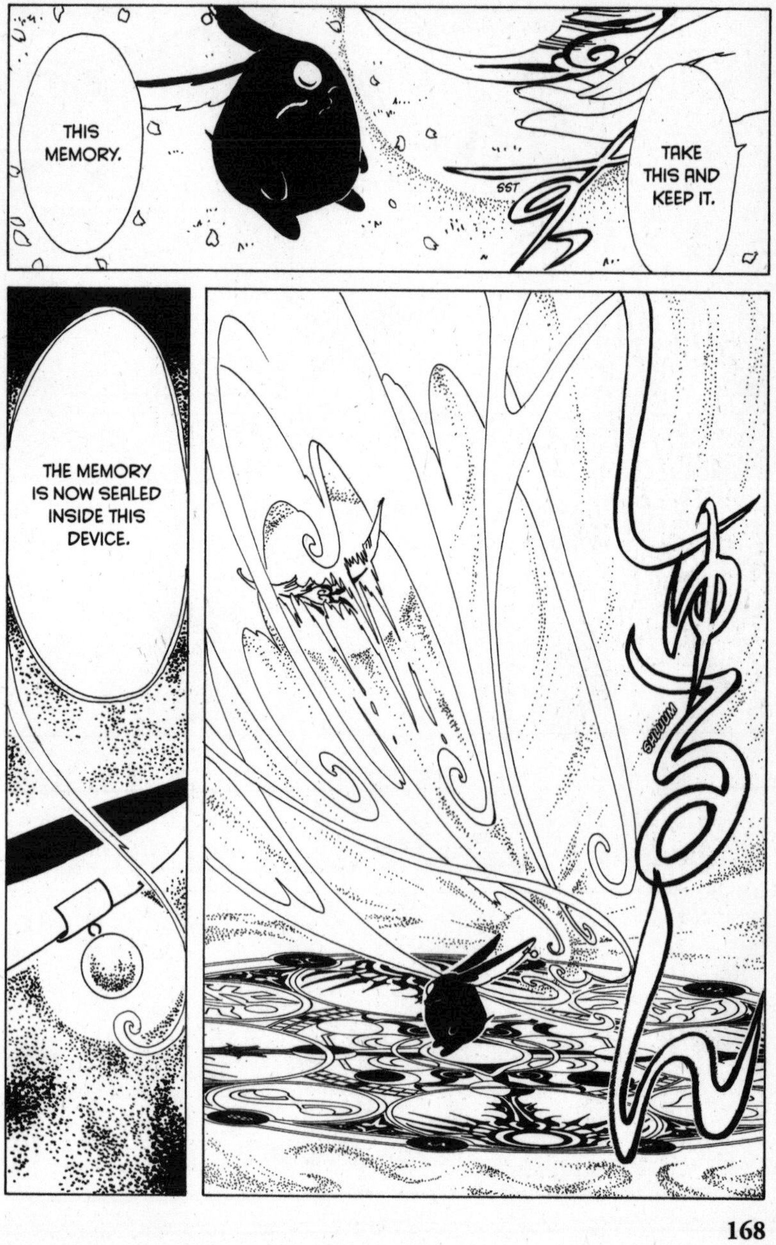
TAKE THIS AND KEEP IT.
SST
THIS MEMORY.
SHUUUN
THE MEMORY IS NOW SEALED INSIDE THIS DEVICE.

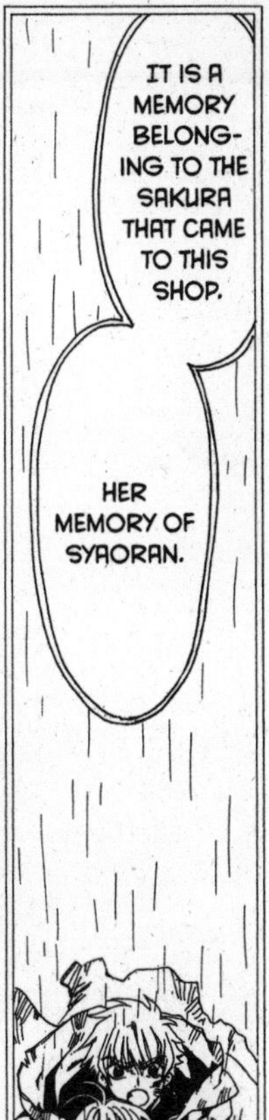
IT IS A MEMORY BELONGING TO THE SAKURA THAT CAME TO THIS SHOP.
HER MEMORY OF SYAORAN.
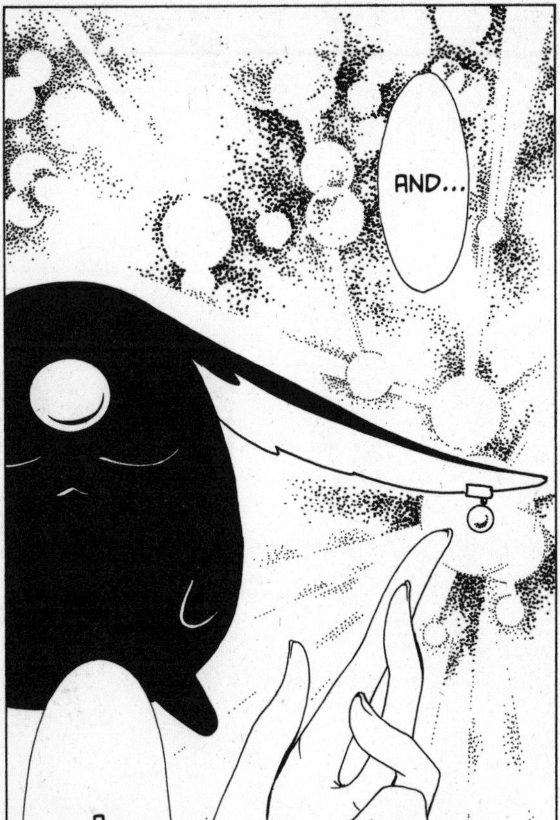
AND...
...A MEMORY OF WATANUKI'S.

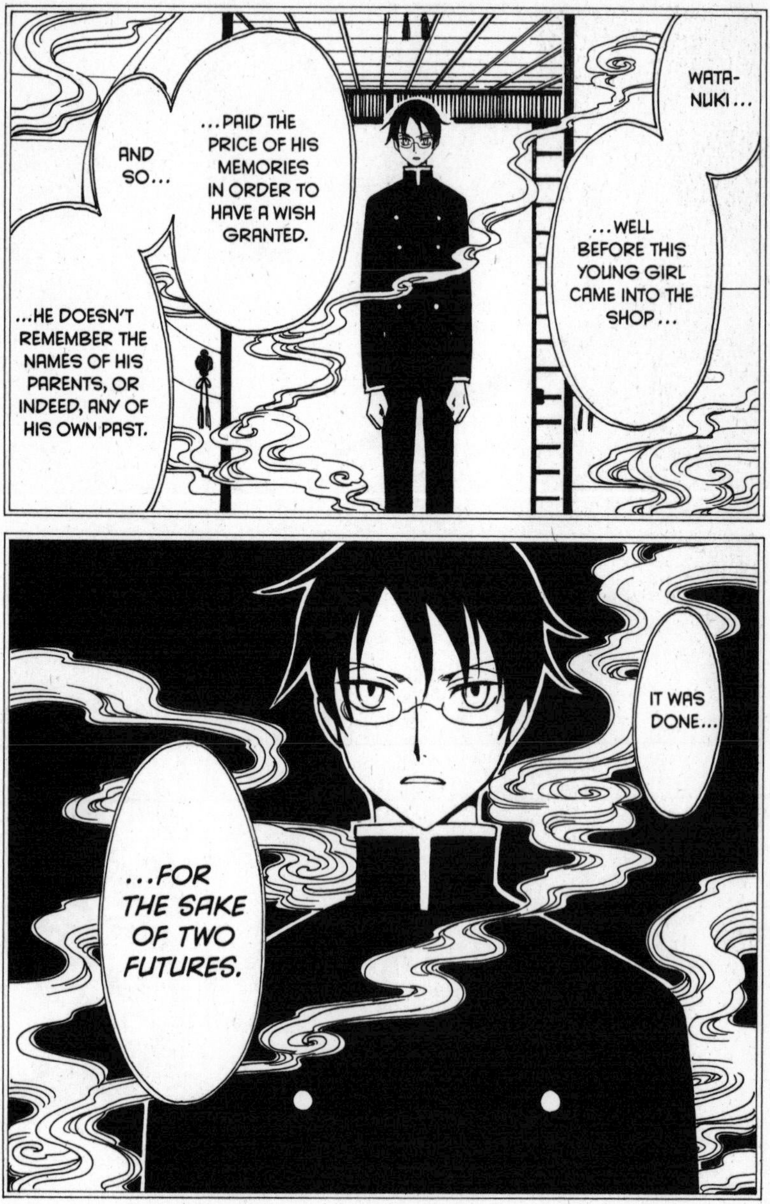
WATA-NUKI...
...WELL BEFORE THIS YOUNG GIRL CAME INTO THE SHOP...
...PAID THE PRICE OF HIS MEMORIES IN ORDER TO HAVE A WISH GRANTED.
AND SO...
...HE DOESN'T REMEMBER THE NAMES OF HIS PARENTS, OR INDEED, ANY OF HIS OWN PAST.
IT WAS DONE...
...FOR THE SAKE OF TWO FUTURES.

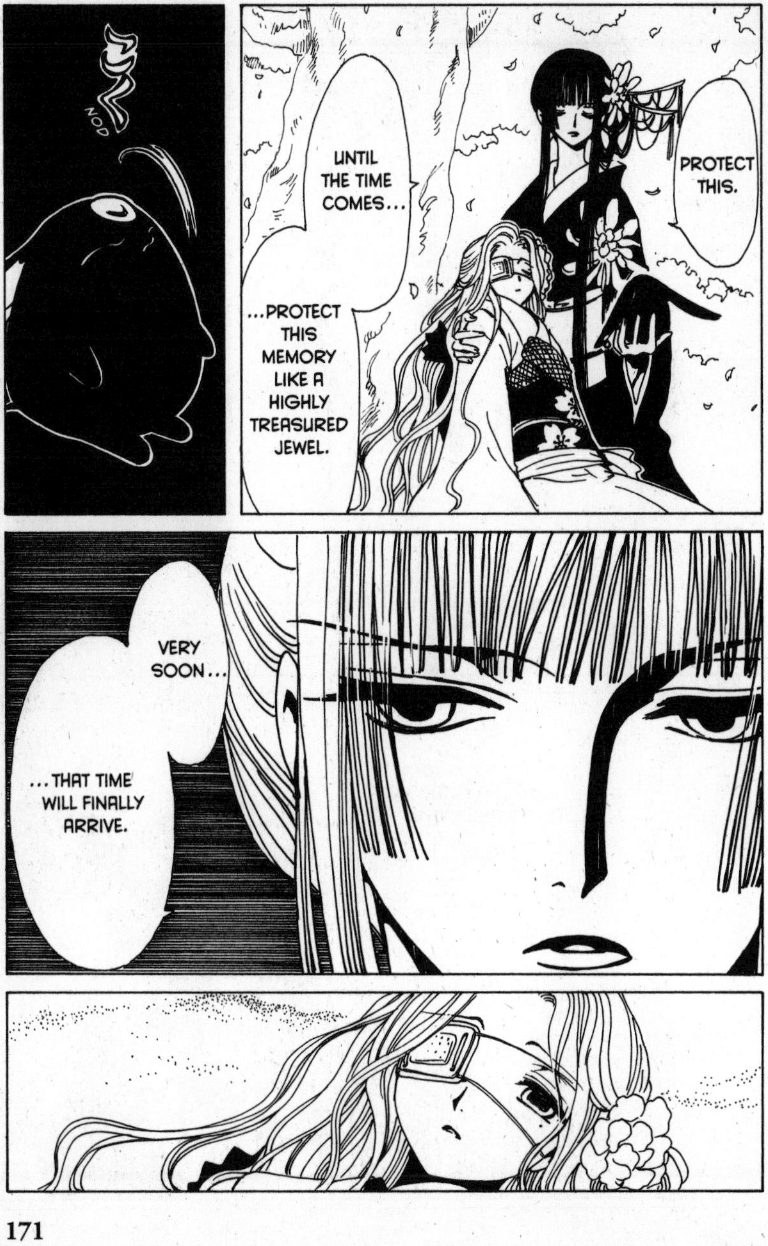
PROTECT THIS.
UNTIL THE TIME COMES...
...PROTECT THIS MEMORY LIKE A HIGHLY TREASURED JEWEL.
NOD
VERY SOON...
...THAT TIME WILL FINALLY ARRIVE.

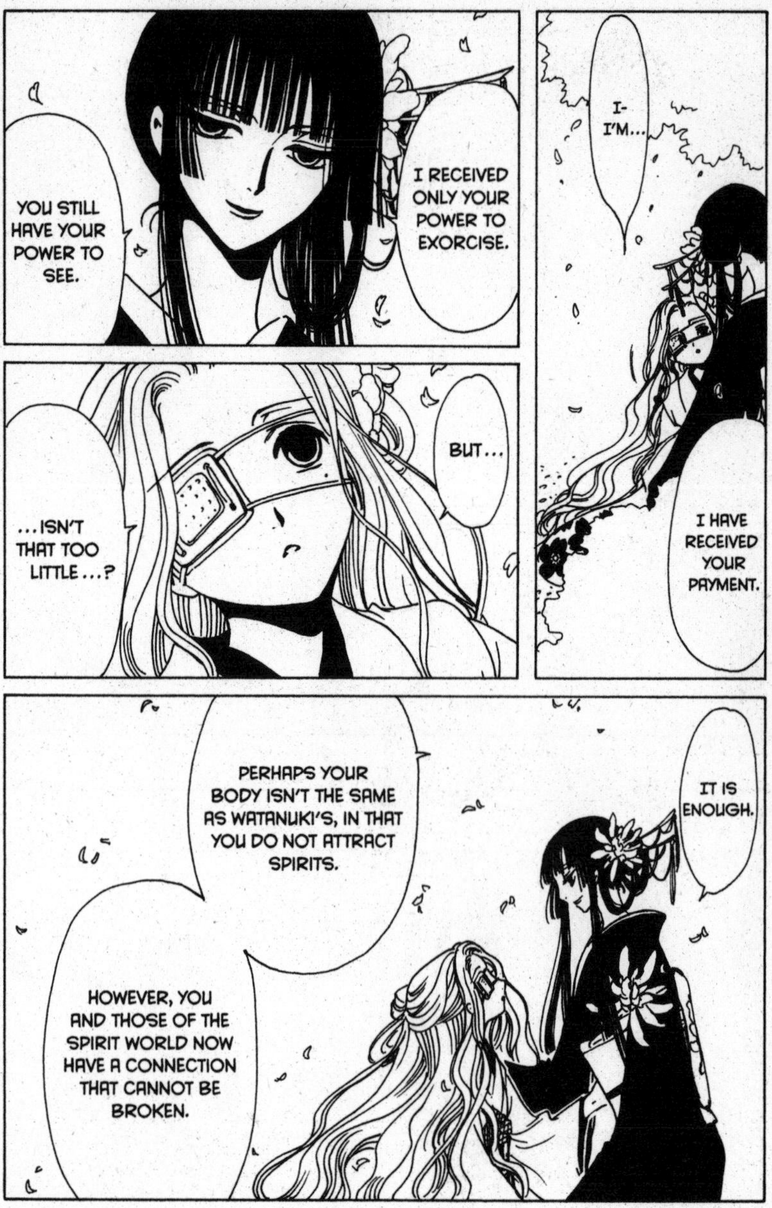
I-
I'M...
I HAVE RECEIVED YOUR PAYMENT.
I RECEIVED ONLY YOUR POWER TO EXORCISE.
YOU STILL HAVE YOUR POWER TO SEE.
BUT...
...ISN'T THAT TOO LITTLE...?
IT IS ENOUGH.
PERHAPS YOUR BODY ISN'T THE SAME AS WATANUKI'S, IN THAT YOU DO NOT ATTRACT SPIRITS.
HOWEVER, YOU AND THOSE OF THE SPIRIT WORLD NOW HAVE A CONNECTION THAT CANNOT BE BROKEN.

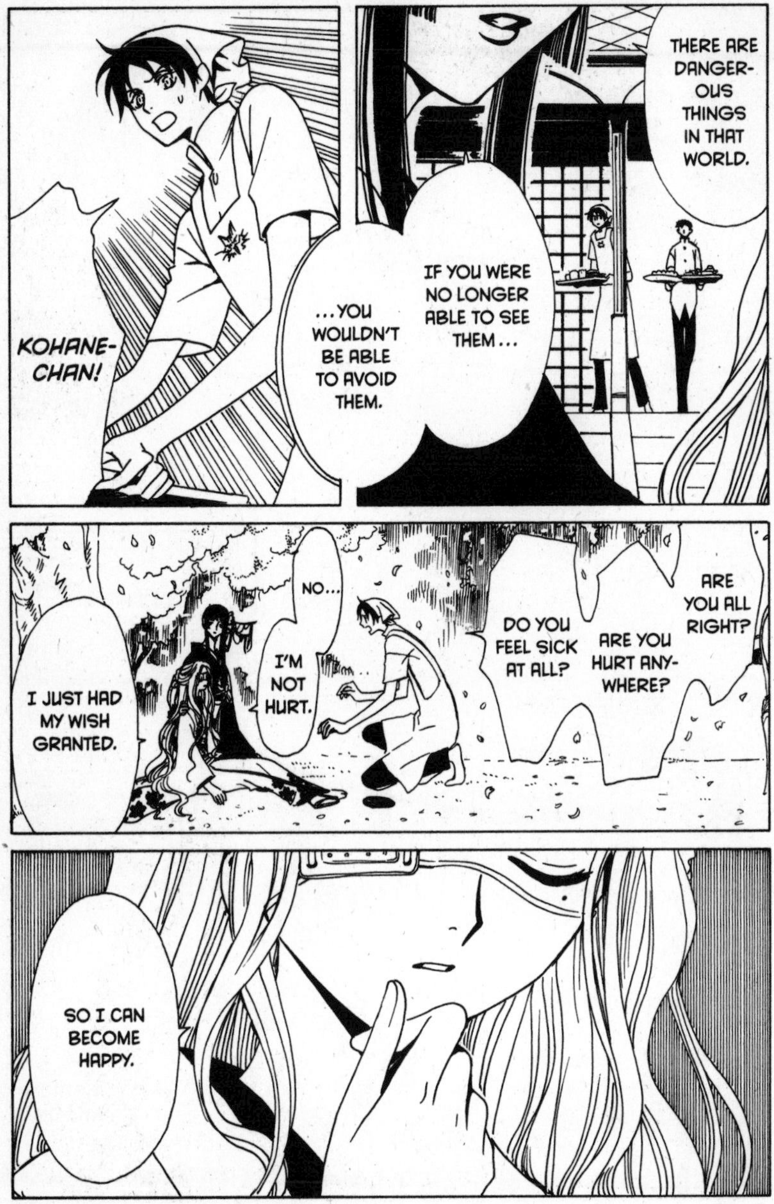
THERE ARE DANGEROUS THINGS IN THAT WORLD.
IF YOU WERE NO LONGER ABLE TO SEE THEM...
...YOU WOULDN'T BE ABLE TO AVOID THEM.
KOHANE-CHAN!
ARE YOU ALL RIGHT?
ARE YOU HURT ANYWHERE?
DO YOU FEEL SICK AT ALL?
NO...
I'M NOT HURT.
I JUST HAD MY WISH GRANTED.
SO I CAN BECOME HAPPY.

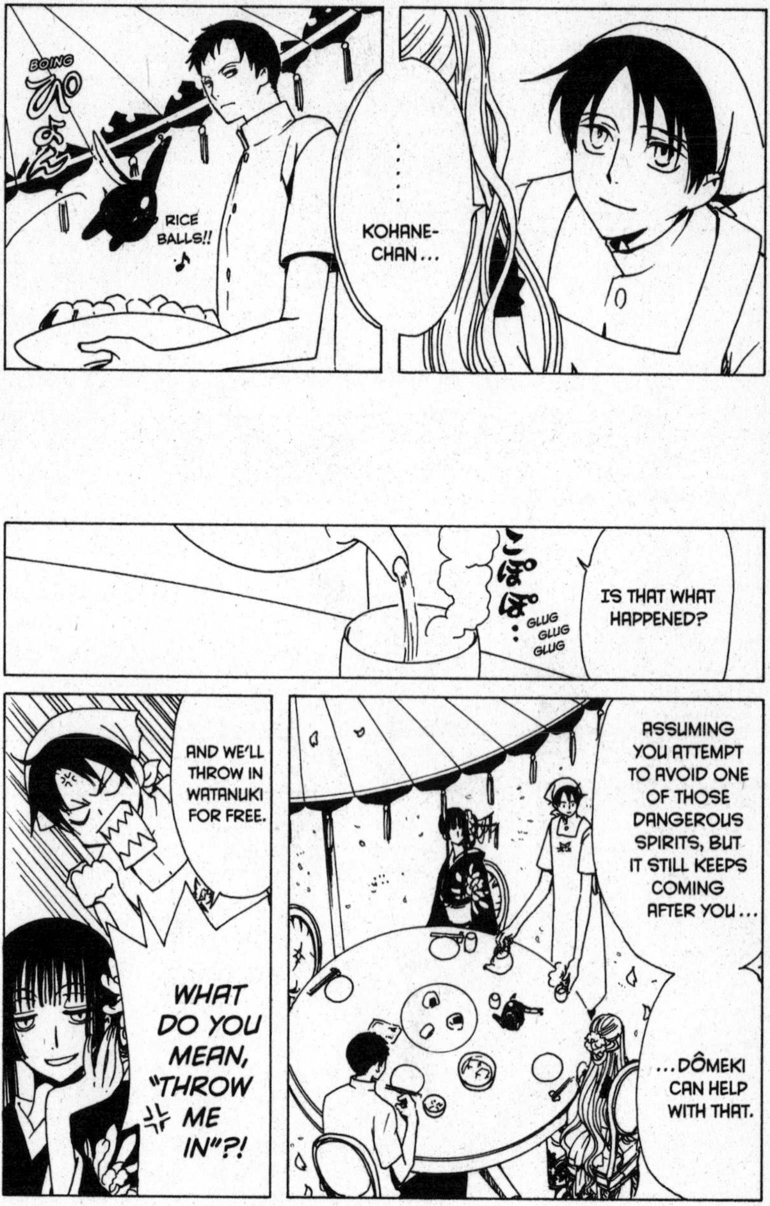
.....
KOHANE-CHAN...
ぴょん
BOING
RICE BALLS!!
IS THAT WHAT HAPPENED?
こぽぽ…
GLUG GLUG GLUG
ASSUMING YOU ATTEMPT TO AVOID ONE OF THOSE DANGEROUS SPIRITS, BUT IT STILL KEEPS COMING AFTER YOU...
...DÔMEKI CAN HELP WITH THAT.
AND WE'LL THROW IN WATANUKI FOR FREE.
WHAT DO YOU MEAN, "THROW ME IN"?!

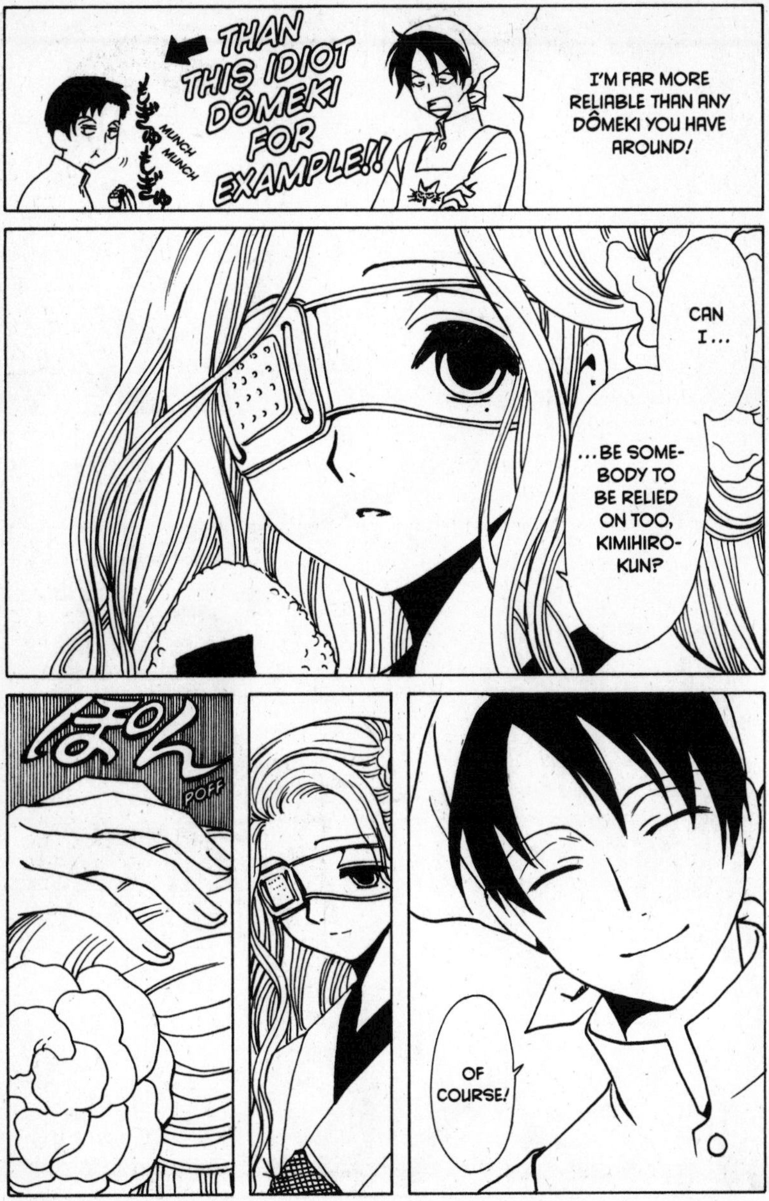
I'M FAR MORE RELIABLE THAN ANY DÔMEKI YOU HAVE AROUND!
THAN THIS IDIOT DÔMEKI FOR EXAMPLE!!
もぎゅもぎゅ
MUNCH MUNCH
CAN I...
...BE SOME-BODY TO BE RELIED ON TOO, KIMIHIRO-KUN?
OF COURSE!
ぽん
POFF

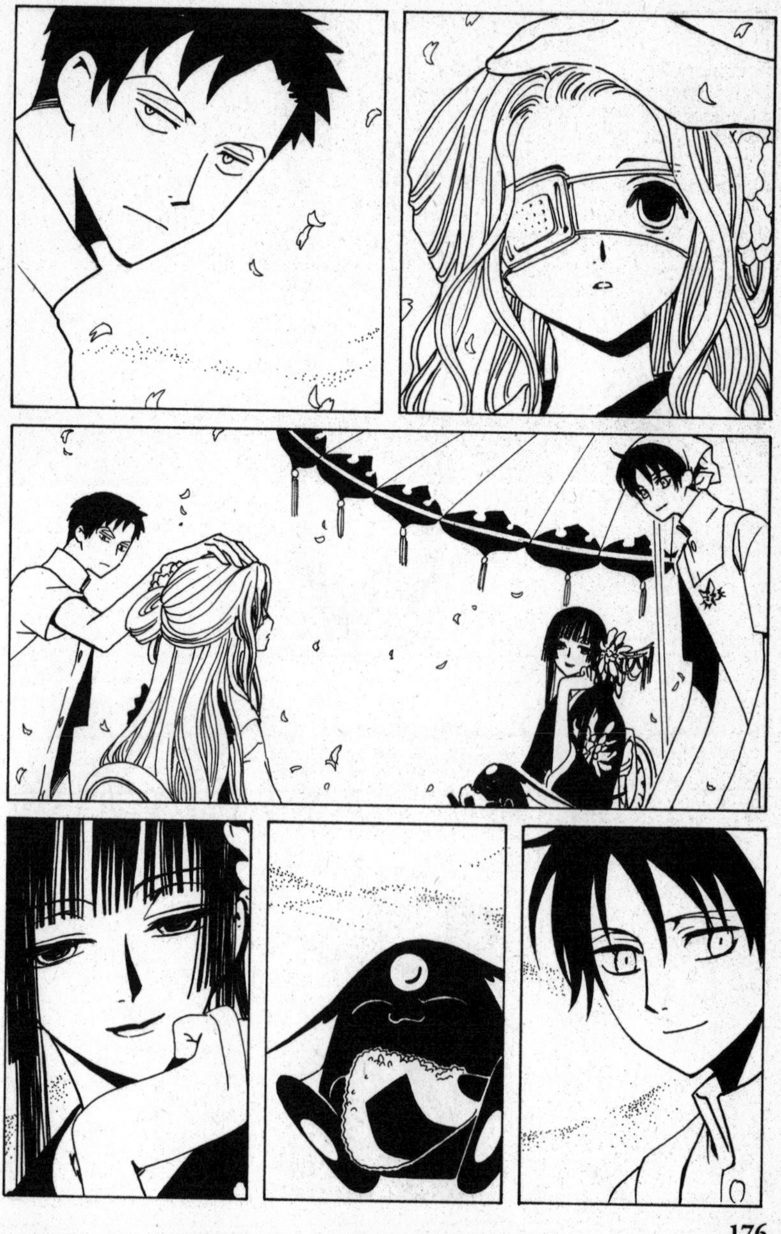

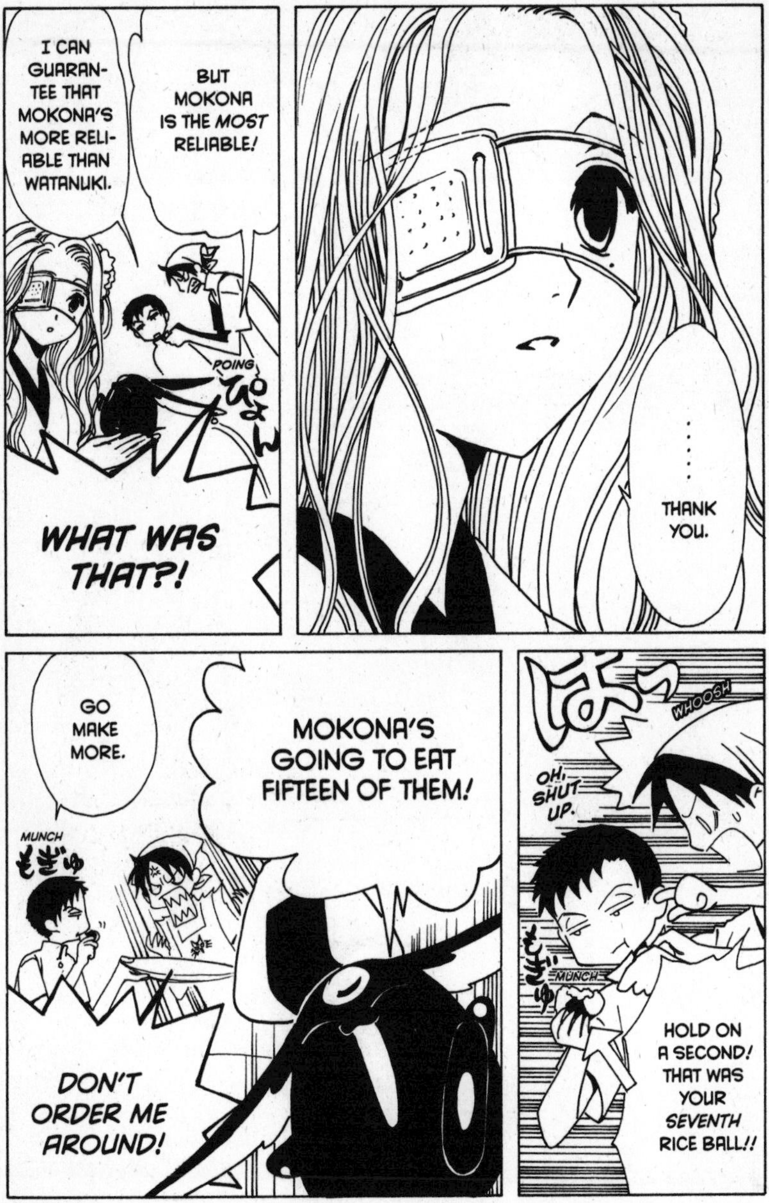
......
THANK YOU.
BUT MOKONA IS THE MOST RELIABLE!
I CAN GUARANTEE THAT MOKONA'S MORE RELIABLE THAN WATANUKI.
POING
ぴょん
WHAT WAS THAT?!
ぱっ
WHOOSH
OH, SHUT UP.
もぎゅ
MUNCH
HOLD ON A SECOND! THAT WAS YOUR SEVENTH RICE BALL!!
MOKONA'S GOING TO EAT FIFTEEN OF THEM!
GO MAKE MORE.
MUNCH
もぎゅ
DON'T ORDER ME AROUND!

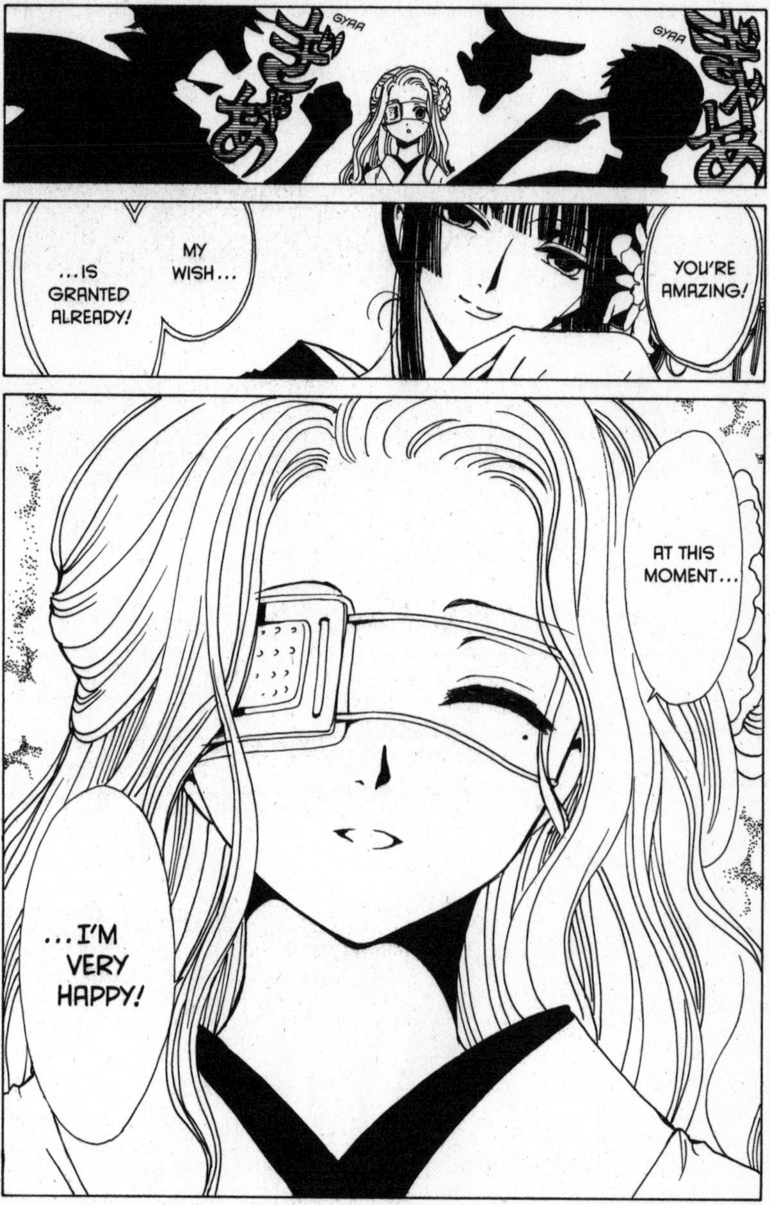
GYAA
GYAA
YOU'RE AMAZING!
MY WISH...
...IS GRANTED ALREADY!
AT THIS MOMENT...
...I'M VERY HAPPY!

# ⇥ Continued ⇤

in *xxxHOLiC*, volume 14

# About the Creators

CLAMP is a group of four women who have become the most popular manga artists in America—Satsuki Igarashi, Tsubaki Nekoi, Mokona, and Ohkawa Nanase. They started out as *doujinshi* (fan comics) creators, but their skill and craft brought them to the attention of publishers very quickly. Their first work from a major publisher was RG Veda, but their first mass success was with *Magic Knight Rayearth*. From there, they went on to write many series, including Cardcaptor Sakura and Chobits, two of the most popular manga in the United States. Like many Japanese manga artists, they prefer to avoid the spotlight, and little is known about them personally.

CLAMP is currently publishing three series in Japan: Tsubasa and xxxHOLiC with Kodansha and Gohou Drug with Kadokawa.

# Translation Notes

Japanese is a tricky language for most Westerners, and translation is often more art than science. For your edification and reading pleasure, here are notes on some of the places where we could have gone in a different direction or where a Japanese cultural reference is used.

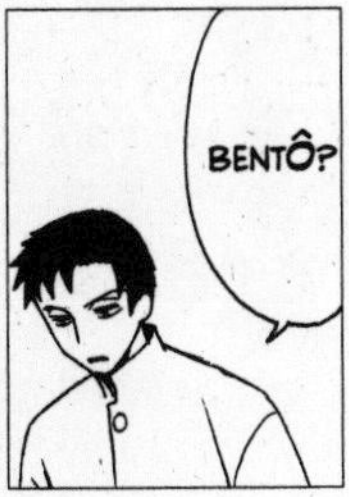
BENTÔ?

**Page 10, *Bentô***

As explained in previous notes, *bentô* is a boxed lunch. In its most traditional form, the meal is decorated with foods cut into shapes to make it pleasing to the eye as well as delicious.

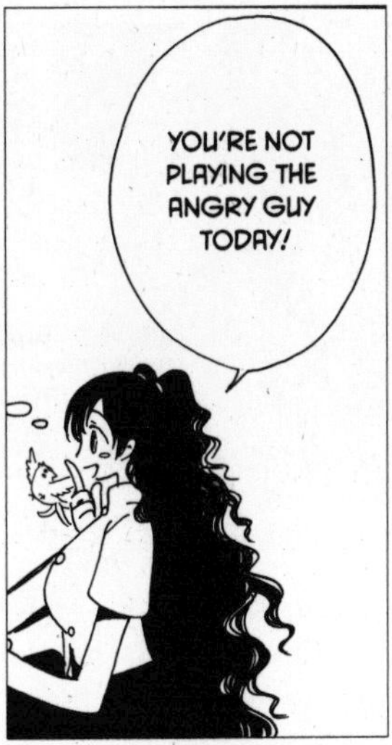
YOU'RE NOT PLAYING THE ANGRY GUY TODAY!

**Page 13, Angry Guy (*Tsukkomi*)**

As described in the notes for volume 6, a standard comedy two-man act called *manzai* is made up of the angry guy (*tsukkomi*) and the dumb guy (*boké*). As the angry guy, Watanuki is constantly snapping at Dômeki.

## Page 15, Cream Crab-cake Croquettes

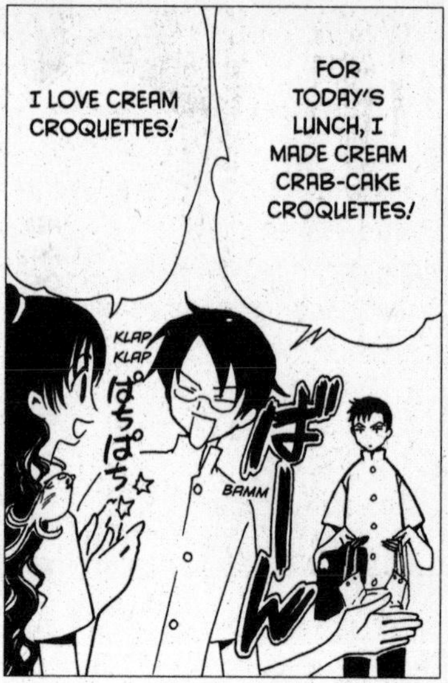
FOR TODAY'S LUNCH, I MADE CREAM CRAB-CAKE CROQUETTES!
I LOVE CREAM CROQUETTES!
ばーん
BAMM
ぱちぱち
KLAP KLAP

Croquettes (pronounced *kurokke* in Japanese) are fried potato patties with all sorts of different foods that can be added or substituted for flavoring. Cream crab-cake croquettes have a crunchy breaded outside and a crab-based cream sauce filling. They are a little hard to eat, since the sauce is a bit more liquid than most croquette fillings, but certainly delicious.

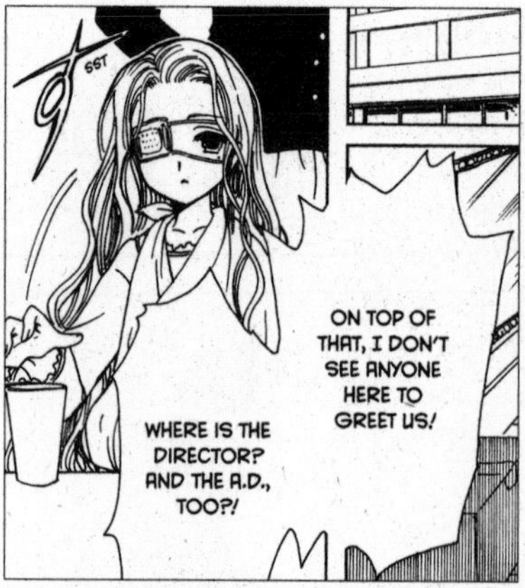
SST
WHERE IS THE DIRECTOR? AND THE A.D., TOO?!
ON TOP OF THAT, I DON'T SEE ANYONE HERE TO GREET US!

## Page 44, TV station greetings, A.D.

Reportedly, a television station's director and assistant director (called A.D. in both Japan and in the West) are expected to come to the guest's dressing room with a greeting—usually filled with flattery about how important the guest is to the show. In many cases, the quality of greeting can indicate a person's standing on the show. The fact that the director and A.D. have not come to Kohane's dressing room is a hint at how precarious her position is on the show.

I READ ALL ABOUT IT IN THE WEEKLY MAGAZINES.
HOW HER HUSBAND ABANDONED THEM. AND WHO CAN BLAME HIM?

## Page 63, Weekly magazines

The United States has its tabloids and Japan has its weeklies. Some of the weeklies print only hard news, but most dabble or even wallow in celebrity scandal, stories of the supernatural, salacious photos, and any other trick possible to attract readers. Due to Japan's train-based commuter culture and magazine kiosks at almost every station, it can be a very lucrative endeavor.

## Page 88, Put her mother on camera

PUT HER MOTHER ON CAM-ERA!

As with most Western non-news shows, the producers must have a signed waiver to put anyone on camera. Most of a celebrity's troupe (manager, agent, etc.)—and in this case, a stage mother—are not signed to appear on camera. But since this is a live broadcast, the director wants Kohane's mother on camera to help improve the show's ratings, and his way around the lack of a waiver is to make the shot appear like an accident.

## Page 115, Kohane

IT WAS SNOWING ON THE DAY I MARRIED YOUR FATHER, AND IT LOOKED LIKE MILLIONS OF TINY FEATHERS WERE FALLING TO THE GROUND.

As Kohane told Watanuki in volume 9, her name means "small feather" (or "feathers"). The significance of this name is revealed only in this volume.

## Page 136, Rice balls

HOW MANY RICE BALLS CAN YOU EAT?
FIVE.

*O-nigiri*, often translated to "rice balls" in English, are foods that are especially made as an easy meal to transport and eat with one's fingers. The "standard" rice ball is a lump of rice about three inches high and about two inches thick formed into a triangular shape. It often has a rectangular piece of dried seaweed wrapped around one of the triangle's sides as a place to hold the ball, and buried in its center is a pickled plum (*umeboshi*) that not only gives the rice ball a sharp taste to contrast with the rice, but also helps to preserve the rice ball without refrigeration. However, rice balls are popular in Japan, and there are as many recipe variations as there are cooks. Some of the variations suggested by Dômeki are possible replacements for the pickled plum.

## Page 136, *Ikura*

*Ikura* are salmon eggs. They are most commonly found as a topping in high-quality sushi dishes, but they are used in many other Japanese dishes as well. *Ikura* is very popular with the Japanese.

## Page 137, *Tarako*, *Tori-Soboro*, and *Irijako*

*Tarako* is cod eggs, and has a reputation for being a very spicy flavoring. *Tori-soboro* is a kind of minced chicken that is often mixed into tofu-based dishes or other sauces to give them a meaty texture. *Irijako* are tiny fish that are pan-fried in oil to a crispy dryness.

# TOMARE!

## [STOP!]

You're going the wrong way!

Manga is a completely different type of reading experience.

To start at the *beginning*, go to the *end*!

That's right! Authentic manga is read the traditional Japanese way—from right to left. Exactly the *opposite* of how American books are read. It's easy to follow: Just go to the other end of the book, and read each page—and each panel—from right side to left side, starting at the top right. Now you're experiencing manga as it was meant to be!

**MLib**